Camping Georgia

A Comprehensive Guide to the State's Best Campgrounds

Jimmy Jacobs and Polly Dean

FALCONGUIDES

ESSEX, CONNECTICUT

FALCONGUIDES®

An imprint of Globe Pequot, the trade division of The Rowman & Littlefield Publishing Group, Inc.
4501 Forbes Blvd., Ste. 200
Lanham, MD 20706
www.rowman.com

Falcon and FalconGuides are registered trademarks and Make Adventure Your Story is a trademark of The Rowman & Littlefield Publishing Group, Inc.

Distributed by NATIONAL BOOK NETWORK

Copyright © 2023 The Rowman & Littlefield Publishing Group, Inc.

Photos by the authors unless noted otherwise.

Maps by The Rowman & Littlefield Publishing Group, Inc.

British Library Cataloguing in Publication Information available

Library of Congress Cataloging-in-Publication Data available

ISBN 978-1-4930-7015-2 (paper : alk. paper)
ISBN 978-1-4930-7016-9 (electronic)

♾™ The paper used in this publication meets the minimum requirements of American National Standard for Information Sciences—Permanence of Paper for Printed Library Materials, ANSI/NISO Z39.48-1992.

The authors and The Rowman & Littlefield Publishing Group, Inc. assume no liability for accidents happening to, or injuries sustained by, readers who engage in the activities described in this book.

To Polly Dean for providing great photography,
constant support, and needed critique,
while exploring the state's camping resources.

Contents

USDA Forest Service

Chattooga River Ranger District **42**

Georgia State Parks and Historic Sites Division

Georgia Power Company

USDA Forest Service

PIEDMONT REGION **59**

Alabama to Atlanta.. **63**

Georgia State Parks and Historic Sites Division

County Parks

Georgia Power Company

US Army Corps of Engineers

USDA Forest Service

Georgia State Parks and Historic Sites Division

Georgia State Authority

County Parks

US Fish and Wildlife Service

National Park Service

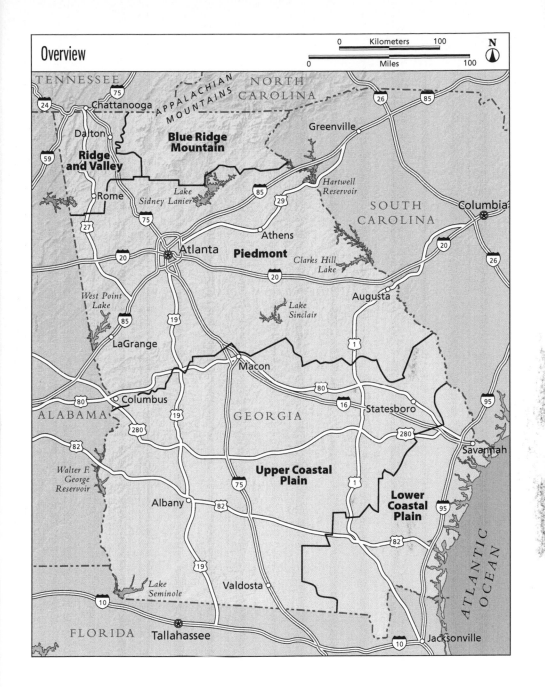

Acknowledgments

Without the efforts of the local, state, and federal government agencies and Georgia Power Company that oversee the public campgrounds of the Peach State and the wild places in which they are located, this book could not have been produced.

Special thanks are due to the Georgia State Parks and Historic Sites Division, their park managers, park staffs, and in particular Public Affairs Coordinator Kim Hatcher for first-rate support provided in making our travels around the state possible.

Meet Your Guides

Jimmy Jacobs is a native Georgian and was for a quarter century the editor of *Georgia Sportsman* magazine. He has been fishing, hiking, and camping across the breadth of the state for more than half a century. He is a member of the Georgia Outdoor Writers Association and was a member of the Florida Outdoor Writers Association, and Southeastern Outdoor Press Association, having received more than four dozen Excellence in Craft awards from those groups. His bibliography includes guidebooks to trout and bass fishing in the Peach State, as well as regional books on trout and saltwater fishing. Jimmy is a 2017 inductee into the Fly Fishing Museum of the Southern Appalachians Hall of Fame in the Communicator Category and a member of the Georgia Outdoor Writers Association Hunting and Fishing Hall of Fame.

Polly Dean is an award-winning writer and photographer, whose passion for fly fishing has led her to camp along the shores of a wide variety of waters throughout the south. She was a member of the Florida Outdoor Writers Association and the Southeastern Outdoor Press Association, as well as past president of the Georgia Outdoor Writers Association.

Your guides were well positioned to produce *Camping Georgia*, having previously worked on two editions of *Hiking Georgia*. The miles of trekking in all regions of the state in writing those editions often put them in many of the campgrounds covered in this present book.

All photographs in the book are by Polly Dean.

Introduction

To say that camping is a popular pastime in Georgia would be a great understatement. Simply put, the state is located in a region where folks spend a lot of time enjoying the outdoors. Setting up a tent or heading out in an RV provides an excellent way to put you right in the midst of all the scenery and recreational opportunities the Peach State offers.

In the case of the many developed campgrounds, during the peak vacation months of summer and changing of the leaves in fall, finding a vacant site may be a chore. Even many of the more primitive campgrounds are also busy. Planning ahead is always a good idea, whenever possible.

In traveling throughout the state of Georgia, despite having spent my entire life here, I am still constantly struck by the great diversity of terrain, flora, and fauna encountered. Sidney Lanier, Georgia's most famed 19th-century poet, described the variety offered by the state in his poem *Song of the Chattahoochee*, describing that river's course southward through the regions of Georgia. Additionally, his *Marshes of Glynn* highlighted the picturesque vistas of the coastal area.

The Blue Ridge Mountains of northeast Georgia range up to elevations of more than 4,000 feet, topped off by the peak of Brasstown Bald at 4,784 feet. This is an area of rushing mountain streams tumbling down to river valleys.

The Ridge and Valley Region of northwest Georgia, though still elevated, is much more akin to the limestone area of the Cumberland Plateau. Pigeon Mountain, named for its once abundant population of the now extinct passenger pigeons that inhabited it, and the dramatic rock formations of Cloudland Canyon, sculpted by erosion of the softer stone found there, are major features of the area.

Georgia's Piedmont Region spans the area covering the foothills of the mountains just north of the capital city of Atlanta, down to the vicinity of Macon in the mid-state. It also stretches from the Alabama border just north of Columbus, across to South Carolina at Augusta. This is a region of rolling terrain with rich soils and abundant wildlife. Much of that fauna is congregated along the number of river valleys that lead to both the Atlantic Ocean and Gulf of Mexico.

You enter the Upper Coastal Plain as you drop over the Fall Line that stretches from Augusta on the South Carolina border down to Columbus at the Alabama line. This feature marks an ancient seacoast and creates long shoal areas where the rivers rush over it. This also separates the Piedmont's fertile terrain from the sandy soils of the long-gone seabed.

Finally reaching the Lower Coastal Plain puts you in subtropical clime, along a saltwater shore fringed by vast flooded prairies of Spartina grass, broken up by a maze of tidal creeks, rivers, and sounds. A string of barrier islands lies beyond the marshes, facing the Atlantic Ocean. These isles range from wilderness areas to others hosting quaint coastal villages with long histories or beachfront family vacation playgrounds.

Whitetail deer are plentiful in the Peach State, especially in the Piedmont Region.

Weather: Georgia obviously has some varied weather patterns due to its more than 400-mile span from north to south and varied elevations. Thus, it is possible to face sweltering South Georgia heat, while atop Brasstown Bald the conditions are much the same as found in Massachusetts. Picking the best time to enjoy pleasant weather for a camping trip very much depends on where in the state you are headed.

The Ridge and Valley and Blue Ridge Mountain areas present the best conditions in the months of April through November. In the spring months of April and May, average temperatures range from the mid-40-degree level up to the high 70s. During June through September the temperatures rise to the low 60s to mid-80s, with the fall temperatures in October and November falling back to match those of the spring. Rainfall on average also is at its lowest levels in April and May and October through November.

These mountainous regions range in temperature on average from the low 30s to mid-60s in winter, which also is a wetter portion of the year. That precipitation can present snow conditions as well. As a result, many public campgrounds in these areas are seasonal, generally closing from late October to mid-March.

Georgia's mid-state Piedmont Region presents some differing conditions. Here the camping season is year-round, with a caveat. Temperatures range from the mid-70s to more than 90 degrees in June through September, which also receives the most precipitation. Rain falls an average of 29 days during this period and humidity often rises to uncomfortable levels. The only campgrounds that are crowded at this time are located on a river or large reservoir.

Piedmont temperatures in March through May and October through November range from the mid-40s to low 80s. Winter temperatures are in the mid-30- to mid-60-degree range.

Both Coastal Plain regions of the Peach State fairly closely mirror the weather of the Piedmont. With regard to temperatures, the only difference is it generally warms up by early March in the spring, and winter does not arrive in full force until mid-December. Also, expect the humidity to seem unbearable at times. Again, campgrounds on lakes and rivers are most comfortable in the summer, along with those on the seacoast that benefit from ocean breezes.

Flora and fauna: In the mountainous north of the state, trout streams flow down the valleys of this region beneath canopies of hickory, oak, white pine, and hemlock trees, while the top of the food chain is dominated by a strong population of black bears.

In the mid-state region, the terrain is of the Piedmont Plateau variety, offering verdant mixed hardwood and pine forests and fertile river valleys. Expect to see lots of pastureland, interspersed with vast stands of loblolly pines, both of which have replaced the small family farms of a bygone era. This is a land of plenty for wildlife, where white-tailed deer and wild turkeys have made amazing comebacks from the brink of extinction in the late 19th and early 20th centuries, to now provide regular sightings when you visit the woodlands. Above the lakes and rivers of this part of Georgia, sightings of osprey and bald eagles are frequent.

Once into the Upper Coastal Plain, the flora of this region was once dominated by longleaf pines with an understory of wiregrass. Efforts are ongoing to revive that greatly reduced ecosystem. Meanwhile, huge stands of loblolly pines, broken up by agricultural fields, stretch for miles. Here again, deer and turkey are abundant, and it's a region where the call of the bobwhite quail still echoes over the fields.

Along the Lower Coastal Plain white-tailed deer are abundant, though stunted in size, due to the lack of fertility in the soil. Here myriad seabirds inhabit the marshes and beaches, while summertime sightings of dolphins and manatees occur in the waters.

Recreation: Recreational activities for campers across Georgia are dependent on these weather conditions just discussed. In the Blue Ridge Mountain highlands, the most dependable year-round activity is hiking the many trails of the region. With the exception of the periods of snowfall, access to the trailheads remains available in winter, while the lack of leaves on the trees provides impressive vistas of the mountains.

The trail system in the mountain counties runs the gamut from short wildflower walks in the spring to multiday adventures on the 80 miles of the Appalachian Trail in the state. Other popular long hikes are found on the Benton McKaye or Bartram Trails. Some of the most popular short trails lead to the many waterfalls scattered across the region. You can totally get away from civilization by taking to the Jacks River or Conasauga River Trails in northwest Georgia. These paths and their connector trails snake their way for a total of more than 30 miles through the 42,000 acres of a federally mandated roadless tract in the Cohutta Wilderness Area.

Campers also take advantage of water sports and fishing on nine major reservoirs spanning from Carters Lake in the west to Hartwell Lake on the Savannah River at the South Carolina border. If you prefer trout fishing in moving water, this region offers more than 4,000 miles of streams and rivers, many of which are regularly stocked in the warmer months. Additionally, included in that stream total are 1,500 miles of water that hold wild, reproducing populations of rainbow, brown, or brook trout. Some of those rivers, such as the upper Chattahoochee and Chattooga also provide paddlers with challenging whitewater canoe, kayak, and rafting adventures.

For lovers of history, the North Georgia mountains have several sites of interest. These include the Foxfire Museum in Mountain City with exhibits of pioneer living in the highlands; the Dahlonega Gold Museum that details the area's gold rush of the 1830s; the Byron Herbert Reece Farm and Heritage Center near Blairsville that celebrates the life and work of the writer the state legislature named as Georgia's Appalachian Poet/Novelist in 2005; and the Civilian Conservation Corps Museum in Vogel State Park that tells the story of that Depression Era organization that did the original construction on many of the state's public campgrounds. All of these sites are located in close proximity to state park campgrounds.

Several natural wonders in this region that should not be missed are Georgia's highest point atop Brasstown Bald, with its view of four states: the raging rapids of the Chattooga River on the South Carolina border, where the bulk of the classic movie *Deliverance* was filmed in the 1970s; and 2-mile-long, 1,000-foot-deep Tallulah Gorge that has attracted tourists since the Victorian Era.

While offering some unique features, the Ridge and Valley Region of northwest Georgia also matches many of the recreational activities found in the mountain region. The similar options are long hikes on Georgia's portion of the multistate Pinhoti Trail, shorter walks on the heights of Pigeon Mountain or into the depths of Cloudland Canyon State Park's 1,000-foot-deep Sitton Gulf to view its twin waterfalls along the way. The state park also offers spelunking adventures in its cave system. For water sports in this region, campgrounds on the shores of the US Army Corps of Engineers' Carters Lake provide access to boating, swimming, fishing, and other activities. The 3,200-acre lake formed by the highest earthen dam east of the Mississippi River is the deepest in Georgia, as it plunges to depths of more than 400 feet.

If you are a history buff, the Ridge and Valley area offers plenty of attractions. The Civil War battlefields of Chickamauga and Resaca lie along General William Sherman's 1864 march toward Atlanta. Even earlier this section of Georgia was part of the Cherokee Nation. Their last tribal capital in the southeast was located at New Echota and is now open for tours as a state historic site. Another state historic site near Chatsworth, the Chief Vann House also is open for tours. The house was built by James Vann and occupied by him and later by his son Joseph, who were both tribal leaders. The structure was the first brick house erected in the Cherokee Nation.

The Peach State Piedmont's main attractions for campers are its numerous major reservoirs. Many campgrounds on these large bodies of water provide swimming beaches as well as headquarters for some great angling for largemouth bass, crappie, or catfish. These lakes also offer plenty of room for sailing, powerboating, or personal watercraft action, along with canoeing, kayaking, or paddleboard ventures.

Located in this area is the Kennesaw Mountain National Battlefield, with more than 17 miles of hiking trails along the best-preserved system of original trenches and earthen fortifications in the nation. The region offers whitewater paddling adventures on the Chattahoochee River near Atlanta and in downtown Columbus. In the eastern part of the Piedmont, paddlers can challenge the rapids on the Savannah River or enjoy a lazy ride down the antebellum era Augusta Canal that bypasses the shoals.

In the Peach State's Coastal Plains Regions, from west to east, the most dramatic natural wonders are Providence Canyon near the Alabama border that has walls festooned with multicolored clay strata. Near Waycross, the 438,000 acres of the Land of the Trembling Earth in the Okefenokee Swamp National Wildlife Refuge beckon you into a subtropical landscape that is home to black bears and alligators. The Cumberland Island National Seashore borders the Atlantic Ocean. You can board the daily ferry from the historic seaport village of St. Marys to explore the island's history that centered around the Carnegie family or venture into the 9,800 acres of federally protected wilderness area.

The bottom line is, regardless of the region of Georgia in which you plan a camping trip, you will find plenty of activities, wonders, and attractions to keep you entertained.

How to Use This Guide

With any tool or piece of machinery, to take full advantage of it you need an instruction manual explaining its function. This guide is no different. The following sections will walk you through the process of getting the most value from the information provided.

To begin with, let's explore what the book offers and how it is arranged to deliver on that promise. Georgia is the largest state east of the Mississippi River. The state covers a total of 37 million acres of land and water. Of that total, more than 67 percent is composed of forests, thus it provides plenty of room to explore and enjoy the outdoors.

The more than 200 public campgrounds in the Peach State provide excellent headquarters and jumping-off points for exploring this vast state. These facilities range from well-maintained and well-operated RV parks to very rustic primitive areas that offer only sparse to nonexistent amenities. Those are operated by a host of local, state, and federal agencies and governmental departments.

To make navigating this maze of information possible, we are breaking Georgia into the five geophysical regions recognized in the state. Those are the Blue Ridge Mountain Region in the northeast, the Ridge and Valley Region of the northwest, the Piedmont Region that spans the mid-state area, the Upper Coastal Plain Region of southwest and south-central Georgia, and the Lower Coastal Plain Region in the southeast. Each of these regions offers differing flora, fauna, elevations, and ecosystems, which in turn make visiting each of the campgrounds a unique experience.

As we delve into these regions, you will find several standardized points discussed. A map of the region will be provided, followed by a table broken down by the agencies managing the campgrounds. The table also will offer information on the amenities and activities found at each site. Next will be a brief overview of the region, then in separate sections, short overviews of the individual campgrounds in the region.

About cell service: The question of whether cell phone service is available in specific campgrounds is not dealt with individually. In more remote mountain areas, it tends to be nonexistent. In most other areas, campgrounds are designed to get you away from the populated areas where such service is readily available. In many state and county parks, there may be service, but that usually depends on which carrier supplies your service. The bottom line is, you are best served to call ahead to your destination for that information if cell service is important during your venture.

Maps: The regional maps will indicate the locations of all campgrounds in that portion of the state. These have key numbers that match up with numbers found on the descriptions of each campground found later in the text.

While these maps are not drawn to scale and the site of each facility is only an approximation, they will give you a general idea of the position of the campground within the region. That information, combined with "Finding the campground" details provided with the individual descriptions of the campgrounds, will make locating the sites easy.

Be aware also that having some other maps may be useful. It is best not to be too dependent on your cell phone or the GPS unit in your vehicle. Not all Forest Service (FS) roads show up on those electronic devices. For old-school backup, the *DeLorme Atlas & Gazetteer* for Georgia can be a very useful tool to have available.

Overview: This section is another that can help you home in on where you want to camp. It provides some detail on points of interest and a lay-of-the-land for each region. This will be information such as, if you want to go whitewater paddling, where are the mountain areas that offer the rushing rivers needed for the sport.

Campgrounds-at-a-glance chart: Regional charts provide a list of the campgrounds in the region broken down by the agencies that manage them, along with details on the most important information you need to pick an appropriate destination for your camping trip. When you have a specific activity in mind, these details are quite helpful in picking an appropriate camping site for your venture, whether it involves cycling, boating, hiking, or any of the other outdoor activities.

Campground descriptions: Here you find each campground described, along with a number corresponding to the site's location on the map. You also get the following information on each campground:

Location: The name of a close-by town or city is provided, along with the general direction for traveling to the site and driving miles.

Season: The dates the various campgrounds are open are listed here. Particularly in the North Georgia mountains and around major reservoirs, many of the campgrounds are not open in the winter months. The dates they are open are provided as a range of months. The specific day on which they open or close changes from year to year. Additionally, some sites remain open in winter, but the water supply and flush toilets are turned off.

Total sites: Here the total number of campsites available is provided, along with the hookups available. Be aware that these may vary slightly from published information from the managing agencies because some sites may be reserved for the use of volunteer hosts. Also, remodeling and expansions are ongoing, particularly in state parks, so the number of sites and hookups may have changed.

Group sites: The total number of group (usually described as pioneer) sites provided. These ordinarily are primitive tent camping areas offering drinking water and vault toilets, but in the case of state parks, may be more developed facilities.

Hookup sites: The number of sites providing hookups, including the type of hookups offered.

Maximum RV length: The maximum length of RV the campground can accommodate. Be aware that in some cases only one or two sites may offer that maximum size.

Facilities: This section provides a list of facilities and amenities found in the campground or in close proximity in the park or recreation area. Some items listed are the presence of restrooms, showers, laundries, drinking water, and recreational activities.

Fees: List of fees per night for staying in the campground as an approximate dollar amount is provided. Also, whether there is a daily parking fee.

Reservations: Can you make reservations for camping? Y = Yes or N = No.

Finding the campground: Here you will find detailed directions and mileages for finding the campgrounds. These will originate at nearby towns or, in the case of more rural areas, at major highway intersections that are easily located.

GPS coordinates: These are provided for fans of electronics.

About the campground: This section provides the important details on each of the campgrounds covered. Here will be described any natural or man-made features that make this a desirable destination for a visit, such as lakes, waterfalls, or historic sites. Other information includes the topography, condition of roads and sites within the campground, the availability of shade, and whether the sites are in an open communal setting or have understory vegetation that make them more private.

Campgrounds At-A-Glance Chart Key

Hookups: W = Water, E= Electricity, S = Sewer, N = None
Maximum RV length: Given in feet, N = Any length, NA = Not applicable
Dump Station: Y = Yes, N = None
Toilets: F = Flush toilets, V = Vault toilets, C = Chemical flush toilets, N = No toilets
Showers: Y = Yes, N = None
Drinking Water: Y = Yes, N = None
ADA compliant: Y = Some sites available, N= No

Fee Range:

N	$0
$	$1–$10
$$	$11–$20
$$$	$21–$30
$$$$	$31–$40
$$$$$	more than $40

Reservations: Y = Yes, N = No

Camping in Georgia

Wilderness restrictions/regulations: Georgia has seven entities that manage public camping areas. At the federal level, the USDA Forest Service, US Fish and Wildlife Service, and the US Army Corps of Engineers oversee lands in which camping are permitted. Two divisions within the Georgia Department of Natural Resources are in control at the state level. Those are the Wildlife Resources Division and the State Parks and Historic Sites Division. The Georgia Power Company also provides campgrounds on the shores of the major reservoirs it operates. Additionally, some public campgrounds are maintained by either county or city governments.

As would be expected, rules and regulations for camping vary, depending on the agency setting them. Some regulations are rather standard, being utilized by all the agencies, though they may vary a bit in application. These cover such things as lengths of stay, restrictions on alcoholic beverages, tent placement, quiet hours, and some other details. These will be covered in depth as the actual camping areas are discussed in later chapters.

In the case of local management by cities and counties, there are no "wilderness" regulations, since these sites tend to be in civilized, urban to suburban areas.

With regard to areas under state park management, camping is only allowed in designated campsites. These range from developed RV parks with full amenities to backcountry walk-in and backpacking sites. While these latter sites are quite primitive, with minimal to no facilities, they are designated areas. These backcountry sites often require obtaining a permit prior to venturing to the sites. The purpose is to allow you to experience the natural areas, but to reduce as much as possible the impact on the flora and fauna within the parks.

In the case of the state's Wildlife Management Areas maintained by the Wildlife Resource Division, camping rules are a bit more lenient. The state oversees more than 100 WMAs throughout Georgia, with over 100,000 acres of land available for hunting, hiking, and camping. The general rule that applies is you may camp anywhere except in designated no camping areas. You are, however, encouraged to utilize sites that obviously have been used previously by campers. This is to lessen the impact on the natural areas.

Throughout the WMA system there are some spots that are specifically designated for camping, but these are described as dispersed camping areas. Generally, that means a clearing in the forest, some of which may have a fire ring or vault toilet, but in most cases have no facilities at all. Since there are literally hundreds of these clearings, they are not covered in this guide.

In the public campgrounds regulated by the Georgia Power Company, that corporation sets the rules. Here the regulations are much the same as for other developed camping areas, but there are some variations. These will be covered in later chapters as well.

At the federal level you find some of the most stringent regulations for camping, but that depends on the agency overseeing the sites. Georgia has no national parks within its borders, but the National Park Service does administer some national battlefield parks, historic sites, and recreation areas. None of those, however, maintain campgrounds.

On the other hand, the National Forest Service has a large number of sites spread across the more than 700,000 acres of the Chattahoochee and Oconee National Forests in North and Middle Georgia. These range from areas with quite liberal regulations on where you can camp to others requiring you to camp only in designated areas. Additionally, in the agency's official Wilderness Areas, only foot or horseback access is allowed, so usage is limited to only backpack camping.

The US Fish and Wildlife Service does maintain some campgrounds in several National Wildlife Refuges, including the 438,000 acres of the Okefenokee Swamp in South Georgia. Additionally, the National Park Service administers the campsites in the Cumberland Island National Seashore on the Peach State coast. Generally, these camping areas are rather primitive, offering minimal amenities.

The US Army Corps of Engineers oversees campgrounds situated on the shores of the major reservoirs it maintains in Georgia. These range from full-service RV parks to primitive locations.

All these federal campgrounds will be covered in detail in the following chapters.

Be prepared: Being well supplied for a camping adventure is essential to make it an enjoyable experience. Having the wrong clothing, footwear, or sleeping setup can make for uncomfortable days and long, sleepless nights. Also, expect your appetites to be keen when outdoors. Being constantly hungry or thirsty is an additional annoyance to avoid.

If you are venturing out in an RV, your chore is simplified. You likely have enough storage to bring along most of the amenities you enjoy at home. But, whether in a trailer or tent, your attire matters.

Layering of clothing is important in Georgia anytime and anywhere, with the exception of South Georgia in the summer months of June through August. From the mountains down to oceanfront, the temperature can change quickly in fall, winter, and spring. You also want good walking or hiking footwear to comfortably take advantage of all the trails available around the campgrounds.

As for sleeping gear, especially in tents, if you opt for an inflatable mattress, go ahead and spend the money to get a heavy-duty one. Saving money can mean waking in the night to find yourself sleeping on a "flat tire." The other option is to go with a solid foam sleeping pad or even a cot.

As noted, be sure to have plenty of food and water with you. When in the primitive campgrounds, you won't have a camp store available and primitive probably means being in an area where any stores are scarce. Additionally, some campgrounds don't even have water supplies. As for cooking, you are best advised to have a fuel-fired camp stove with you. Having electric outlets available or easily accessible is not guaranteed when camping.

Tossing food to a wild animal, such as this alligator, is just inviting it to hang around the campsites.

Safety: The most important tip regarding safety when camping is always to be aware of your surroundings. Part of the appeal of being outdoors is discovering the unexpected. But you don't want those surprises to be unexpected dangers.

A very important point to remember is that you should never feed wildlife while camping. Also, don't leave food where the critters can get to it on their own. That is simply an annoyance with regard to raccoons, mice, or squirrels. On the other hand, in the Georgia woods or on the water, it can become dangerous when involving bears or alligators. The northern mountains as well as some Middle and South Georgia swamps host black bears. These animals have keen senses of smell when it comes to food sources. Leave your food in the open and you may get unexpected visitors.

Around water in the southern half of the state, you likely are never far from alligators. Feeding them is courting danger for yourself, and even more so for your pets. The gators will gladly make a meal of Fido, if your dog gets in or near waters where the reptiles are present. And tossing marshmallows to a gator is inviting him to hang around your campsite.

Even if you are not injured in encounters with either of those animals due to making food available to them, wildlife managers have a saying that "a fed bear is a dead bear." That also applies to alligators. If those animals become accustomed to being fed, they pose a risk to anyone crossing paths with them. For that reason, they usually have to be trapped and euthanized. Bottom line is, don't kill them by feeding them.

If you are inclined to go trekking the trails in Georgia, always have a compass handy. Today we often are so addicted to technology that we forgo that basic gear in favor of a GPS unit or cell phone. Unfortunately, there are places in the Peach State where you won't get a signal for either one of those devices.

The layering of clothing mentioned earlier is important to ward off hypothermia and heat exhaustion, both of which can be encountered in Georgia. Also have plenty of water along when venturing out of camp to lessen the chances of encountering dehydration.

Of course, anytime you are in wild places in our state, you run the risk of encountering poison oak or ivy. Again, be aware of your surroundings and be careful of what you touch. Also, use plenty of bug repellant to ward off the abundant mosquitoes of the lowlands. Additionally, along the coast, you will encounter sand flies, known locally as no-see-ums. These tiny biting insects can make you miserable in a hurry.

Georgia is also home to five varieties of venomous snakes. Statewide you may encounter copperheads, while the northern portion of the state also holds timber rattlesnakes. Farther south the lowlands are home to diamondback rattlesnakes, water

The great majority of snakes in the state are nonvenomous such as this common water snake.

Camping etiquette is a two-way street.

moccasins, and coral snakes. Your best defense against these is again to be vigilant regarding your surroundings.

Probably the two most feared of all these dangers for most people are the snakes and bears. But there are two others that cause more injuries and deaths in the southeast every year than either of those. That would be yellow jackets and rocks. Swarms of the stinging wasps can be and have been lethal. Also, people taking that proverbial "one step closer" to cliffs and waterfalls have been sent hurdling off slippery rocks to injury or death at a far higher rate than from wildlife encounters.

Camping etiquette: Camping etiquette is a two-way street. If you have camped very much, you undoubtedly have a tale or two of how other discourteous campers have annoyed you. It is best to remember such events and make sure that you don't inflict that same atmosphere on anyone setting up camp near you.

Always check out the rules that apply to a campground you plan to visit and stick to them. While the purpose of some of the regulations may not be abundantly clear to you at the time, rest assured that past experience has guided the managers who put the rules in place.

Some of the regulations you will encounter are lengths of stay, limits on the number of campers on a site, how many and where vehicles may be parked, and the imposition of quiet hours.

Regarding the length of stay, in most RV parks, there will be a host or manager on site to remind you of when you need to vacate the site. In most of the primitive areas, this is not the case, so a bit of self-discipline is called for. Despite how much you are enjoying the campground, when time is up you need to move on. The same goes for having a lot of extra people and vehicles on hand. Remember that many of your fellow campers probably are trying to get away from crowds, not into one. Also, be cognizant when pitching tents or parking vehicles to not block any paths or driveways.

Having a bit of your favorite music playing can make your camp brighter, but keep in mind that your neighbor may not have the same tastes, so keep the volume at a reasonable level. That is especially true during designated quiet hours. There is nothing worse than trying to sleep while your tent or RV reverberates with a resonating bass line coming from a nearby campsite.

If you are camping with children or pets, we all realize that they may be the cutest and friendliest of their kind. Your neighboring campers may find them to be a joy to have visit their site. But make sure that those other campers make the first move to welcome them over. Otherwise keep the kids and animals under control and on your site.

At the heart of it, campground etiquette is nothing more than applying a bit of common sense and courtesy to your time in camp.

Map Legend

Transportation

≡⟨20⟩≡ Interstate Highway

≡⟨27⟩≡ US Highway

≡⟨53⟩≡ State Highway

Symbols

① Campground

⊛ Capital

○ City/Town

— - — - State Border

Water Features

Body of Water

Land Management

Region Area

Ridge and Valley Region

The Ridge and Valley Region of Georgia is located in the state's northwest corner, abutting the borders of Alabama on the west and Tennessee to the north. Topographically this area is dominated by the southern spine of Lookout Mountain, stretching down from Chattanooga, Tennessee, along with Taylor Ridge and Johns Mountain to the east. The western portion of the Conasauga Ranger District of the Chattahoochee National Forest protrudes into this region as well.

Calhoun, Dalton, Lafayette, and Rome are the major cities within this region, with all but Lafayette located in the wide, fertile valley to the east of the highlands and running from Dalton down toward Atlanta. That valley served as the conduit for Gen. William Tecumseh Sherman during his March to Atlanta during the Civil War. The battlefields at Chickamauga and Resaca during that campaign now are historic parks, with the former operated by the National Park Service and the latter in development by the State Parks and Historic Sites Division.

A yet earlier era of history is chronicled in the Native American sites located here. New Echota was the last capital of the Cherokee Nation and is now open to visitors under state management, as is the Chief Vann House in Spring Place. Portions of the original path of the Trail of Tears that forcibly took the native people to Oklahoma are also marked throughout the region.

The Etowah Indian Mounds State Historic Site is also located at the southern end of this region. This 54-acre complex of ceremonial mounds dates back at least 1,200 years, having been built by the people of the Mississippian Period.

The area is in the upper drainage of the Coosa River, which is formed in Rome at the junction of the Oostanaula and Etowah Rivers. The city has a history as an old riverboat town and sister city to Rome, Italy

Also located in Rome is Berry College, featuring the largest campus in the world at 27,000 acres. Founded by Martha Berry and financed in great part by Henry Ford, the fully accredited institution includes a working farm.

The geology of this region is composed of elongated parallel ridges underlain by Paleozoic sedimentary rocks. Those stone formations were laid down on the bottom of an inland sea that covered the region in ancient times. The ability of moving water

to wear away these softer rocks allowed the formation of Cloudland Canyon in this area. The canyon, which also is called Sitton Gulf, is the major feature of its namesake state park. Besides great vistas of the region, you also find a trail down into the canyon that features 587 stone or metal steps, going past two waterfalls.

This abandoned marble mine, with a small waterfall and reflecting pool, is a popular attraction in the state park.

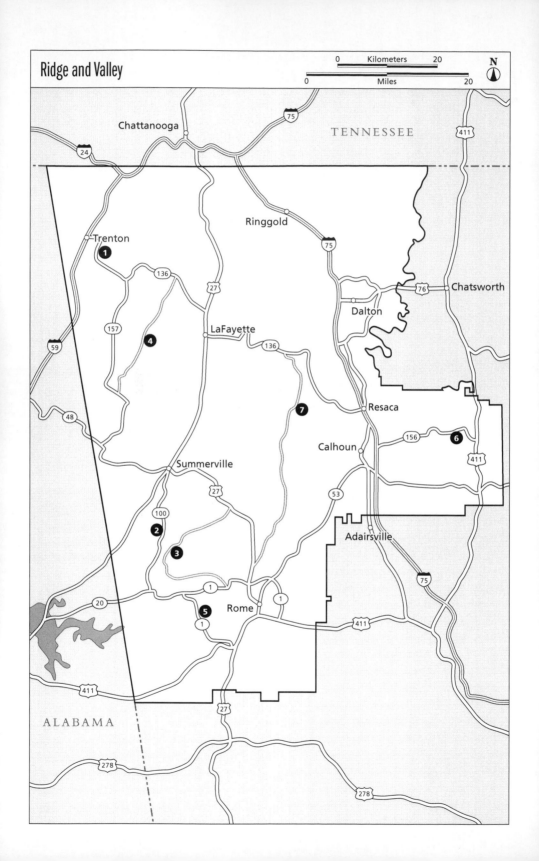

Ridge and Valley Region

Campgrounds At-A-Glance

#	Name	Total Sites	Group Sites	Hookup Sites	Hookups	Maximum RV Length	Dump Station	Toilets	Showers	Drinking Water	ADA	Fees	Reservations
Georgia State Parks and Historic Sites Division													
1	Cloudland Canyon State Park	119	4	72	WE	50	Y	F	Y	Y	Y	$-$$$$$	Y
2	James H. "Sloppy" Floyd State Park	28	0	24	WE	50	Y	F	Y	Y	Y	$$-$$$$$	Y
Georgia Wildlife Resources Division													
3	Rocky Mountain Recreation Area	45	0	36	WE	45	Y	F	Y	Y	Y	$$-$$$$$	Y
4	Sawmill Lake RV Campground	8	0	0	N	Any	N	N	N	N	N	N	N
County Parks													
5	Lock and Dam Park	31	0	31	WES	50	N	F	Y	Y	Y	$$$-$$$$	Y
6	Salacoa Creek Park	35	0	32	WE	45	Y	F	Y	Y	Y	$$	Y
USDA Forest Service													
7	The Pocket Recreation Area	28	0	0	N	26	N	F	N	Y	N	$$	N

See Amenities Chart key on page xxi.

1 Cloudland Canyon State Park

Recreation: Hiking, fishing, biking, playground, horseback riding
Location: 6 miles southeast of Trenton; 122 Cloudland Canyon Park Road, Rising Fawn 30738
GPS: N34 84.03' / W85 48.29'
Facilities and amenities: Flush toilets, showers, laundry, grills, fire rings, water, picnic tables, picnic pavilion, dump station, hiking, mountain biking and equestrian trails, disc golf, geocaching, caving (by permit only), fishing pond, playground, gift shop, interpretive center
Elevation: 1,764
Road conditions: Paved roads
Hookups: Water, electric
Sites: 62 standard RV/tent sites, 10 premium RV/tent sites, 30 walk-in tent sites, 13 backcountry tent sites, 4 pioneer campsites, 1 group lodge, 16 cottages, 10 yurts

Maximum RV length: 50

Season: Year-round, Apr–Nov peak season

Fees: Premium RV/tent site $42–$44, standard RV/tent site $38–$40, walk-in tent site $22, backcountry tent site $10, pioneer site $60, group lodge $240, 2-bedroom cottage $185–$220, 3-bedroom cottage $225, yurt $115, daily parking fee $5, annual pass $50

Maximum stay: 14 days

Management: Georgia State Parks and Historic Sites Division, 2610 Highway 155 SW, Stockbridge; (770) 389-7286; www.gastateparks.org

Reservations: (800) 864-7275; www.gastateparks.org/reservations

Pets: Dogs on 6-foot leashes allowed

Quiet hours: 10 p.m.–7 a.m.

Alcohol restrictions: Unlawful in public areas

ADA compliant: Yes

Finding the campground: From the intersection of GA 193, GA 136, and US 27 in LaFayette, take GA 136 north and follow the route for 20.8 miles. The park entrance is on the right.

About the campground: At 3,538 acres, Cloudland Canyon is one of Georgia's largest state parks. It is situated on the western edge of Lookout Mountain. The park features a 1,000-foot-deep canyon, two waterfalls, a cave system and miles of scenic hiking trails that provide overlooks into the canyon. There also is a full range of facilities and activities for the entire family.

The park has two RV/tent loops, one on the east rim near the visitor center and the other on the west rim of the canyon. The east loop is rather open, with sites tightly spaced and not offering much privacy. The west loop is more spacious, with the sites more separated. All the sites offer at least partial shade.

The walk-in tent campground is on the west rim, providing spacious, private settings.

2 James H. "Sloppy" Floyd State Park

Recreation: Hiking, fishing, boating, paddling, birding, playground

Location: 3.5 miles south of Summerville; 2800 Sloppy Floyd Lake Road, Summerville 30747

GPS: N34 43.99' / W85 33.73'

Facilities and amenities: Flush toilets, showers, laundry, fire rings, picnic tables, dump station, picnic areas and pavilions, playground, hiking trails, lakes, fishing docks, boat ramps, historic site

Elevation: 883

Road conditions: Paved roads

Hookups: Water, electric

Sites: 9 premium pull-through RV/tent sites, 15 standard RV/tent sites, 4 backcountry tent sites, 4 cottages

Maximum RV length: 50

Season: Year-round, Apr–Nov peak season

Fees: Premium RV/tent site $38, standard RV/tent site $34, backcountry tent site $15, cottage $180, daily parking fee $5, annual pass $50

Maximum stay: 14 days

Management: Georgia State Parks and Historic Sites Division, 2610 Highway 155 SW, Stockbridge; (770) 389-7286; www.gastateparks.org

Popular with visitors to Cloudland Canyon are the overlooks into the 1,000-foot-deep canyon.

Reservations: (800) 864-7275; www.gastateparks.org/reservations
Pets: Dogs on 6-foot leashes allowed
Quiet hours: 10 p.m.–7 a.m.
Alcohol restrictions: Unlawful in public areas
ADA compliant: Yes
Finding the campground: From the junction of US 27 and GA 48 in Summerville, go east on US 27 (Rome Boulevard) for 3 miles. Turn right on Sloppy Floyd Lake Road. At 3.1 miles the park entrance is on the right.
About the campground: James H. "Sloppy" Floyd State Park is named for a longtime local legislator, who got his nickname for the way his high school football uniform hung on his slender frame. The park covers 561 acres of land, containing two lakes, in the northwest quadrant of the state. It also was the site of mining operations in earlier times, with an abandoned marble mine featuring a small waterfall and reflecting pool, offering a major attraction along one of its hiking trails.

The park's RV campground is located in a shaded, forest area, with the sites well-spaced and offering privacy. The four backcountry tent sites are located on a spur trail off the park's Marble Mine Trail. The park also features four rental cottages.

3 Rocky Mountain Recreation Area

Recreation: Hiking, fishing, boating, paddling, biking, swimming, playground
Location: 17 miles northwest of Rome; 4054 Big Texas Valley Road, Rome 30165
GPS: N34 36.09' / W85 31.62'
Facilities and amenities: Flush toilets, showers, grills, water, picnic tables, picnic pavilion, picnic area, playground, dump station, hiking and mountain biking trails, archery range, geocaching, lakes, fishing pier, hunting, boat ramp, swimming beach, historic site
Elevation: 904
Road conditions: Paved roads
Hookups: Water, electric
Sites: 34 standard RV/tent sites, 2 double RV/tent sites; 9 walk-in tent sites
Maximum RV length: 45
Season: Year-round, Apr–Nov peak season
Fees: Standard RV/tent site $25, double RV tent site $50, walk-in tent site $12, pioneer site $55, daily parking fee $5, annual pass $30
Maximum stay: 14 days
Management: Georgia Wildlife Resources Division, 2067 US Highway 278 SE, Social Circle; (706) 557-3333; www.georgiawildlife.com
Reservations: (800) 336-2661; www.gooutdoorsgeorgia.com
Pets: Dogs on 6-foot leashes allowed
Quiet hours: 10 p.m.–7 a.m.
Alcohol restrictions: Alcohol allowed only in the campground
ADA compliant: Yes
Finding the campground: From Rome, go 10.4 miles north on US 27. Turn left on Sike Storey Road for 0.4 mile. Turn left onto Big Texas Valley Road for 5.4 miles. The entrance is on the left.

Visitors to James H. Floyd State Park can fish or kayak either of two stocked lakes or hike the 5 miles of trails within the park.

About the campground: Rocky Mountain Recreation Area is a 5,000-acre tract in west Georgia, owned by Oglethorpe Power Company and managed by the Georgia Department of Natural Resources as a Public Fishing Area. The area contains 357-acre Antioch Lake and 202-acre Heath Lake.

Fishing is the main attraction of the area, but it also has a range of other options for family activities. The area is open to waterfowl and archery hunting in the fall and winter. There is a commercial trading post and bait shop just across Big Texas Valley Road from the area entrance.

The campground is located on the shore of Antioch Lake, with some RV and tent sites on the water. The campground gates close at 10 p.m. with no admittance until sunrise without special arrangements with the camp host. Only registered campers are allowed after the gates close.

4 Sawmill Lake RV Campground

Recreation: Hiking
Location: 11.4 miles southwest of LaFayette; Rocky Lane, Crockford-Pigeon Mountain Wildlife Management Area
GPS: N34 66.86' / W85 39.20'
Facilities and amenities: Fire rings, picnic tables
Elevation: 1,860

Road conditions: Steep, winding, gravel, dirt road

Hookups: None

Sites: 8 RV/tent sites

Maximum RV length: Any

Season: Year-round, Apr–Nov peak season

Fees: None

Maximum stay: None

Management: Georgia Wildlife Resources Division, 2067 US Highway 278 SE, Social Circle; (706) 557-3333; www.georgiawildlife.com

Reservations: No

Pets: Only hunting dogs allowed

Quiet hours: 10 p.m.–7 a.m.

Alcohol restrictions: Alcohol allowed only in the campground

ADA compliant: No

Finding the campground: From US 27 in LaFayette, go west on GA 193 for 3.5 miles. Turn left onto Chamberlain Road and go 3.5 miles. Turn right on Rocky Lane. At 6.7 miles the campground is on the right.

About the campground: The campground is located in Crockford-Pigeon Mountain Wildlife Management Area, which covers 20,657 acres atop its namesake mountain. The WMA is named for Jack Crockford, a former director of the old Georgia Game and Fish Commission and for the now extinct passenger pigeons that inhabited the mountain.

The campground consists of a large open, grassy field surrounded by eight campsites. These are quite primitive, offering virtually no facilities, except level ground for parking RVs. This is a site used by hunters in the fall and winter or those who really like to get away from civilization.

The drive to Pigeon Mountain is steep in places and the vistas can be spectacular. Another field a few hundred yards to the east offers very primitive tent camping, and small Sawmill Lake is nearby.

5 Lock and Dam Park

Recreation: Hiking, fishing, boating, paddling, playground

Location: 9.7 miles southeast of downtown Rome; 181 Lock and Dam Road, Rome 30161

GPS: W34 19.92' / N85 25.57'

Facilities and amenities: Flush toilets, picnic tables, fire pits, grills, showers, laundry, dump station, playground, horseshoe pits, pavilion, amphitheater, boat ramp, fishing, trading post, bait shop, exhibit center, historic site

Elevation: 582

Road conditions: Level, paved roads

Hookups: Water, electric, sewer

Sites: 8 RV sites with full hookups, 21 RV/tent sites with water and electric hookups, 2 tent sites with water and electric hookups

Maximum RV length: 50

Season: Year-round, Mar–Nov peak season

Fees: Premium RV sites $34, standard RV/tent sites $32, tent sites $28, $2 daily parking pass

Maximum stay: 14 days
Management: Rome–Floyd County Parks and Recreation Department, 1 Shorter Avenue, Rome; (706) 291-0766; www.rfpra.com
Reservations: (706) 234-5601; www.BookYourSite.com; credit cards only
Pets: Dogs on 6-foot leashes allowed
Quiet hours: 10 p.m.–7 a.m.
Alcohol restrictions: No alcohol allowed
ADA compliant: Yes
Finding the campground: From the junction of US 411 and US 27 in south Rome, go west on US 411 for 0.8 mile. Turn right onto GA 1 (West Rome By-pass) and drive 4 miles to Blacks Bluff Road. Turn right and go 1 mile to Lock and Dam Road on the left. The park is 0.4 mile down this road.
About the campground: The park is on the site of the old Mayo Bar Lock and Dam on the Coosa River that dates from 1915. This facility allowed navigation upriver to Rome. The dam has now been partially removed and the lock serves as a fishing pier. The striped bass and crappie fishing is some of the best in the state and a major draw for the campground. The entire complex is on the National Registry of Historic Landmarks.

The campground offers some sites overlooking the river with small pavilions. All the sites are closely spaced on level ground. The overstory of trees provides full, partial, or no shade depending on the site you choose.

6 Salacoa Creek Park

Recreation: Hiking, fishing, boating, paddling, swimming, playground
Location: 6.4 miles northwest of Ranger; 388 Park Drive, Ranger 30734
GPS: N34 53.21' / W84 75.92'
Facilities and amenities: Flush toilets, showers, fire ring, picnic table, wooden deck, dump station, picnic pavilion, swimming beach, boat launch, rental boats, fishing dock, playgrounds, nature trail, concessions
Elevation: 669
Road conditions: Paved with some steep grades
Hookups: Water, electric
Sites: 32 RV sites with water and electric hookups, 3 primitive tent sites
Maximum RV length: 45
Season: Apr–Nov
Fees: RV site $18, tent site $11, $3 day-use fee
Maximum stay: 14 days
Management: Gordon County Parks and Recreation Department, 201 North Wall Street, Calhoun; (706) 629-3795; www.gordoncounty.org
Reservations: (706) 629-3490; www.gordoncounty.org/departments/salacoa-creek-park/
Pets: Dogs on 6-foot leashes allowed
Quiet hours: 10 p.m.–7 a.m.
Alcohol restrictions: No alcohol allowed
ADA compliant: Yes

Finding the campground: From exit 315 on I-75, go west on GA 156 (Red Bud Road) for 10 miles. Turn right on Park Drive. The park entrance is at 0.4 mile.

About the campground: Salacoa Creek Park covers 364 acres of rolling hills in northwest Georgia. The major attraction of this county-owned facility is 126-acre Salacoa Lake (also identified as Defoor Walters Lake), which makes it a favorite with anglers. The park also features activities for the entire family and allows day use by visitors for a fee. The nature trail and swimming beach are two of the most popular attractions.

The campground is rather hilly, with sites close together. Some of those overlook the lake and all are shaded. Each of the sites has a picnic table, fire ring, and wooden deck.

7 The Pocket Recreation Area

Recreation: Hiking, fishing
Location: 13 miles northwest of Calhoun; Pocket Campground Road, Johns Mountain Wildlife Management Area
GPS: N34 58.48' / W85 08.53'
Facilities and amenities: Flush toilets, water, picnic tables, fire rings, picnic area, hiking, fishing
Elevation: 944
Road conditions: Level and paved
Hookups: None
Sites: 28 RV/tent sites
Maximum RV length: 26
Season: Apr–Oct 31
Fees: RV/tent site $15
Maximum stay: 14 days
Management: USDA Forest Service, Conasauga Ranger District, 3941 US Highway 76, Chatsworth; (706) 695-6736; www.fs.usda.gov/recarea/conf/recarea/?recid=10460
Reservations: No
Pets: Dogs on 6-foot leashes allowed
Quiet hours: 10 p.m.–6 a.m.
Alcohol restrictions: No alcohol allowed
ADA compliant: Yes
Finding the campground: From US 41 in Calhoun, go west on GA 156 (Roland Mayes Parkway) for 11.8 miles. Turn right on Everett Springs Road. At 11.6 miles the campground is on the right.
About the campground: This recreation area is located within both the Chattahoochee National Forest and the state's Johns Mountain Wildlife Management Area. Along the drive to the campground, you pass some dispersed campsites on Johns Creek along Everett Springs Road. The campground is on the site formerly used by Camp F-16 of the Civilian Conservation Corps.

The main attractions of this campground are hiking the 2.8-mile loop of The Pocket Trail, springs that bubble up within the campground, and the trout fishing in nearby Johns Creek.

The campground itself is on level ground in a single loop. The sites are well spaced and all provide shade.

Blue Ridge Mountain Region

The Blue Ridge Mountain Region of Georgia stretches across the highlands in the north-central and northeastern portions of the state. An imaginary line drawn down US 411 from the Tennessee border to the town of Chatsworth, then turning east through Ellijay, Gainesville, and Toccoa before reaching the South Carolina border would roughly define this region.

The bulk of the Chattahoochee National Forest's 750,000 acres of land lies within that area, composed of the Blue Ridge Ranger District in the west and Chattooga River Ranger District to the east. This vast domain is home to black bears, white-tailed deer, wild turkeys, and a host of smaller animals. It also contains a number of river drainages that are home to both stocked and wild rainbow, brown, and brook trout. Needless to say, this is a paradise for hunters and anglers alike.

Equally appealing to anglers and water sports enthusiasts, this mountain realm holds half a dozen large man-made reservoirs, around which are found myriad campgrounds, boat ramps, and day-use areas. Carters Lake is on the western edge of this region, situated on the Coosawattee River, a tributary of the Etowah. Although the classic movie *Deliverance* was filmed in northeast Georgia, James Dickey's novel that spawned the film was actually based on the author's canoeing adventures on the Coosawattee prior to the building of Carters Lake.

The other river names like Toccoa, Etowah, Chattahoochee, Tallulah, and Chattooga harken back to the time when the Cherokee tribe ruled the area. Petroglyphs from even earlier Native Americans are found on the rocks of Track Rock Gap, along with the rocky face of Yonah Mountain, Stone Pile Gap, and the mounds in Nacoochee Valley all figuring in the Indian lore as well. Another highlight on the western edge of the region is Fort Mountain, located in the state park bearing the same name. Across its top a stone wall gives the peak its moniker. Who built this fortification has been lost in history, since it predates even the Cherokee Tribe.

The region also is traversed by a maze of hiking, mountain biking, and equestrian trails. Among these are the first 80 miles of the Appalachian Trail (AT), as it begins its long journey to Maine. Sharing portions of the same pathway in Georgia, the Benton McKaye Trail—named for the driving force behind the establishment of the

AT—winds through the western portion of the region, passing into East Tennessee on a 240-plus-mile course to rejoining the AT in the Great Smoky Mountains National Park. The eastern portion of the region is crossed by the Bartram Trail, which tracks the travels of naturalist William Bartram as he explored the area from 1773 to 1777. Along the way, this 35-mile path crosses Georgia's second highest peak on 4,696-foot Rabun Bald, then descends to continue down the valley of the Chattooga River National Wild and Scenic River Corridor. It was on this portion of the river that Burt Reynolds, Jon Voight, Ned Beatty, and crew actually filmed much of the film *Deliverance*.

In the western part of the region, the burgeoning vacation town of Blue Ridge has been named the Trout Capital of Georgia by the state's General Assembly. Driving east past Amicalola Falls, the third-highest waterfall east of the Mississippi River at 729 feet, puts you in the mid-portion of the region. Here you find Dahlonega, the site of a gold rush in the 1830s and '40s. The old courthouse is now the Dahlonega Gold Museum State Historic Site and is well worth a visit, or you might want to take an underground tour in the historic Consolidated Gold Mine. Farther east, Helen morphed from a sawmill town into a faux Bavarian village, tourist attraction, and home to Oktoberfest each fall. Anchoring the eastern end of the region are the towns of Clayton and Dillard along US 441. The Foxfire Museum is situated between those villages in several restored period farm structures, offering a peek into pioneer life, folklore, and mountain crafts through their nationally acclaimed oral history projects.

◀ *Lake Trahlyta's 22 acres offer a variety of recreational opportunities on the water, including a swimming beach and pedal-boat rental.*

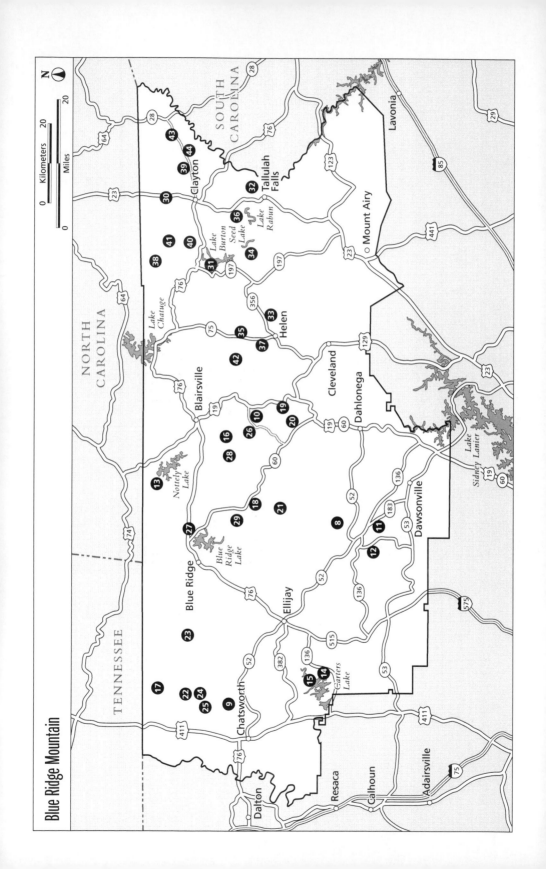

Blue Ridge Ranger District

Campgrounds At-A-Glance

#	Name	Total Sites	Group Sites	Hookup Sites	Hookups	Maximum RV Length	Dump Station	Toilets	Showers	Drinking Water	ADA	Fees	Reservations
Georgia State Parks and Historic Sites Division													
8	Amicalola Falls State Park	24	0	24	WE	92	Y	F	Y	Y	Y	$$$$$	Y
9	Fort Mountain State Park	83	3	66	WE	50	Y	F	Y	Y	Y	$$-$$$$$	Y
10	Vogel State Park	98	1	79	WE	40	Y	F	Y	Y	Y	$$$-$$$$$	Y
Georgia Wildlife Resources Division													
11	Lindsey Ford Amicalola River Access Campground	6	0	0	N	NA	N	N	N	N	N	N	N
12	Wildcat Campground	3	0	0	N	24	N	N	N	N	N	N	N
County Parks													
13	Poteete Creek Campground	59	0	54	WES	40	Y	F	Y	Y	Y	$$-$$$$	Y
US Army Corps of Engineers													
14	Doll Mountain Campground	57	1	37	WE	62	Y	F	Y	Y	Y	$$-$$$$$	Y
15	Woodring Branch Campground	42	1	30	WE	40	Y	F	Y	Y	Y	$$-$$$	Y
USDA Forest Service													
16	Cooper Creek Recreation Area	14	1	0	N	35	N	V	N	Y	Y	$$-$$$	Y
17	Cottonwood Patch Campground	8	0	0	N	20	N	V	N	N	Y	$	N
18	Deep Hole Recreation Area	9	0	0	N	35	N	V	N	N	Y	$$	Y
19	DeSoto Falls Recreation Area	23	0	0	N	40	N	F	Y	Y	Y	$-$$$$	Y
20	Dockery Lake Recreation Area	10	0	0	N	24	N	V F	N	Y	Y	$	N
21	Frank Gross Recreation Area	8	0	0	N	35	N	V	N	N	Y	$	Y
22	Hickey Gap Campground	5	0	0	N	24	N	V	N	N	Y	N	N

Campgrounds At-A-Glance

#	Name	Total Sites	Group Sites	Hookup Sites	Hookups	Maximum RV Length	Dump Station	Toilets	Showers	Drinking Water	ADA	Fees	Reservations
23	Jacks River Fields Campground	7	0	0	N	24	N	V	N	N	Y	$	N
24	Lake Conasauga Recreation Area	31	0	0	N	24	N	F	N	Y	Y	$$	Y
25	Lake Conasauga Overflow Campground	6	0	0	N	NA	N	V	N	N	Y	$	N
26	Lake Winfield Scott Recreation Area	31	1	5	WE	40	N	F	Y	Y	Y	$$$–$$$$$	Y
27	Morganton Point Recreation Area	37	2	37	WE	30	Y	F	Y	Y	Y	$$$–$$$$$	Y
28	Mulky Campground	11	0	0	N	35	N	V	N	Y	Y	$–$$	Y
29	Toccoa River Sandy Bottoms Recreation Area	4	0	0	N	NA	N	V	N	N	N	$	N

See Amenities Chart key on page xxi.

8 Amicalola Falls State Park

Recreation: Hiking, fishing, playground
Location: 13.5 miles northwest of Dawsonville; 418 Amicalola Falls Road, Dawsonville 30534
GPS: N34 56.27' / W84 24.76'
Facilities and amenities: Flush toilets, showers, laundry, dump station, picnic tables, fire rings, water, hiking and fitness trails, fishing, archery range, geocaching, zip lines, rock climbing wall, playground, picnic areas, waterfall, lodge, gift shop, restaurant, visitor center
Elevation: 1,877
Road conditions: Paved roads. The road up to the campground is very steep at a 25 percent grade
Hookups: Water, electric
Sites: 24 standard RV/tent sites with hookups; 14 cabins, 57-guest-room lodge
Maximum RV length: 92
Season: Year-round, Apr–Oct peak season
Fees: Standard RV/tent site $47, cabins $289, lodge rooms $169, daily parking fee $5, annual pass $50
Maximum stay: 14 days

The cascading 729-foot Amicalola Falls is the third tallest waterfall east of the Mississippi River.

Management: Georgia State Parks and Historic Sites Division, 2610 Georgia Highway 155 SW, Stockbridge; (770) 389-7286; www.gastateparks.org
Reservations: (706) 344-1500; www.amicalolafallslodge.com
Pets: Dogs on 6-foot leashes allowed
Quiet hours: 10 p.m.–7 a.m.
Alcohol restrictions: Unlawful in public areas
ADA compliant: Yes
Finding the campground: From US 76 / GA 515 in Ellijay, travel 19.2 miles east on GA 52. The park entrance is on the left.
About the campground: Amicalola Falls State Park takes its name from the 729-foot cascade located on Little Amicalola Creek within its boundaries. This is the third-tallest waterfall east of the Mississippi River. The park is also the jumping-off point for the Appalachian Trail. A roughly 8-mile path leads from the park up to Springer Mountain and the official beginning of that 2,180-plus mile pathway running to Mount Katahdin in Maine. The park covers a total of 829 acres, offering a wide range of activities for the entire family.

The approach up the mountain to the top of the falls and the campground is on a paved road, but it is very steep. The campground is on relatively level ground, with sites offering at least partial shade.

⑨ Fort Mountain State Park

Recreation: Hiking, fishing, boating, paddling, biking, swimming, playground, horseback riding
Location: 7.5 miles east of Chatsworth; 181 Fort Mountain Park Road, Chatsworth 30705
GPS: N34 76.13' / W84 70.27'
Facilities and amenities: Flush toilets, showers, laundry, dump station, water, grills, picnic tables, cable TV hookups, hiking/biking/equestrian trails, geocaching, miniature golf, swimming beach, playground, boat rentals, historic sites, gift shop, 17-acre lake
Elevation: 2,579
Road conditions: Paved roads throughout the campground, steep winding approaches from both east and west
Hookups: Water, electric
Sites: 37 premium RV/tent sites with hookups, 29 standard RV/tent sites with hookups, 4 walk-in tent sites, 6 platform tent sites, 4 backcountry tent sites, 3 pioneer campsite, 15 cottages
Maximum RV length: 50
Season: Year-round, Apr–Nov peak season
Fees: Premium RV/tent site $37–$39, standard RV/tent site $35–$37, walk-in tent site $20, platform tent site $14, backcountry tent site $12, 2-bedroom cottage $200, 3-bedroom cottage $300, daily parking fee $5, annual pass $50
Maximum stay: 14 days
Management: Georgia State Parks and Historic Sites Division, 2610 Georgia Highway 155 SW, Stockbridge; (770) 389-7286; www.gastateparks.org
Reservations: (800) 864-7275; www.gastateparks.org/reservations
Pets: Dogs on 6-foot leashes allowed
Quiet hours: 10 p.m.–7 a.m.

The 17-acre lake is popular for cooling off from the summertime heat.

Alcohol restrictions: Unlawful in public areas
ADA compliant: Yes
Finding the campground: From US 411 in Chatsworth, travel 7.5 miles east on GA 52 (East Fort Street). The park entrance is on the left.
About the campground: Fort Mountain State Park covers 3,712 acres atop its namesake mountain at the western end of the Cohutta Mountain Range. The park elevation is 2,850 feet above sea level, as it towers above the Ridge and Valley Region to the west. The park opened in 1936, with many of the features within constructed by the Civilian Conservation Corps during the Great Depression.

The park is home to an 855-foot-long stone wall thought to have been built between 500 and 1500 AD by a race the Cherokee tribe called the Moon-eyed people. Virtually nothing is known about those folks or why they constructed the wall. It did, however, provide the name for the mountain and park.

The other major features of the park are a four-story, stone fire tower and 17-acre Fort Mountain Lake, both constructed by the CCC. Additionally, the park offers a variety of amenities that make it attractive to families and outdoor groups.

The adjacent Lake Side and Creek Side loops make up the campground. Seven premium sites in the Lake Side area are positioned on the lake, as are the six platform tent sites. The four backcountry tent sites are located along the 8.2-mile Gahuti Trail that circles the mountaintop, while the four walk-in sites are in the Creek Side loop.

10 Vogel State Park

Recreation: Hiking, fishing, paddling, biking, swimming, playground
Location: 11 miles south of Blairsville; 405 Vogel State Park Road, Blairsville 30512
GPS: N34 76.59' / W83 92.54'
Facilities and amenities: Flush toilets, showers, laundry, grills, water, picnic tables, picnic pavilion, dump station, swimming beach, canoe, kayak, paddleboard/pedal boat rentals, amphitheater, hiking/mountain biking trails, miniature golf, playground, trading post, CCC museum, visitor center
Elevation: 2,328
Road conditions: Paved roads
Hookups: Water, electric
Sites: 38 premium RV/tent sites with hookups, 41 standard RV/tent sites with hookups, 18 walk-in tent sites, 1 pioneer site, 34 cottages
Maximum RV length: 40
Season: Year-round, Apr–Nov peak season
Fees: Premier RV/tent site $42–$44, standard RV/tent site $38–$40, walk-in tent site $30, pioneer site $60, efficiency cottage $135, 1-bedroom cottage $155, 2-bedroom cottage $230, 3-bedroom cottage $260, daily parking fee $5, annual pass $50
Maximum stay: 14 days
Management: Georgia State Parks and Historic Sites Division, 2610 Georgia Highway 155 SW, Stockbridge; (770) 389-7286; www.gastateparks.org
Reservations: (800) 864-7275; www.gastateparks.org/reservations
Pets: Dogs on 6-foot leashes allowed
Quiet hours: 10 p.m.–7 a.m.
Alcohol restrictions: Unlawful in public areas
ADA compliant: Yes
Finding the campground: From the Cleveland town square take US 129 for 21 miles north. The park entrance is on the left.
About the campground: Vogel is one of Georgia's oldest state parks and is considered by many to be the best in the system. Created in 1931 by the Civilian Conservation Corps during the Great Depression, it covers 233 acres and contains within its boundaries 22-acre Lake Trahlyta, the CCC Museum, and Trahlyta Falls on Wolf Creek. The park offers a wide variety of activities and amenities for the entire family, including the trailhead for the 13-plus-mile Coosa Backcountry Trail.

The campground spreads along either side of Wolf Creek in the relatively level stream valley. The sites are mostly shaded, but they are grouped quite close together.

11 Lindsey Ford Amicalola River Access Campground

Recreation: Fishing, boating, paddling
Location: 12 miles northwest of Dawsonville; Amicalola Church Road, Marble Hill 30148
GPS: N34 47.52' / W84 24.29'
Facilities and amenities: Tent pads, fire rings, picnic tables, lantern posts, canoe and kayak launch

The aerial view of Lake Trahlyta is quite stunning any time of the year.

Elevation: 1,375
Road conditions: Approach roads from the north and south as well as in the campground are dirt and gravel
Hookups: None
Sites: 6 tent sites with no hookups
Maximum RV length: NA
Season: Year-round, Apr–Oct peak season
Fees: Annual Public Land-use pass $30
Maximum stay: 14 days
Management: Georgia Wildlife Resources Division, 2067 US Highway 278 SE, Social Circle; (706) 557-3333; www.georgiawildlife.com
Reservations: No
Pets: Dogs on 6-foot leashes allowed
Quiet hours: 10 p.m.–6 a.m.
Alcohol restrictions: Alcohol allowed only in the campground
ADA compliant: No
Finding the campground: From the junction of GA 9 and GA 53 in Dawsonville, go west on GA 53 for 10.8 miles. Turn right onto Steve Tate Highway and proceed 4.3 miles. Turn right on Afton Road and at 1.5 miles turn right onto gravel Amicalola Church Road. At 0.4 mile the campground entrance is on the left.
About the campground: The campground at Lindsey Ford is a primitive setting with minimal facilities. Despite the camping area's name, it is on the shore of upper Amicalola Creek, which is large enough to be a river by North Georgia mountain standards.

This site in the Dawson Forest Wildlife Management Area is used almost exclusively by anglers trout fishing on the creek and paddlers using the canoe or kayak launch for trips on the stream. The Amicalola's rapids are known to be second only to those on the Chattooga River among Peach State whitewater runs.

All users must have a hunting or fishing license or a Public Land-use pass.

12 Wildcat Campground

Recreation: Hiking, fishing
Location: 16 miles northwest of Dawsonville; Wildcat Campground Road, Dawson Forest Wildlife Management Area
GPS: N34 48.53' / W84 28.09'
Facilities and amenities: Fire ring, picnic tables, hiking trails
Elevation: 1,525
Road conditions: The dirt road from Steve Tate Highway to the campground is very rough and suitable only for vehicles with high suspension or 4-wheel drive.
Hookups: None
Sites: 3 RV/tent sites with no hookups
Maximum RV length: 24
Season: Year-round, Apr–Nov peak season
Fees: Users must have a hunting or fishing license or an annual Public Land-use pass $30

Maximum stay: 14 days

Management: Georgia Wildlife Resources Division, 2067 US Highway 278 SE, Social Circle; (706) 557-3333; www.georgiawildlife.com

Reservations: No

Pets: Dogs on 6-foot leashes allowed

Quiet hours: 10 p.m.–6 a.m.

Alcohol restrictions: Alcohol allowed only in the campground

ADA compliant: No

Finding the campground: From the junction of GA 53 and GA 9 in Dawsonville, travel west for 10.8 miles. Turn right on Steve Tate Highway and go 7.2 miles. Make a left turn onto Wildcat Campground Road and drive 0.9 mile to its end in the campground.

About the campground: This small, primitive camping area is on the Amicalola Tract of the Dawson Forest Wildlife Management Area. Though it offers minimal facilities, it is popular with hikers due to the extensive trail system that begins there. Also, seasonal trout fishing is available in Amicalola Creek on which it is located, while the area is open to managed hunts in the fall and winter.

A few points to note are that camping here is free, but you must possess a hunting or fishing license or a Public Land–use pass in order to be on the WMA property. Those can be obtained at www.gooutdoorsgeorgia.com, however, internet service is poor at the campground, so make your purchase before arriving. Additionally, some sources list the campground as being on Red Fox Drive, which is incorrect. Google Maps shows it twice, once at that location, as well as having it in its proper position. Finally, the last mile of road from Steve Tate Highway is dirt, and the Georgia Wildlife Resources Division recommends vehicles traversing it to have high suspension clearance or 4-wheel drive.

Despite those concerns, the campground is appealingly clean, with an open understory. In addition to the three marked sites, there is room for tent camping here, which is also allowed. The entire campground is heavily wooded and shaded.

13 Poteete Creek Campground

Recreation: Swimming, fishing, boating

Location: 13.5 miles northwest of Blairsville; 1040 Poteete Creek Road, Blairsville 30512

GPS: N34 94.83' / W84 09.48'

Facilities and amenities: Flush toilets, showers, grills, water, picnic tables, picnic pavilion, dump station, swimming beach, horseshoe pits, boat ramp

Elevation: 1,786

Road conditions: Gravel lanes within the campground

Hookups: Water, electric, sewer

Sites: 3 premium RV sites with full hookups, 11 premium RV/tent sites with water and electric hookups, 40 standard RV/tent sites with water and electric hookups, 5 tent sites with no hookups

Maximum RV length: 40

Season: Apr 1–Oct 15

Fees: Premium RV/tent site $35, standard RV/tent site $30, tent site $20, $5 daily parking pass required

Maximum stay: Entire season

Management: Union County Parks and Recreation Department, 519 Industrial Boulevard, Blairsville 30512; www.unioncountyga.gov/parks-recreation/poteete-creek-camp-ground-cap/
Reservations: (706) 439-6103
Pets: Limit of 2 dogs allowed on 6-foot leashes
Quiet hours: 11 p.m.–7 a.m.
Alcohol restrictions: No alcohol allowed
ADA compliant: Yes
Finding the campground: From Blairsville go 7.5 miles west on US 76 / GA 515. Turn right on Nottely Dam Road (GA 325). Proceed 7.5 miles and turn right on Poteete Creek Road. The campground is on the right at 1.1 miles.
About the campground: The campground is on the shore of 4,180-acre Nottely Lake, a Tennessee Valley Authority reservoir on the Nottely River. The Poteete Creek complex is very popular and allows daily, weekly, monthly, and season rentals. Reservations are recommended, since the facility stays booked up. It is a family-friendly campground with no alcoholic beverages allowed and strict quiet times. Also, the main gate is locked from 10 p.m. to 7 a.m. nightly.

There are 14 lakeside campsites very near the water, with the rest located up a slight rise overlooking the lake. All sites are shaded to partially shaded, with all the amenities located close by.

14 Doll Mountain Campground

Recreation: Fishing, boating, playground
Location: 13 miles southwest of Ellijay; 1362 Doll Mountain Road, Ellijay 30540
GPS: N34 36.48' / W84 37.26'
Facilities and amenities: Flush toilets, showers, dump station, water, grills, picnic tables, playground, boat ramp
Elevation: 1,105
Road conditions: Paved roads, entrance drive has a steep downhill grade
Hookups: Water, electric
Sites: 36 standard RV/tent sites with hookups, 1 tent site with hookups, 19 tent sites with no hookups, 1 group site
Maximum RV length: 62
Season: Apr–Oct
Fees: Standard RV/tent site $28, tent site with hookups $24, tent site with no hookups $18, group site $100
Maximum stay: 14 days
Management: US Army Corps of Engineers, 1850 Carters Dam Road, Chatsworth; (706) 334-2248; www.recreation.gov/camping/campgrounds/232575?tab=info
Reservations: (877) 444-6777; www.recreation.gov
Pets: Dogs on 6-foot leashes allowed
Quiet hours: 10 p.m.–6 a.m.
Alcohol restrictions: No alcohol allowed
ADA compliant: Yes

Finding the campground: From GA 515 at Talking Rock, take GA 136 west for 9 miles. Turn right on GA 382 and go 3.4 miles to Doll Mountain Road on the left. Follow Doll Mountain Road for 1.4 miles to the campground entrance.

About the campground: Camping at Doll Mountain is by reservation only and no drive-throughs or sightseeing is allowed. The access road in the campground has a steep downhill grade.

The campground is on the shore of 3,200-acre Carters Lake. According to the Army Corps of Engineers, the lake reaches depths in excess of 450 feet and is one of the deepest reservoirs east of the Mississippi River. The lake offers fishing and boating access. There are no private homes or development on the lakeshore, thus it remains in a very natural state.

Although some campsites provide lake views, the sites are far up on the steep hillside. The entire campground is heavily wooded, shading all the sites. Four of those are pull-through sites.

15 Woodring Branch Campground

Recreation: Hiking, fishing, boating, biking, swimming, playground
Location: 18.5 miles southwest of Ellijay; 5026 Woodring Branch Road, Ellijay 30540
GPS: N34 40.14' / W84 32.60'
Facilities and amenities: Flush toilets, showers, dump station, water, grills, picnic tables, lantern posts, playground, hiking and mountain biking trails, boat ramp, swimming beach
Elevation: 1,183
Road conditions: Paved roads
Hookups: Water, electric
Sites: 30 standard RV/tent sites with hookups, 10 tent sites with no hookups, 2 group sites
Maximum RV length: 40
Season: May–Sep
Fees: Standard RV/tent site with hookups $28, tent-only site with no hookups $18, group sites $20
Maximum stay: 14 days
Management: US Army Corps of Engineers, 1850 Carters Dam Road, Chatsworth; (706) 334-2248; www.recreation.gov/camping/campgrounds/232751?tab=info
Reservations: (877) 444-6777; www.recreation.gov
Pets: Dogs on 6-foot leashes allowed
Quiet hours: 10 p.m.–6 a.m.
Alcohol restrictions: No alcohol allowed
ADA compliant: Yes
Finding the campground: From the junction with Old GA 5 in Ellijay, travel 12.4 miles west on US 76. Turn left onto Woodring Branch Road and drive 4.3 miles to the recreation area entrance.
About the campground: Located in the Woodring Branch Recreation Area, the campground is on the shore of 3,200-acre Carters Lake. According to the Army Corps of Engineers, the lake reaches depths in excess of 450 feet and is one of the deepest reservoirs east of the Mississippi River. The lake offers fishing and boating access. There are no private homes or development on the lakeshore, thus it remains in a very natural state.

Although some campsites provide lake views, the sites are far up on the steep hillside. The entire campground is heavily wooded, shading all the sites.

16 Cooper Creek Recreation Area

Recreation: Hiking, fishing
Location: 25 miles southwest of Blairsville; FS 236, Blue Ridge Wildlife Management Area
GPS: N34 76.28' / W84 06.83'
Facilities and amenities: Vault toilet, grills, water, picnic tables, lantern posts, hiking trails
Elevation: 2,209
Road conditions: Roads from the east and west are gravel and dirt, as are the ones in the campground
Hookups: None
Sites: 13 RV/tent sites, 1 tent-only site, 1 group site
Maximum RV length: 35
Season: Year-round, Apr–Oct peak season, water is cut off Nov 1–Mar 31
Fees: RV/tent site $15, tent-only site $15, group site $30
Maximum stay: 14 days
Management: USDA Forest Service, Blue Ridge Ranger District, 2042 Georgia Highway 515 West, Blairsville; (706) 745-6928; www.recreation.gov/camping/campgrounds/10156125?tab=info
Reservations: (877) 444-6777; www.recreation.gov
Pets: Dogs on 6-foot leashes allowed
Quiet hours: 10 p.m.–6 a.m.
Alcohol restrictions: No alcohol allowed
ADA compliant: Yes
Finding the campground: From Dahlonega go 26 miles north on GA 60. Turn right onto FS 4 (Cooper Creek Road, but changes name to Mulky Gap Road at the bridge over Sea Creek). The campground is at 6 miles on the right at the junction with FS 236. Be aware that a long portion of the approach on Forest Service property is on a gravel road.
About the campground: Cooper Creek Campground is closely associated with the nearby Mulky Campground. Those two facilities share a camp host, who is located at the Cooper Creek site. Also, the numbering of the campsites is in combination. Sites 1 to 11 are at Mulky, while 12 to 25 are at Cooper Creek.

The Cooper Creek Campground is situated on the shore of its namesake stream. This creek is one of the most heavily stocked and fished trout streams in the Peach State. Also, nearby are several long and short hiking trails within the Cooper Creek Wildlife Management Area.

Some campsites here are right on the creek bank, while others are a bit back up on the hill overlooking the creek. All these back-in sites are in a wooded area and enjoy full shade. This is a popular site for families and for anglers in the summer months.

17 Cottonwood Patch Campground

Recreation: Hiking, fishing, biking, horseback riding
Location: 21 miles northeast of Chatsworth; 5000 Old Georgia Highway 2, Cisco 30708
GPS: N34 98.06' / W84 63.88'

Facilities and amenities: Vault toilet, fire ring, picnic tables, lantern posts, horse troughs, hitching posts, hiking and equestrian trails
Elevation: 980
Road conditions: Last 6 miles of approach road are gravel and dirt
Hookups: None
Sites: 8 RV/tent sites with no hookups
Maximum RV length: 20
Season: Year-round, Apr–Nov peak season
Fees: $8
Maximum stay: 14 days
Management: USDA Forest Service, Conasauga Ranger District, 3941 US Highway 76, Chatsworth; (706) 695-6736; www.fs.usda.gov/recarea/conf/recreation/camping-cabins/recarea/?recid=10457&actid=29
Reservations: No
Pets: Dogs on 6-foot leashes allowed
Quiet hours: 10 p.m.–6 a.m.
Alcohol restrictions: No alcohol allowed
ADA compliant: Yes
Finding the campground: From US 411 in Cisco, travel east on Old GA 2 for 7.8 miles. Turn left into the campground drive.
About the campground: The Cottonwood Patch Campground is on the banks of the Conasauga River near the border with Tennessee and on the edge of both the Cohutta Wildlife Management Area and the 42,000-acre federal Cohutta Wilderness Area.

The eight partially shaded and well-spaced campsites offer few amenities and are mostly used by hikers, horseback riders, mountain bikers, anglers, and hunters. Trailers are limited to 20-foot lengths due to curvy roads and small bridges.

18 Deep Hole Recreation Area

Recreation: Fishing, paddling
Location: 25 miles southwest of Blairsville; Deep Hole Campground Road, Suches 30572
GPS: N3473.97' / W84 14.01'
Facilities and amenities: Vault toilet, grills, picnic tables, lantern posts, fishing, paddling, ADA accessible fishing pier, canoe/kayak launch
Elevation: 1,990
Road conditions: Gravel roads within the campground
Hookups: None
Sites: 9 RV/tent sites
Maximum RV length: 35
Season: Year-round, Apr–Nov peak season
Fees: $15
Maximum stay: 14 days
Management: USDA Forest Service, Blue Ridge Ranger District, 2042 Georgia Highway 515 West, Blairsville; (706) 745-6928; www.recreation.gov/camping/campgrounds/10075391

Reservations: (877) 444-6777; www.recreation.gov
Pets: Dogs on 6-foot leashes allowed
Quiet hours: 10 p.m.–6 a.m.
Alcohol restrictions: No alcohol allowed
ADA compliant: Yes
Finding the campground: From Dahlonega go 27 miles north on GA 60. The 0.5-mile gravel entrance drive is on the left.
About the campground: The Deep Hole campground is situated on a bend in the Toccoa River that, unsurprisingly, creates a deep hole. It also is a spot that is heavily stocked with trout in spring through fall by the Georgia DNR. A wooden fishing platform that is wheelchair accessible overlooks the pool.

Deep Hole is also the start of the 13.8-mile Toccoa River Canoe Trail, which ends at the Toccoa River Sandy Bottoms Recreation Area. A sloped launching area is provided for paddlers venturing onto the river.

The nine primitive campsites that have no hookups or drinking water are by reservation only. They are spacious, in a wooded setting, and shaded.

19 DeSoto Falls Recreation Area

Recreation: Hiking, fishing
Location: 14.5 miles northwest of Cleveland; 18365 US Highway 129, Cleveland 30528
GPS: N34 70.57'/ W83 91.48'
Facilities and amenities: Flush toilets, showers, water, picnic tables, fire rings, grills, lantern posts
Elevation: 2,050
Road conditions: Paved roads
Hookups: None
Sites: 20 RV/tent sites, 1 double RV/tent site, 2 tent-only sites
Maximum RV length: 40
Season: Year-round, Apr–Oct peak season
Fees: RV/tent and tent-only sites $20 peak, $10 non-peak, double site $40 peak, $20 non-peak
Maximum stay: 14 days
Management: USDA Forest Service, Blue Ridge Ranger District, 2042 Georgia Highway 515 West, Blairsville; (706) 745-6928; www.recreation.gov/camping/campgrounds/240242?start=2
Reservations: (877) 444-6777; www.recreation.gov
Pets: Dogs on 6-foot leashes allowed
Quiet hours: 10 p.m.–6 a.m.
Alcohol restrictions: No alcohol allowed
ADA compliant: Yes
Finding the campground: From the courthouse square in Cleveland, go north on US 129 for 14.6 miles. The entrance to the campground is on the left.
About the campground: DeSoto Falls Recreation Area is located on the banks of Frogtown Creek. The location gets its name from some Spanish armor supposedly discovered in the area and attributed to Hernando DeSoto's exploration party that passed through the vicinity in the 1500s.

Anglers are attracted to Frogtown Creek, which is stocked with trout during the spring and summer months.

Today the major attractions of the site are twin waterfalls on streams feeding into Frogtown Creek and positioned along the area's hiking trails. Additionally, anglers are attracted by the trout stocked in Frogtown annually during the April to Labor Day period.

The campground is composed of Upper and Lower Loops in a heavily wooded area. The individual sites are well spaced and receive full shade; some are located on the creek shore. The showers at the comfort station are in stalls outside the building. All water is cut off in the campground, including for the toilets, during non-peak times. Non-flush vault toilets are available during those months.

20 Dockery Lake Recreation Area

Recreation: Hiking, fishing, boating, paddling
Location: 13 miles north of Dahlonega; Dockery Lake Road, Cleveland 30528
GPS: N34 66.41' / W83 98.13'
Facilities and amenities: Flush toilets, vault toilets, grills, picnic tables, lantern post, lake, picnic area
Elevation: 2,402
Road conditions: GA 60 is a paved, but steep winding road. The final mile of Dockery Creek Road is a rough, steep, and narrow dirt track.
Hookups: None
Sites: 10 RV/tent sites with no hookups
Maximum RV length: 24
Season: Peak season Apr 1–Oct 31, off-season Nov 1–Jan 1, closed Jan 2–Mar 31
Fees: $8 peak season, $4 off-season
Maximum stay: 14 days
Management: USDA Forest Service, Blue Ridge Ranger District, 2042 Georgia Highway 515 West, Blairsville; (706) 745-6928; www.fs.usda.gov/recarea/conf/recreation/camping-cabins/recarea/?recid=10545&actid=29
Reservations: No
Pets: Dogs on 6-foot leashes allowed
Quiet hours: 10 p.m.–6 a.m.
Alcohol restrictions: No alcohol allowed
ADA compliant: No
Finding the campground: From the Dahlonega town square, go 13 miles north on GA 60. After turning left (northwest) on GA 60, turn right onto Dockery Lake Road that ends in the campground at 1 mile.
About the campground: Dockery Lake Recreation Area's campground spreads along the shore of its 6-acre, namesake pond. The Georgia Wildlife Resources Division stocks the lake in the spring months with rainbow trout. Anglers targeting those fish are the most frequent campers at this site. There are, however, a couple of hiking trails that originate at the recreation area and draw some visitors.

No swimming is allowed in the lake, but canoes, kayaks, and small boats with electric motors may be used. There is no boat ramp, but a section of sloped shoreline is available for carrying vessels to the water.

The campsites are in a heavily wooded area, with thick ground vegetation making them rather private. Also, the tree canopy provides full shade.

21 Frank Gross Recreation Area

Recreation: Fishing
Location: 24 miles southwest of Blairsville; FS 69 (Rock Creek Road), Blue Ridge Wildlife Management Area
GPS: N34 70.15' / W84 14.94'
Facilities and amenities: Vault toilet, grills, picnic tables, lantern posts, hiking trails, trout hatchery
Elevation: 2,275
Road conditions: The last 4 miles of Rock Creek Road are a rough gravel track and the drive within the campground also is gravel.
Hookups: None
Sites: 8 RV/tent sites
Maximum RV length: 35
Season: Mid-Mar–Nov 30
Fees: $8
Maximum stay: 14 days
Management: USDA Forest Service, Blue Ridge Ranger District, 2042 Georgia Highway 515 West, Blairsville; (706) 745-6928; www.fs.usda.gov/recarea/conf/recreation/hiking/recarea/?recid=10526&actid=29
Reservations: (877) 444-6777; www.recreation.gov
Pets: Dogs on 6-foot leashes allowed
Quiet hours: 10 p.m.–6 a.m.
Alcohol restrictions: No alcohol allowed
ADA compliant: Yes
Finding the campground: From Dahlonega go 27 miles north on GA 60. Turn left onto FS 69 (Rock Creek Road) for 5.2 miles to the campground on the right. The final 4 miles are on a rough gravel road.
About the campground: The Frank Gross Campground is in a rather isolated area, far from paved roads. The camping is primitive in a wooded area with plenty of shade, but with minimal amenities. The campground is located right on Rock Creek, which is a very heavily stocked and popular trout stream.

The Chattahoochee National Fish Hatchery is located 0.25 mile downstream of Frank Gross and is open for self-guided tours of the rearing runs daily from 8 a.m. to 3:30 p.m., Monday through Friday. Also, Rock Creek Lake is 1.6 miles south along FS 69. This 13-acre reservoir on the creek is periodically stocked with trout, has no boat ramp, but allows non-gasoline powered boats.

22 Hickey Gap Campground

Recreation: Fishing, biking
Location: 16.5 miles northeast of Chatsworth; 7001 Mill Creek Road, Chatsworth 30705
GPS: N34 89.41' / W84 67.25'
Facilities and amenities: Vault toilet, grills, picnic tables, lantern posts, mountain biking, fishing, hunting

Elevation: 1,825

Road conditions: Last 6.5 miles are on a twisting dirt road. The entrance drive to the campground is quite steep and the camping loop is on a gravel track.

Hookups: None

Sites: 5 RV/tent sites

Maximum RV length: 24

Season: Year-round, Apr–Oct peak season

Fees: None

Maximum stay: 14 days

Management: USDA Forest Service, Conasauga Ranger District, 3941 US Highway 76, Chatsworth; (706) 695-6736; www.fs.usda.gov/recarea/conf/recreation/camping-cabins/recarea/?recid=10458&actid=29

Reservations: No

Pets: Dogs on 6-foot leashes allowed

Quiet hours: 10 p.m.–6 a.m.

Alcohol restrictions: No alcohol allowed

ADA compliant: Yes

Finding the campground: From Chatsworth, go 9 miles north on US 411. Turn right on Grass Street. At the end of the road turn right and go 100 feet. Turn left on Mill Creek Road (FS 630). At 6.5 miles, the campground is on the right.

About the campground: Hickey Gap Campground is located on the shore of Mill Creek on USDA Forest Service property within the state's Cohutta Wildlife Management Area. It contains five sites that are shaded by hardwoods in the summer months, but there are minimal amenities.

This location is popular with mountain bikers, anglers pursuing trout that are stocked in Mill Creek in the spring, and hunters in the fall and winter. The size limit of 24 feet for campers is dictated by the 6.5-mile drive on a twisting dirt road that ends with a quite steep driveway down to the campground. On the plus side, the drive to the campground parallels scenic Mill Creek for the entire distance.

23 Jacks River Fields Campground

Recreation: Hiking, fishing, biking, horseback riding

Location: 19 miles west of Blue Ridge; FS 64, Cohutta Wildlife Management Area, Epworth

GPS: N 3486.34' / W84 52.01'

Facilities and amenities: Vault toilet, grills, picnic tables, lantern posts, hitching posts, hiking / mountain biking / equestrian trails

Elevation: 2,700

Road conditions: Last 5.7 miles of approach is over a rough dirt and gravel road. The campground has dirt drive as well.

Hookups: None

Sites: 7 RV/tent sites

Maximum RV length: 24

Season: Year-round, Apr–Oct peak season

Fees: $5

Maximum stay: 14 days
Management: USDA Forest Service, Conasauga Ranger District, 3941 US Highway 76, Chatsworth; (706) 695-6736; www.fs.usda.gov/recarea/conf/recarea/?recid=10459
Reservations: No
Pets: Dogs on 6-foot leashes allowed
Quiet hours: 10 p.m.–6 a.m.
Alcohol restrictions: No alcohol allowed
ADA compliant: Yes
Finding the campground: From US 76 in Blue Ridge, go 3.8 miles north on GA 5. Turn left on GA 2 (Watson Road). Go 10.2 miles to Watson Gap and turn left on FS 64. At 4 miles the campground is on the left. During winter months the campground is only accessible from the east using these directions. Be aware the last 5.7 miles are on a rough dirt and gravel road.
About the campground: The campground is located on the headwaters of the South Fork of the Jacks River, on the edge of the 42,000-acre Cohutta Wilderness Area. It is a popular area for horse camping.

The elevation here is around 2,700 feet, with surrounding ridges and mountains rising to 3,000-plus feet. You can expect cooler temperatures here year-round.

The camping area is fairly open with some shade provided by the yellow poplar, oak, hickory, and white pines amid which it is located. The campground basically is rather primitive, more suited for hikers, equestrians, and anglers targeting the trout in the South Fork.

24 Lake Conasauga Recreation Area

Recreation: Hiking, fishing, boating, paddling, swimming
Location: 20 miles northeast of Chatsworth; FS 68, Cohutta Wildlife Management Area
GPS: N34 85.96' / W84 65.14'
Facilities and amenities: Flush toilets, water, grills, picnic tables, lantern posts, hiking trails, boat ramp
Elevation: 3,175
Road conditions: Last 14.5 miles of approach are on a winding dirt and gravel road, ending in a narrow entrance drive.
Hookups: None
Sites: 31 RV/tent sites
Maximum RV length: 24
Season: Mid-Apr–Oct 31
Fees: $15
Maximum stay: 14 days
Management: US Forest Service, Blue Ridge Ranger District, 2042 Georgia Highway 515 West, Blairsville; (706) 745-6928; www.fs.usda.gov/recarea/conf/recreation/bicycling/recarea/?recid=10461&actid=29
Reservations: (877) 444-6777; www.recreation.gov
Pets: Dogs on 6-foot leashes allowed
Quiet hours: 10 p.m.–6 a.m.
Alcohol restrictions: No alcohol allowed

The main attraction of Lake Conasauga Recreation Area is the 19-acre spring-fed lake from which it takes its name.

ADA compliant: Yes

Finding the campground: From GA 515 in Ellijay, go west for 6.5 miles on GA 52. Turn right on Gates Chapel Road. At 4 miles the road changes to dirt and gravel; continue another 1.2 miles and go right on Wilderness Road (FS 18). After another 1.6 miles turn right on Old CCC Camp Road (FS 68) and climb steeply for 3.2 miles to the junction with FS 64 on Potato Patch Mountain. Turn left to remain on FS 68, which now is Lake Conasauga Road. At 4.3 miles turn right into the recreation area.

About the campground: The main attraction of Lake Conasauga Recreation Area is the 19-acre, spring-fed lake from which it takes its name. This man-made structure is at the highest elevation of any lake in Georgia. The site also hosts the trailhead to a historic fire tower and scenic vista from the top of Grassy Mountain.

Canoes, kayaks, and small fishing boats may be carried down to the lake, but only electric motors are allowed. The area also offers access to several hiking trails. A grass swimming beach is provided as well.

The campground offers well-spaced and shaded campsites, situated on two gravel loop roads. Some of the sites overlook the lake.

25 Lake Conasauga Overflow Campground

Recreation: Hiking, fishing, boating, paddling, biking
Location: 20 miles northeast of Chatsworth; FS 68, Cohutta Wildlife Management Area
GPS: N34 85.59' / W84 64.96'
Facilities and amenities: Vault toilet, picnic tables, lantern posts, hiking trails
Elevation: 3,150
Road conditions: Last 14.5 miles of approach are on a winding dirt and gravel road. Parking is in a gravel lot across the road from the camping area.
Hookups: None
Sites: 6 tent sites
Maximum RV length: NA
Season: Mid-Mar–Dec 31
Fees: $8
Maximum stay: 14 days
Management: US Forest Service, Blue Ridge Ranger District, 2042 Georgia Highway 515 West, Blairsville; (706) 745-6928; www.fs.usda.gov/recarea/conf/recreation/recarea/?recid=10463&actid=29
Reservations: (877) 444-6777; www.recreation.gov
Pets: Dogs on 6-foot leashes allowed
Quiet hours: 10 p.m.–6 a.m.
Alcohol restrictions: No alcohol allowed
ADA compliant: Yes
Finding the campground: From GA 515 in Ellijay, go west for 6.5 miles on GA 52. Turn right on Gates Chapel Road. At 4 miles the road changes to dirt and gravel; continue another 1.2 miles and go right on Wilderness Road (FS 18). After another 1.6 miles turn right on Old CCC Camp Road (FS 68) and climb steeply for 3.2 miles to the junction with FS 64 on Potato Patch Mountain. Turn left to remain on FS 68, which now is Lake Conasauga Road. At 5.1 miles take the left fork onto FS 49 and continue 0.4 mile to the overflow parking lot on the left and camping area on the right.
About the campground: This overflow area is not on the main Lake Conasauga Campground loop, but rather it is connected to it via a trail system. The overflow campground consists of six primitive tent sites, a parking area, and a single vault toilet. The sites are in a wooded area with full shade.

26 Lake Winfield Scott Recreation Area

Recreation: Hiking, fishing, boating, paddling, playground
Location: 17 miles south of Blairsville; 439 Lake Winfield Scott Road, Suches 30572
GPS: N34 73.38' / W83 97.43'
Facilities and amenities: Flush toilets, showers, grills, water, picnic tables, lantern posts, water, 18-acre lake, hiking trails, carry-down boat launch, grass swimming beach, bathhouse, playground, pavilions
Elevation: 2,900

Road conditions: Paved roads

Hookups: Water, electric

Sites: 31 RV/tent sites, 1 group site, 1 cabin

Maximum RV length: 40

Season: Year-round for North Loop, mid-Apr–Oct 31 for South Loop

Fees: RV/tent site $24 peak season, off-peak $12; double site $48 peak season, $24 off-season; group site $75; cabin $125; daily parking fee $5

Maximum stay: 14 days

Management: US Forest Service, Blue Ridge Ranger District, 2042 Highway 515 West, Blairsville; (706) 745-6928; www.fs.usda.gov/recarea/conf/recarea/?recid=10528

Reservations: (877) 444-6777; www.recreation.gov

Pets: Dogs on 6-foot leashes allowed

Quiet hours: 10 p.m.–6 a.m.

Alcohol restrictions: No alcohol allowed

ADA compliant: Yes

Finding the campground: From Blairsville, drive south on US 19/129 for 10 miles and turn right on GA 180. At 7 miles turn left into the recreation area on Lake Winfield Scott Road.

About the campground: Lake Winfield Scott Campground is composed of two loops near its namesake body of water. However, neither the North nor South Loop is on the shore. The facility is easily one of the least standardized in the Peach State. Sites range from electric and water

You are offered recreational activities centered around beautiful Lake Winfield Scott.

hookups to tent sites that don't even have fire rings, as well as ones falling in between with regard to amenities. Your best bet is to check the recreation.gov link for Lake Winfield Scott to see the range of sites offered. All sites are in fully shaded, woodland settings.

Reservations are accepted for campsites in the South Loop, while the North Loop is first-come, first-served. The South Loop is open from mid-April to the end of October. The North Loop remains open year-round, but from November to mid-April the water is cut off in both loops. The vault toilets remain open year-round. There is no dump station on site. One rental cabin is available in the recreation area.

Lake Winfield Scott is stocked with trout annually and private boats are allowed. The launch area, however, is carry-down. Only electric motors are allowed. No fishing is permitted in the designated swimming area.

27 Morganton Point Recreation Area

Recreation: Hiking, fishing, boating, paddling, swimming
Location: 9 miles east of Blue Ridge; 475 Lake Drive, Morganton 30560
GPS: N34 86.92' / W84 24.94'
Facilities and amenities: Flush toilet, showers, dump station, grills, water, picnic tables, pavilion, lantern posts, hiking trails, boat ramp, swimming beach, kayak/paddleboard rentals
Elevation: 1,728
Road conditions: Paved roads
Hookups: Water, electric
Sites: 24 RV/tent sites with hookups, 13 tent sites with no hookups, 2 group sites
Maximum RV length: 30
Season: Year-round, Apr–Oct peak season
Fees: RV/tent site $33, double site $48, tent-only site $24, group site $51, $5 daily parking fee
Maximum stay: 14 days
Management: US Forest Service, Blue Ridge Ranger District, 2042 Georgia Highway 515 West, Blairsville; (706) 745-6928; www.fs.usda.gov/recarea/conf/recreation/wateractivities/recarea/?recid=10529&actid=82
Reservations: (877) 444-6777; www.recreation.gov
Pets: Dogs on 6-foot leashes allowed
Quiet hours: 10 p.m.–6 a.m.
Alcohol restrictions: No alcohol allowed
ADA compliant: Yes
Finding the campground: From Blue Ridge go 4 miles north on US 76 / GA 515. Turn right on GA 60 and go to the stop sign. Turn left and continue on GA 60 for 1.5 miles to Morganton. Turn right on Lake Drive and go 1 mile to the recreation area.
About the campground: Morganton Point is located on the shore of 3,290-acre Blue Ridge Lake. This Tennessee Valley Authority impoundment on the Toccoa River provides boating, fishing, swimming, and other water sports at the campground.

The campsites with hookups are clustered overlooking the lake with water views, but up on the hillside. Some of the walk-in tent sites are down on the shoreline. All the sites are shaded, with the exception of tent sites A to F near the water.

Tent sites 31 to 37 are along a very rough drive on the east side of the campground. These seven sites are on a first-come, first-served basis.

Rental kayaks and paddleboards are available at The Point concession site within the recreation area.

28 Mulky Campground

Recreation: Hiking, fishing
Location: 25 miles southwest of Blairsville; FS 4, Blue Ridge Wildlife Management Area
GPS: N34 76.18' / W84 07.41'
Facilities and amenities: Vault toilet, grills, water, picnic tables, lantern posts, hiking trails, fishing
Elevation: 2,227
Road conditions: Roads from the east and west are gravel and dirt, as are the ones in the campground
Hookups: None
Sites: 11 RV/tent sites
Maximum RV length: 35
Season: Year-round, Apr–Oct peak season
Fees: $15 peak season, $7.50 off season
Maximum stay: 14 days
Management: US Forest Service, Blue Ridge Ranger District, 2042 Georgia Highway 515 West, Blairsville; (706) 745-6928; www.fs.usda.gov/recarea/conf/recarea/?recid=10530
Reservations: (877) 444-6777; www.recreation.gov
Pets: Dogs on 6-foot leashes allowed
Quiet hours: 10 p.m.–6 a.m.
Alcohol restrictions: No alcohol allowed
ADA compliant: Yes
Finding the campground: From Dahlonega go 26 miles north on GA 60. Turn right onto FS 4 (Cooper Creek Road, but the name changes to Mulky Gap Road as it crosses the bridge over Sea Creek). The campground is at 5 miles on the left. Be aware that a long portion of the approach on Forest Service property is on a gravel road.
About the campground: Mulky Campground is often associated with the nearby Cooper Creek Campground. Those two facilities share a camp host, who is located at the Cooper Creek site, as well as the numbering of their campsites being in combination. Sites 1 to 11 are at Mulky, while 12 to 25 are at Cooper Creek.

Mulky is situated just across the Forest Service road from Cooper Creek. This stream is one of the most heavily stocked and fished trout streams in the Peach State. Also, nearby are several long and short hiking trails within the Cooper Creek Wildlife Management Area.

The campsites here are in a level area along an entrance drive near the vault toilet and centrally positioned water faucet. Some sites, however, are connected directly to the forest road. All these back-in sites are in a wooded area and enjoy full shade.

The campground has a varied fee schedule. From the first of April to the end of October, peak season rates apply. The rest of the year the cost drops to half the peak season rate, but the water supply to the campground is cut off for the winter.

29 Toccoa River Sandy Bottoms Recreation Area

Recreation: Fishing, paddling
Location: 17.5 miles southeast of Blue Ridge; Old Dial Road, Morganton 30560
GPS: N34 78.62' / W84 23.97'
Facilities and amenities: Vault toilet, grills, picnic tables, lantern posts, fishing, paddling, canoe/kayak launch
Elevation: 1,825
Road conditions: Paved roads
Hookups: None
Sites: 4 tent sites
Maximum RV length: NA
Season: Year-round, Mar–Dec peak season
Fees: Tent site $8, $3 parking fee
Maximum stay: 14 days
Management: US Forest Service, Blue Ridge Ranger District, 2042 Georgia Highway 515 West, Blairsville; (706) 745-6928; www.fs.usda.gov/recarea/conf/recreation/recarea/?recid=10531&actid=29
Reservations: No
Pets: Dogs on 6-foot leashes allowed
Quiet hours: 10 p.m.–6 a.m.
Alcohol restrictions: No alcohol allowed
ADA compliant: No
Finding the campground: From Blue Ridge go south on Aska Road for 13.2 miles. Turn left on Newport Road. Cross the Toccoa River, and at the end of the road, turn left on Old Dial Road. At 2.6 miles the campsites are on the right.
About the campground: The Sandy Bottoms camping area is located across Old Dial Road from the Toccoa River. The canoe/kayak launch is adjacent upriver. The landing serves as the end of the Toccoa River Canoe Trail that starts 13.8 miles upstream at the Deep Hole Recreation Area.

The river is stocked with trout year-round, but from November to mid-May delayed-harvest regulations apply. Only artificial lures and flies may be used then, and all trout must be immediately released. The rest of the year trout may be harvested, and regular statewide trout rules apply.

The four primitive campsites that have no hookups or drinking water are available on a first-come, first-served basis. They are arranged as two sets of adjoining sites and all are shaded.

Be aware there is another Forest Service campground with the same Sandy Bottoms name on the Tallulah River in the Chattooga River Ranger District.

Chattooga River Ranger District

Campgrounds At-A-Glance

#	Name	Total Sites	Group Sites	Hookup Sites	Hookups	Maximum RV Length	Dump Station	Toilets	Showers	Drinking Water	ADA	Fees	Reservations
Georgia State Parks and Historic Sites Division													
30	Black Rock Mountain State Park	61	1	44	WE	50	Y	F	Y	Y	Y	$$–$$$$$	Y
31	Moccasin Creek State Park	50	0	50	WES	50	Y	F	Y	Y	Y	$$$$	Y
32	Tallulah Gorge State Park	52	1	48	WE	50	Y	F	Y	Y	Y	$$–$$$$$	Y
33	Unicoi State Park	104	0	52	WES	40	Y	F	Y	Y	Y	$$–$$$$$	Y
Georgia Power Company													
34	Seed Lake Campground	12	0	0	N	NA	N	F	N	Y	N	N	N
USDA Forest Service													
35	Andrews Cove Campground	10	0	0	N	24	N	F	N	Y	Y	$$	N
36	Lake Rabun Campground	83	0	37	WE	35	Y	F	Y	Y	Y	$$$–$$$$$	Y
37	Low Gap Campground	13	0	0	N	28	N	V	N	Y	N	$$	N
38	Sandy Bottoms Campground	13	0	0	N	47	N	V	N	Y	Y	$$	N
39	Sarah's Creek Campground	22	0	0	N	28	N	V	N	N	N	$	N
40	Tallulah River Campground	19	0	0	N	98	N	V	N	Y	Y	$$	N
41	Tate Branch Campground	19	0	0	N	28	N	V	N	Y	N	$$	N
42	Upper Chattahoochee River Campground	19	0	0	N	24	N	C	N	N	Y	$$	N
43	West Fork Campground	5	0	0	N	NA	N	V	N	N	N	$	N
44	Willis Knob Horse Campground	9	0	0	WE	60	N	V	N	Y	Y	$$–$$$$	Y

See Amenities Chart key on page xxi.

30 Black Rock Mountain State Park

Recreation: Hiking, fishing, playground
Location: 6.2 miles northwest of Clayton; 3085 Black Rock Mountain Parkway, Mountain City 30562
GPS: N34 90.69' / W83 40.84'
Facilities and amenities: Flush toilets, showers, laundry, dump station, grills, tables, picnic shelters, picnic areas, playground, hiking trails, lake, geocaching, gift shop
Elevation: 3,250
Road conditions: Paved roads
Hookups: Water, electric
Sites: 3 premium RV/tent sites, 41 standard RV/tent sites, 12 walk-in tent sites, 4 backcountry tent sites, 1 pioneer site, 10 cottages
Maximum RV length: 50
Season: Year-round, Apr–Nov peak season
Fees: Premium RV/tent site $38, standard RV/tent site $36, walk-in tent site $25, backcountry tent site $20, pioneer site $135, 2-bedroom cottage $225, 3-bedroom cottage $255, daily parking fee $5, annual pass $50
Maximum stay: 14 days

Being Georgia's highest state park, Black Rock's views offer 80-mile vistas.

Management: Georgia State Parks and Historic Sites Division, 2610 Georgia Highway 155 SW, Stockbridge; (770) 389-7286; www.gastateparks.org

Reservations: (800) 864-7275; www.gastateparks.org/reservations

Pets: Dogs on 6-foot leashes allowed

Quiet hours: 10 p.m.–7 a.m.

Alcohol restrictions: Unlawful in public areas

ADA compliant: Yes

Finding the campground: From US 441 in Mountain City, go west on Black Rock Mountain Parkway for 3.1 miles. The visitor center is on the left.

About the campground: Black Rock Mountain's 1,743 acres sit at an elevation of 3,640 feet, making it Georgia's highest state park. For that reason, it offers great 80-mile vistas of the surrounding area. Halfway up the mountain, Black Rock Lake is within the park, providing angling opportunities for bass, bream, and seasonally stocked trout.

The campground is composed of two sections at either end of a loop road, situated in Hickory Cove. The sites are shaded by rhododendron and gnarly oak trees.

Be aware that Black Rock Mountain Parkway offers a quite steep approach to the park. Additionally, the driveway down to the campground is very steep, as well as being narrow, as it runs amid the hilly campsites.

31   Moccasin Creek State Park

Recreation: Fishing, boating, paddling, playground

Location: 14.5 miles west of Clayton; 3655 Georgia Highway 197, Clarkesville 30523

GPS: N34 84.49' / W83 58.81'

Facilities and amenities: Flush toilets, showers, laundry, picnic tables, fire rings, dump station, picnic area and shelter, playgrounds, geocaching, horseshoe pits, boat ramps, fishing docks, fish cleaning station, canoe/kayak/paddleboard rentals

Elevation: 1,900

Road conditions: Paved roads

Hookups: Water, electric, sewer

Sites: 9 premium RV sites with full hookups, 7 premium RV/tent sites with water and electric hookups, 34 standard RV/tent sites with water and electric hookups

Maximum RV length: 50

Season: Year-round, Apr–Oct peak season

Fees: Premium site $40, standard site $38, daily parking fee $5, annual pass $50

Maximum stay: 14 days

Management: Georgia State Parks and Historic Sites Division, 2610 Georgia Highway 155 SW, Stockbridge; (770) 389-7286; www.gastateparks.org

Reservations: (800) 864-7275; www.gastateparks.org/reservations

Pets: Dogs on 6-foot leashes allowed

Quiet hours: 10 p.m.–7 a.m.

Alcohol restrictions: Unlawful in public areas

ADA compliant: Yes

The heavily stocked trout stream is a popular draw for senior campers.

Finding the campground: From the junction of GA 17 and GA 197 in Clarkesville, drive 23.5 miles north on GA 197. The park entrance is on the right.

About the campground: Moccasin Creek State Park covers just 32 acres on the shore of 2,775-acre Lake Burton. The major attractions of the park are boating on the lake and trout fishing in its namesake stream that flows through the park. That latter option is limited to fishing by children 11 and younger or seniors 65 or older. The creek is heavily stocked with trout from the adjacent Lake Burton Trout Hatchery. Other visitors may fish in the park's waters on Lake Burton.

The campground is on a level area with a single-loop paved drive. The sites range from full to partial shade, with no understory of plants, resulting in a communal setting.

32 Tallulah Gorge State Park

Recreation: Hiking, fishing, boating, paddling, biking, swimming, playground, rock climbing
Location: 11.5 miles south of Clayton; 338 Jane Hurt Yarn Drive, Tallulah Falls 30573
GPS: N34 73.98' / W83 39.52'
Facilities and amenities: Flush toilets, showers, laundry, dump station, water, grills, picnic tables, picnic areas and shelters, playgrounds, hiking and bike trails, tennis courts, archery range, geo-caching, swimming beach, boat ramp, historic sites, gift shop, 63-acre lake

The major feature of this state park is the spectacular Tallulah Gorge.

Elevation: 1,575

Road conditions: Paved roads

Hookups: Water, electric

Sites: 11 premium RV/tent sites with hookups, 37 standard RV/tent sites with hookups, 3 Adirondack backcountry shelters, 1 pioneer site

Maximum RV length: 50

Season: Year-round, Apr–Oct peak season

Fees: Premium RV/tent site $40, standard RV/tent site $36, Adirondack shelter $20, pioneer site $45, daily parking fee $5, annual pass $50

Maximum stay: 14 days

Management: Georgia State Parks and Historic Sites Division, 2610 Georgia Highway 155 SW, Stockbridge; (770) 389-7286; www.gastateparks.org

Reservations: (800) 864-7275; www.gastateparks.org/reservations

Pets: Dogs on 6-foot leashes allowed

Quiet hours: 10 p.m.–7 a.m.

Alcohol restrictions: Unlawful in public areas

ADA compliant: Yes

Finding the campground: From the junction of Main Street and US 441 in Tallulah Falls, go 0.5 mile north on US 441. Turn right onto Jane Hurt Yarn Drive to enter the park.

About the campground: The major feature of this park is 2-mile long, 1000-foot-deep Tallulah Gorge and its waterfalls. This site has been drawing tourists since the Victorian Era and continues to enthrall visitors with its natural beauty.

Water releases are periodically done from Tallulah Falls Dam for kayaking in the gorge, as well as presenting vistas of the canyon as it was before the dam and 63-acre Tallulah Falls Lake were built. Hiking trails lead into the gorge, as well as skirting both sides of the rim, and a 200-foot suspension bridge spans the gorge. The remains of the towers used by Karl Wallenda to tightrope across the canyon in the 1970s are on the rim as well.

Besides water sports on Tallulah Falls Lake, the park has a boat ramp at the foot of the gorge on Lake Tugalo. Be forewarned, however, that gravel Stoneplace Road, which leads to it, is for 4-wheel-drive vehicles only. It is not because the road is rough, but rather it often is at almost 45-degree inclines, making it virtually impossible for 2-wheel-drive vehicles to climb back up.

The park's Terrora Campground is toward the eastern end of the park and composed of a single loop. The campsites are shaded, but rather closely spaced. Two of the park's backcountry Adirondack sites are on the High Bluff Loop, while the third is on the Stoneplace Trail near the end of the gorge.

33 Unicoi State Park

Recreation: Hiking, fishing, boating, paddling, biking, playground

Location: 2.5 miles northeast of Helen; 1788 Georgia Highway 356, Helen 30545

GPS: N34 73.18' / W83 71.78'

Facilities and amenities: Flush toilets, showers, laundry, picnic tables, fire rings, dump station, picnic areas and shelters, playgrounds, geocaching, hiking and mountain biking trails, ziplining, tennis courts, archery and air gun ranges, ax throwing, swimming beach, fishing docks, kayak and paddleboard rentals, amphitheater, lodge, conference center, restaurant

Elevation: 1,734

Road conditions: Paved roads

Hookups: Water, electric, sewer

Sites: 13 RV/tent sites with full hookups, 33 RV/tent sites with water and electric hookups, 6 double RV/tent sites with water and electric hookups, 4 glamping tent sites, 32 walk-in tent sites, 16 squirrel's nest platform sites, 100-room lodge, 29 cabins

Maximum RV length: 40

Season: Year-round, Apr–Oct peak season

Fees: RV/tent site with full hookups $50, RV/tent sites with water and electric hookups $45, double RV/tent sites $60, glamping sites $134–$170, walk-in tent sites $25, squirrel's nest platform sites $15, cabins $239, lodge rooms $149, daily parking fee $5, annual pass $50

Maximum stay: 14 days

Management: Georgia State Parks and Historic Sites Division, 2610 Georgia Highway 155 SW, Stockbridge; (770) 878-2201; www.gastateparks.org

Reservations: (706) 864-7275; www.unicoilodge.com

Pets: Dogs on 6-foot leashes allowed

Quiet hours: 10 p.m.–7 a.m.

Alcohol restrictions: Unlawful in public areas

ADA compliant: Yes

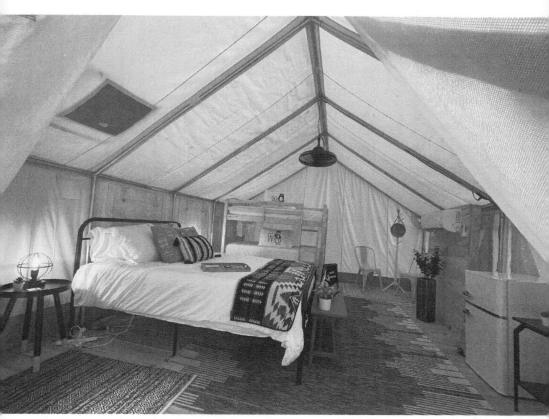

Combining luxury with the great outdoors, Unicoi State Park offers four glamping sites.

Finding the campground: From downtown Helen, go 1.1 miles north on GA 75 (North Main Street). Turn right onto GA 356 and go 1.7 miles to Unicoi Campground Road. Turn left and proceed 1.1 miles to the campground entrance on the left.

About the campground: Unicoi State Park covers 1,029 acres of Blue Ridge Mountain terrain, including 53-acre Unicoi Lake and a portion of Smith Creek's trout-stream habitat. The park also offers an extremely varied array of activities for the entire family. The Bavarian-themed tourism attractions of the town of Helen are located nearby.

The campground is divided into the Big Brook Spur with full hookups, along with Laurel Ridge and the Little Brook Spur that have electric and water hookups. Hickory Hollow has the walk-in tent sites, while the Squirrel's Nest holds the platform tent sites. The four glamping sites are in the Little Brook Spur.

All of these are located in a hardwood forest and are shaded. The sites also range from close together to separated, but there is little understory of plants to provide privacy.

34 Seed Lake Campground

Recreation: Fishing, swimming
Location: 17 miles southwest of Clayton; 3633 Crow Creek Road, Lakemont 30552
GPS: N34 48.70' / W83 31.80'
Facilities and amenities: Flush toilets, swimming beach, fire rings
Elevation: 1,875
Road conditions: Last 3.7 miles of approach on Crow Creek Road are rough, gravel
Hookups: None
Sites: 12 walk-in tent sites
Maximum RV length: NA
Season: Apr–Nov
Fees: None
Maximum stay: 14 days
Management: Georgia Power Company, North Georgia Lake Resource Office, 4 Seed Lake Road, Lakemont; (706) 746-1450; www.georgiapower.com/community/environment/lakes-rivers/north-georgia-lakes.html
Reservations: No
Pets: Dogs on 6-foot leashes allowed
Quiet hours: 10 p.m.–7 a.m.
Alcohol restrictions: No alcohol allowed
ADA compliant: No
Finding the campground: From the junction of US 441 and US 76 in Clayton, go west on US 76 for 7.2 miles. Turn left onto Charlie Mountain Road and continue for 3.6 miles to the end of the road at its junction with Bridge Creek Road. Turn right and go 2 miles to the end of the road at the junction with Burton Dam Road. Turn right and at 0.6 mile, turn left onto Crow Creek Road. The campground is on the left at 3.7 miles.

About the campground: This campground is located on the shores of Georgia Power Company's Seed Lake, a 240-acre impoundment on the Tallulah River. It is a no-frills primitive camping area that is not easily reached; thus, it is a place to really get away from civilization.

The 12 walk-in campsites are quite primitive and spread along a wooded slope overlooking the lake, offering both shade and privacy. Surprisingly for its location, it does have restrooms with flush toilets and drinking water is available. There also is a swimming beach provided.

35 Andrews Cove Campground

Recreation: Hiking, fishing
Location: 6 miles north of Helen; 15000 Georgia Highway 75 North, Helen 30545
GPS: N34 77.69' / W83 73.76'
Facilities and amenities: Flush toilet, water, picnic table, fire ring, lantern post, hiking trail
Elevation: 2,100
Road conditions: Paved roads
Hookups: None
Sites: 5 RV/tent sites, 5 tent-only sites
Maximum RV length: 24
Season: Mid-May–Oct
Fees: Single site $12, double site $17
Maximum stay: 14 days
Management: USDA Forest Service, Chattooga River Ranger District, 9975 US Highway 441, Lakemont; (706) 754-622; www.fs.usda.gov/Internet/FSE_DOCUMENTS/fseprd496058.pdf1
Reservations: No
Pets: Dogs on 6-foot leashes allowed
Quiet hours: 10 p.m.–6 a.m.
Alcohol restrictions: No alcohol allowed
ADA compliant: Yes
Finding the campground: From the junction of GA 75 and GA 356 in Helen, go north on GA 75 for 5.4 miles. The campground entrance is on the right.
About the campground: The campground is in the Andrews Cove Recreation Area, located on a hairpin curve of GA 75. The major attractions of this site are the trailhead of the Andrews Cove Trail that leads up the valley to intersect the Appalachian Trail, along with the cold waters of Andrews Creek, which runs through the campground. This small stream harbors a population of small, wild rainbow trout. Additionally, the Bavarian-themed tourist town of Helen is located close by.

The campground is situated on a paved loop road, with campsites that are shaded and surrounded by vegetation for privacy. Drinking water is supplied by a single, centrally located hand pump.

36 Lake Rabun Campground

Recreation: Hiking, fishing, boating, paddling, swimming
Location: 10 miles northwest of Tallulah Falls; 4726 Lake Rabun Road, Lakemont 30552
GPS: N34 75.56' / W83 48.13'

Facilities and amenities: Flush toilets, showers, dump station, picnic tables, fire rings, swimming beach, hiking trail, boat ramp
Elevation: 1,775
Road conditions: Paved roads
Hookups: Water, electric
Sites: 37 RV/tent sites with water and electric hookups, 45 RV/tent sites with no hookups, 1 group site
Maximum RV length: 35
Season: Mid-Apr–Oct
Fees: Loop 1 sites $24, Loop 2 sites $35, group site $75
Maximum stay: 14 days
Management: USDA Forest Service, Chattooga River Ranger District, 9975 US Highway 441, Lakemont; (706) 754-6221; www.fs.usda.gov/Internet/FSE_DOCUMENTS/fseprd496058.pdf
Reservations: (877) 444-6777; www.recreation.gov
Pets: Dogs on 6-foot leashes allowed
Quiet hours: 10 p.m.–6 a.m.
Alcohol restrictions: No alcohol allowed
ADA compliant: Yes
Finding the campground: From the junction of US 23 / 441 and Old US 441 South, go west on Old US 441 South for 2.7 miles. Turn left on Lake Burton Road. At 5.2 miles the campground entrance is on the right. Although Lake Rabun Road is paved, it is quite narrow with many twists and turns as it follows the lakeshore. Also don't trust your GPS with the campground's address. The address numbers are quite confusing on this road.
About the campground: Located in the Lake Rabun Beach Recreation Area, the campground consists of two connected, paved loop roads. The area features a swimming beach on 835-acre Lake Rabun, as well as a boat ramp. The camping area also is the jumping-off point for walking the 1.7-mile Angel Falls Trail, which leads to two small cascades on Joe Creek.

The 37 campsites on Loop 2 feature water and electric hookups, while the 45 on Loop 1 do not. Loop 1 does have centrally located water faucets. All campsites are well shaded and surrounded by understory that offers privacy. Though you can make reservations, a few of the sites are managed on a first-come, first served basis.

Between the two loops is the Pear Tree Hill Group Camp, offering four primitive sites.

37 Low Gap Campground

Recreation: Fishing
Location: 5.5 miles northwest of Helen; 190 Low Gap Road, Helen 30545
GPS: N34 75.11' / W83 78.28'
Facilities and amenities: Vault toilet, water, picnic table, fire ring
Elevation: 1,875
Road conditions: Chattahoochee River Road is a dirt and gravel track for most of the distance to the campground. The drive to the camping area is also dirt.
Hookups: None
Sites: 13 RV/tent sites

Maximum RV length: 28
Season: Mid-Mar–Oct
Fees: $12
Maximum stay: 14 days
Management: USDA Forest Service, Chattooga River Ranger District, 9975 US Highway 441, Lakemont; (706) 754-6221; www.fs.usda.gov/Internet/FSE_DOCUMENTS/fseprd496058.pdf
Reservations: No
Pets: Dogs on 6-foot leashes allowed
Quiet hours: 10 p.m.–6 a.m.
Alcohol restrictions: No alcohol allowed
ADA compliant: No
Finding the campground: From the junction of GA 75 and GA 75A in Helen, go west on GA 75A for 0.1 mile, crossing the Chattahoochee River. Turn right on Chattahoochee River Road (which soon changes from paved to gravel and dirt) and go 3.7 miles. The campground entrance is on the left.
About the campground: Low Gap Campground is positioned on the banks of the creek of the same name, a tributary of the Chattahoochee River. The main appeal of the site is trout fishing in Low Gap Creek and the nearby river, both of which are stocked with trout in spring through fall.

The campground is in an open wooded situation, with only partial shade on all sites. A single hand pump supplies water to the campground.

The maximum RV length is dictated by the rough, twisting approach to the campground. Also be aware that to reach sites 8 and 13, driving across a low-water ford of the creek is required.

38 Sandy Bottoms Campground

Recreation: Fishing
Location: 17 miles northwest of Clayton; 4841 Tallulah River Road, Clayton 30525
GPS: N34 96.09' / W83 55.77'
Facilities and amenities: Vault toilet, water, picnic table, fire ring, lantern post
Elevation: 2,360
Road conditions: The approach along Tallulah River Road is a curvy, dirt and gravel road. The drive within the campground also is gravel.
Hookups: None
Sites: 13 RV/tent sites
Maximum RV length: 47
Season: Mid-Mar–Oct
Fees: $15, daily parking fee $4
Maximum stay: 14 days
Management: USDA Forest Service, Chattooga River Ranger District, 9975 US Highway 441, Lakemont; (706) 754-6221; www.fs.usda.gov/Internet/FSE_DOCUMENTS/fseprd496058.pdf
Reservations: No
Pets: Dogs on 6-foot leashes allowed
Quiet hours: 10 p.m.–6 a.m.

On the Tallulah River, this campground's main attraction is to anglers targeting the stocked trout.

Alcohol restrictions: No alcohol allowed
ADA compliant: Yes
Finding the campground: From the junction of US 441 and US 76 in Clayton, go west on US 76 for 7.9 miles. Turn right onto Persimmon Road and continue for 4.3 miles. Turn left onto Tallulah River Road. At 1.3 miles it changes to dirt and gravel. Stay on the road for another 2.3 miles to the campground on the left.
About the campground: Sandy Bottoms is a no-frills, rustic camping area on the shores of the Tallulah River, close to the North Carolina border. Its attraction is mainly for anglers targeting the brook, brown, and rainbow trout stocked in the river from spring to fall.

The camping area is level along the riverside and partially shaded. Some of the campsites are right on the shore.

Although the sites can handle larger RVs, the road is rough, with some tight turns and narrow bridges. Getting such campers to the campground may be your problem.

39 Sarah's Creek Campground

Recreation: Hiking, fishing
Location: 11 miles east of Clayton; 1946 Sarah's Creek Road, Clayton 30525
GPS: N34 92.88' / W83 26.42'
Facilities and amenities: Vault toilet, picnic tables, fire rings, lantern posts
Elevation: 2,040
Road conditions: After 0.3 mile, Sarah's Creek Road changes to dirt and gravel.
Hookups: None
Sites: 22 RV/tent sites
Maximum RV length: 28
Season: Year-round, Apr–Oct peak season
Fees: $10
Maximum stay: 14 days
Management: USDA Forest Service, Chattooga River Ranger District, 9975 US Highway 441, Lakemont; (706) 754-6221; www.fs.usda.gov/Internet/FSE_DOCUMENTS/fseprd496058.pdf
Reservations: No
Pets: Dogs on 6-foot leashes allowed
Quiet hours: 10 p.m.–6 a.m.
Alcohol restrictions: No alcohol allowed
ADA compliant: No
Finding the campground: From the junction of US 441 and Warwoman Road in Clayton, go east on Warwoman Road for 9.1 miles. Turn left onto Sarah's Creek Road. At 2 miles the road runs through the campground.
About the campground: Sarah's Creek Campground is mostly a destination for anglers pursuing the trout that are stocked in the creek from spring to fall. The facilities are quite primitive, offering few amenities. The road into and through the camping area is a rough, dirt and gravel track. Most of the sites are best suited for tent camping.

40 Tallulah River Campground

Recreation: Hiking, fishing
Location: 17 miles west of Clayton; 1441 Tallulah River Road, Clayton 30525
GPS: N34 92.27' / W83 54.32'
Facilities and amenities: Vault toilet, water, picnic tables, fire rings, lantern posts, fishing, hiking trail
Elevation: 2,025
Road conditions: Tallulah River Road paved to the campground. Gravel loop drive in the camping area.
Hookups: None
Sites: 15 RV/tent sites, 4 walk-in tent sites
Maximum RV length: 98
Season: Year-round, Apr–Oct peak season

Fees: $15

Maximum stay: 14 days

Management: USDA Forest Service, Chattooga River Ranger District, 9975 US Highway 441, Lakemont; (706) 754-6221; www.fs.usda.gov/Internet/FSE_DOCUMENTS/fseprd496058.pdf

Reservations: No

Pets: Dogs on 6-foot leashes allowed

Quiet hours: 10 p.m.–6 a.m.

Alcohol restrictions: No alcohol allowed

ADA compliant: Yes

Finding the campground: From the junction of US 441 and US 76 in Clayton, go west on US 76 for 7.9 miles. Turn right onto Persimmon Road and continue for 4.3 miles. Turn left onto Tallulah River Road. At 1.3 miles the campground is on the left.

About the campground: This is the best developed of the three campgrounds along the Tallulah River. The sites are placed along a single loop, with some on the river frontage. All are on level terrain and heavily shaded. Several water spigots are spread throughout the camping area. Although the sites are large enough for bigger RVs, the road in may make getting to the campground a bit troublesome.

The main attractions here are fishing for trout in the stocked waters of the Tallulah River or for wild trout in the Coleman River that flows into the Tallulah adjacent to the campground. Also, the Coleman River Trail offers hikes up into the Coleman River Scenic Area.

This is a very popular campground from spring through fall, especially for family groups.

41 Tate Branch Campground

Recreation: Fishing

Location: 17 miles northwest of Clayton; 2040 Tallulah River Road, Clayton 30525

GPS: N34 95.53' / W83 55.21'

Facilities and amenities: Vault toilet, water, picnic table, fire ring, lantern post, fishing

Elevation: 2,300

Road conditions: Tallulah River Road is dirt and gravel, with lots of twists and narrow bridges. It is not very RV friendly. The campground has a gravel drive.

Hookups: None

Sites: 15 RV/tent sites, 4 walk-in tent sites

Maximum RV length: 28

Season: Mid-Mar–Oct

Fees: $15

Maximum stay: 14 days

Management: USDA Forest Service, Chattooga River Ranger District, 9975 US Highway 441, Lakemont; (706) 754-6221; www.fs.usda.gov/Internet/FSE_DOCUMENTS/fseprd496058.pdf

Reservations: No

Pets: Dogs on 6-foot leashes allowed

Quiet hours: 10 p.m.–6 a.m.

Alcohol restrictions: No alcohol allowed

ADA compliant: No

Finding the campground: From the junction of US 441 and US 76 in Clayton, go west on US 76 for 7.9 miles. Turn right onto Persimmon Road and continue for 4.3 miles. Turn left onto Tallulah River Road. At 1.3 miles it changes to dirt and gravel. Stay on the road for another 1.4 miles to the campground.

About the campground: This campground sits on level ground at the mouth of Tate Branch on the Tallulah River, offering a primitive experience to campers. Roughly half the campsites are on the riverfront, with the walk-in sites across Tallulah River Road from the rest.

    The main activity here is fishing for stocked brook, brown, and rainbow trout in the river or venturing up Tate Branch in search of wild, native brook trout.

42 Upper Chattahoochee River Campground

Recreation: Hiking, fishing
Location: 12 miles northwest of Helen; 48 Forest Service Road, Helen 30545
GPS: N34 78.67' / W83 78.29'
Facilities and amenities: Chemical flush toilets, picnic tables, fire rings, lantern posts, picnic area, hiking trails, waterfalls
Elevation: 2,800
Road conditions: The entire drive from GA 75 to the campground, as well as the driveways in the facility are dirt, gravel, and very curvy.
Hookups: None
Sites: 9 RV/tent sites, 10 tent-only sites
Maximum RV length: 24
Season: Mid-Mar–mid-Dec
Fees: $12
Maximum stay: 14 days
Management: USDA Forest Service, Chattooga River Ranger District, 9975 US Highway 441, Lakemont 30552; (706) 754-6221; www.fs.usda.gov/Internet/FSE_DOCUMENTS/fseprd496058.pdf
Reservations: No
Pets: Dogs on 6-foot leashes allowed
Quiet hours: 10 p.m.–6 a.m.
Alcohol restrictions: No alcohol allowed
ADA compliant: Yes
Finding the campground: From the junction of GA 75 and GA 75A in Helen, go north on GA 75 for 7.7 miles. Turn left onto dirt and gravel Wilks Road, which soon changes its name to Chattahoochee River Road. Continue for 4.5 miles to the campground entrance driveway on the right.
About the campground: This campground marks the uppermost approach to Georgia's most famous river near its wellspring in the Chattahoochee Gap close to the Appalachian Trail. Situated on the banks of the river, the facility is the jumping-off point for hiking trails to Horse Trough Falls on one of the river's feeder streams and to Henson Creek Falls, which is actually located on the main river rather than that creek. The river through the campground is stocked with trout during spring to fall, while the portion upstream of Henson Creek Falls holds wild, native brook trout.

    Undergrowth vegetation provides privacy to the campsites, while the overstory of mixed hardwoods, pines, and hemlocks keep the sites fully shaded. Some sites are located right along the river.

Although the RV sites could handle rigs of up to 60 feet, the twisting, rough roads approaching from any direction make smaller units much more practical.

43 West Fork Campground

Recreation: Fishing
Location: 15 miles northeast of Clayton; 919 Overflow Creek Road, Clayton 30525
GPS: N34 94.82' / W83 20.38'
Facilities and amenities: Vault toilet, picnic table, fire ring, lantern post
Elevation: 1,625
Road conditions: Overflow Creek Road leading to the campground is dirt and gravel.
Hookups: None
Sites: 5 walk-in tent sites
Maximum RV length: NA
Season: Year-round, Apr–Oct peak season
Fees: $10
Maximum stay: 14 days
Management: USDA Forest Service, Chattooga River Ranger District, 9975 US Highway 441, Lakemont 30552; (706) 754-6221; www.fs.usda.gov/Internet/FSE_DOCUMENTS/fseprd496058.pdf
Reservations: No
Pets: Dogs on 6-foot leashes allowed
Quiet hours: 10 p.m.–6 a.m.
Alcohol restrictions: No alcohol allowed
ADA compliant: No
Finding the campground: From the intersection of US 441 and Warwoman Road in Clayton, go 13.8 miles east on Warwoman Road. Just across the bridge over the West Fork of the Chattooga River, turn left onto Overflow Creek Road. Drive 0.9 mile to the campground on the left.
About the campground: The West Fork Campground is a small, rustic facility on the bank of the West Fork of the Chattooga River. It provides only minimal amenities for visitors, most of whom are anglers targeting stocked trout released in the river from spring through fall.

A gravel parking lot and chemical vault toilet are available on site.

44 Willis Knob Horse Campground

Recreation: Horseback riding
Location: 14 miles east of Clayton; 1922 Willis Knob Road, Clayton 30525
GPS: N34 53.57' / W83 13.21'
Facilities and amenities: Vault toilet, water, picnic tables, fire rings, lantern posts, cable TV hookup, hitching high-lines, watering troughs, equestrian trails
Elevation: 1,750
Road conditions: Willis Knob Road is a dirt and gravel track.
Hookups: Water, electric

Sites: 6 single RV/tent sites, 3 double RV/tent sites

Maximum RV length: 60

Season: Year-round

Fees: Single site $20, double site $30 or $40

Maximum stay: 14 days

Management: USDA Forest Service, Chattooga River Ranger District, 9975 US Highway 441, Lakemont 30552; (706) 754-6221; www.fs.usda.gov/Internet/FSE_DOCUMENTS/fseprd496058.pdf

Reservations: (877) 444-6777; www.recreation.gov

Pets: Dogs on 6-foot leashes allowed

Quiet hours: 10 p.m.–6 a.m.

Alcohol restrictions: No alcohol allowed

ADA compliant: Yes

Finding the campground: From the junction of US 441 and Warwoman Road in Clayton, go 11.3 miles east on Warwoman Road. Turn right on Willis Knob Road. At 2.1 miles the entrance driveway to the campground is on the left.

About the campground: As the name implies, Willis Knob Horse Camp is designed exclusively for the use of equestrian campers. The camping area is quite open, but the sites are well spaced. The entrance road has a gate that is locked when campers are not present.

The site provides access to the 15-mile Willis Knob Trail for rides through a wilderness setting within the Chattahoochee National Forest.

You are required to clean up manure and hay during your stay. Trailers are provided at the campground for that purpose.

Piedmont Region

The Piedmont Region of Georgia stretches from the foothills just north of Atlanta down to the Fall line at Macon. West to east the region runs from the Alabama border to the South Carolina state line. In many ways, this has been and still is the heartland of the Peach State.

Georgia's total population is just shy of 11 million people, making it the 18th largest state in the Union. Of that total number of residents, roughly 45 percent live in the 11 Metro Atlanta counties that anchor the central portion of the Piedmont Region. Obviously, the more people you have, the more folks you have looking to get outdoors for fun and relaxation, including going camping. As a result, the Piedmont has more public camping areas than the state's vacation areas in the northern mountains or along the Atlantic Coast.

Early in the state's history, the Piedmont also was Georgia's "breadbasket" and home to large plantations, but even more small family farms. That agricultural past left physical marks on the land in the form of cleared fields and pastures that today are subdivisions or have reverted to mixed pine and hardwood forests. The rivers and streams of this central portion of the state are dotted with sites of old grist mills where corn and other grains were made into meal and flour.

This area so rich in the bounty of the fields has attracted invaders since the first colonists spread out from their settlements around Savannah on the coast. Those colonists moved in to replace the Native American peoples. Next it was the British during the Revolutionary War trying to tame the land and Georgians of the eastern Piedmont. Finally, the encroachment of Gen. William T. Sherman during the Civil War laid waste to much of the western and central Piedmont Region. Each of those events left historical sites across Georgia's midsection, many of which spawned parks and recreation areas around which campgrounds are located today.

A more recent feature of the region is major reservoirs on the rivers that provide recreational options in the Piedmont. The Savannah, Oconee, Ocmulgee, Chattahoochee, and Coosa Rivers served first as travel corridors through the region. Now those waterways host ten large Corps of Engineers projects offering hundreds of thousands of acres of water around which campgrounds have sprung up.

Another factor of the fertility of the Piedmont is the wildlife it supports. In many areas of the region, the population of white-tailed deer is large. It is not uncommon to see them grazing along roadways or darting across the asphalt in the evenings. Wild turkeys often are seen foraging in fallow fields, pastures, or even residential yards. Along the swamp corridor of the Ocmulgee River, black bears still are present in the region. Smaller mammals abound, as do the many resident bird species.

In all quarters of the Piedmont, campgrounds abound to allow residents and visitors to the state to enjoy the history, wildlife, and natural beauty of the Piedmont Region.

◀ *Sweetwater State Park's ten yurts are popular with anglers, hikers, and those that just want a getaway so close to metro Atlanta.*

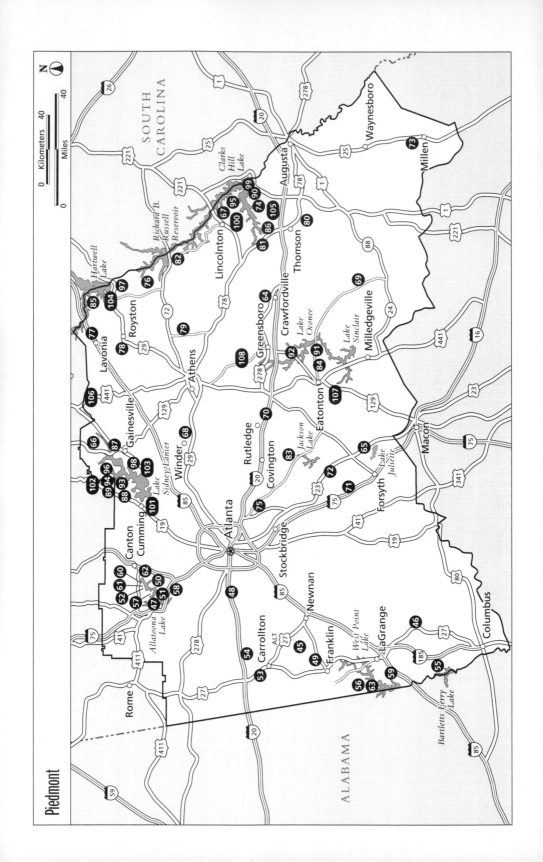

Piedmont

Alabama to Atlanta

Campgrounds At-A-Glance

#	Name	Total Sites	Group Sites	Hookup Sites	Hookups	Maximum RV Length	Dump Station	Toilets	Showers	Drinking Water	ADA	Fees	Reservations
Georgia State Parks and Historic Sites Division													
45	Chattahoochee Bend State Park	64	1	35	WE	40	Y	F	Y	Y	Y	$$-$$$$$	Y
46	Franklin D. Roosevelt State Park	132	5	111	WE	100	Y	F	Y	Y	Y	$$-$$$$$	Y
47	Red Top Mountain State Park	94	1	78	WE	40	Y	F	Y	Y	Y	$$$$-$$$$$	Y
48	Sweetwater Creek State Park	5	0	0	N	NA	N	F	Y	Y	Y	$$$-$$$$$	Y
County Parks													
49	Bush Head Shoals Access Park	6	0	0	N	NA	N	V	N	N	N	N	N
50	Clark Creek North Campground	24	0	24	WE	40	Y	F	Y	Y	Y	$$$$	Y
51	Clark Creek South Campground	40	0	25	WE	40	Y	F	Y	Y	Y	$$$-$$$$	Y
52	Gatewood Park	70	0	58	WE	40	Y	F	Y	Y	Y	$$-$$$	Y
53	John Tanner Park	33	1	32	WE	40	Y	F	Y	Y	Y	$$$-$$$$	Y
54	Little Tallapoosa Park	64	0	64	WES	50	Y	F	Y	Y	Y	$$-$$$	Y
Georgia Power Company													
55	Blanton Creek Campground	51	0	51	WE	42	Y	F	Y	Y	Y	$$$	Y
US Army Corps of Engineers													
56	Holiday Campground	130	2	110	WE	80	Y	F	Y	Y	Y	$$-$$$$$	Y
57	McKaskey Creek Campground	50	0	31	WE	34	Y	F	Y	Y	Y	$$$-$$$$	Y
58	McKinney Campground	149	0	149	WE	60	Y	F	Y	Y	Y	$$$$	Y
59	R. Shaefer Heard Campground	120	0	120	WE	90	Y	F	Y	Y	Y	$$$-$$$$$	Y

#	Name	Total Sites	Group Sites	Hookup Sites	Hookups	Maximum RV Length	Dump Station	Toilets	Showers	Drinking Water	ADA	Fees	Reservations
60	Sweetwater Campground	150	1	108	WE	70	Y	F	Y	Y	Y	$$$–$$$$$	Y
61	Upper Stamp Creek Campground	20	0	18	WE	32	Y	F	Y	Y	Y	$$$–$$$$	Y
62	Victoria Campground	72	0	71	WE	70	Y	F	Y	Y	Y	$$$–$$$$	Y
63	Whitetail Ridge Campground	58	0	58	WE	75	Y	F	Y	Y	Y	$$$–$$$$$	Y

See Amenities Chart key on page xxi.

45 Chattahoochee Bend State Park

Recreation: Hiking, fishing, boating, paddling, biking, playground
Location: 15 miles northwest of Newnan; 425 Bob White Way, Newnan 30263
GPS: N33 42.97' / W84 98.96'
Facilities and amenities: Flush toilets, showers, laundry, water, dump site, picnic tables, fire rings, picnic areas and shelters, playgrounds, hiking and mountain biking trails, boat ramp, canoe/kayak put-in, observation tower, visitor center
Elevation: 665
Road conditions: Paved roads
Hookups: Water, electric
Sites: 5 premium RV/tent sites with hookups, 30 standard RV/tent sites with hookups, 12 walk-in tent sites, 8 platform tent sites, 8 backcountry paddle-in tent sites, 1 Adirondack group site, 3 cottages
Maximum RV length: 40
Season: Year-round, Apr–Oct peak season
Fees: Premium RV/tent site with hookups $36, standard RV/tent site with hookups $32, walk-in tent site $20, platform tent site $17, backcountry paddle-in site $11, Adirondack group site $75, cottage $150, daily parking fee $5, annual pass $50
Maximum stay: 14 days
Management: Georgia State Parks and Historic Sites Division, 2610 Georgia Highway 155 SW, Stockbridge; (770) 389-7286; www.gastateparks.org
Reservations: (800) 864-7275; www.gastateparks.org/reservations
Pets: Dogs on 6-foot leashes allowed
Quiet hours: 10 p.m.–7 a.m.
Alcohol restrictions: Unlawful in public areas
ADA compliant: Yes

Finding the campground: From exit 47 on I-85 at Newnan, go 0.6 mile west on GA 34 (Bullsboro Boulevard). Turn right on GA 34 Bypass (Millard Farmer Industrial Boulevard) and drive 6 miles to a 4-way stop. Turn right on GA 34 (Franklin Road). At 8.2 miles turn right on Thomas Road and proceed 5.5 miles (the road changes names several times, but just continue straight). Turn right on Flat Rock Road, which becomes Bobwhite Way and ends in the park.

About the campground: Chattahoochee Bend is one of Georgia's newest and largest parks. Its 2,910 acres stretch for 7 miles along the east side of the Chattahoochee River in Coweta County near the town of Newnan. The park offers a number of family activities, most of which center on the river and its shores.

The campgrounds are located in two loops at the southern end of the park, both of which are in a mostly pine forest setting. The sites are level, well-spaced in an open understory, and have partial shade. The backcountry paddle-in sites are at the extreme northern end of the park.

46 Franklin D. Roosevelt State Park

Recreation: Hiking, fishing, paddling, birding, swimming, biking, playground
Location: 21 miles southeast of LaGrange; 2070 Georgia Highway 190 East, Pine Mountain 31822
GPS: N32 83.75' / W84 81.56'
Facilities and amenities: Flush toilets, showers, laundry, water, dump station, picnic tables, fire rings, playground, picnic area and pavilion, amphitheater, hiking/biking/equestrian trails, swimming pool, rental boats, fishing pier, trading post, gift shop
Elevation: 1,125
Road conditions: Paved roads
Hookups: Water, electric
Sites: 39 premium RV/tent sites with hookups, 72 standard RV/tent sites with hookups, 16 backcountry tent sites, 4 pioneer campsites, 1 group camp, 21 cottages
Maximum RV length: 100
Season: Year-round, Apr–Oct peak season
Fees: Premium RV/tent site with hookups $42, standard RV/tent site with hookups $36, backcountry tent site $12, pioneer site $75–$150, group camp $500, 2-bedroom premier cottage $190, 2-bedroom cottage $175, 1-bedroom premier cottage $150, daily parking fee $5, annual pass $50
Maximum stay: 14 days
Management: Georgia State Parks and Historic Sites Division, 2610 Georgia Highway 155 SW, Stockbridge; (770) 389-7286; www.gastateparks.org
Reservations: (800) 864-7275; www.gastateparks.org/reservations
Pets: Dogs on 6-foot leashes allowed
Quiet hours: 10 p.m.–7 a.m.
Alcohol restrictions: Unlawful in public areas
ADA compliant: Yes
Finding the campground: From exit 42 on I-185, go east on US 27 for 18 miles. Turn left onto GA 354. At 2.6 miles turn right and go 0.4 mile to the campground drive (Lake Deleanor Road) on the right.

On the north side of Lake Deleanor, many of the campsites enjoy a lake view.

About the campground: This park was named for the 32nd president, who often visited the area while staying at his nearby Little White House or at Warm Springs for treatment of his polio. Today the facility is the largest state park at 9,049 acres and includes the 23-mile Pine Mountain Trail.

The park's campground is on the northern side of 15-acre Lake Deleanor, while the backcountry tent sites are spread along the Pine Mountain Trail. The RV/tent sites are composed of five loops, with some sites on loops 1 and 2 having lake frontage.

Hiking trails connect the campground to the Pine Mountain Trail and the park's iconic Liberty Bell swimming pool that was built by the CCC in the 1930s and is open seasonally.

47 Red Top Mountain State Park

Recreation: Hiking, fishing, boating, paddling, biking, swimming, playground
Location: 6 miles east of Cartersville; 50 Lodge Road, Acworth 30102
GPS: N34 14.35' / W84 70.42'
Facilities and amenities: Flush toilets, showers, laundry, dump station, grills, water, tables, picnic shelters, picnic areas, playgrounds, swimming beach, hiking and mountain biking trails, boat ramps, tennis courts
Elevation: 957

Road conditions: Paved roads

Hookups: Water, electric

Sites: 27 premium RV/tent sites with hookups, 51 standard RV/tent sites with hookups, 15 walk-in tent sites, 1 pioneer site, 6 yurts, 20 cottages

Maximum RV length: 40

Season: Year-round, Apr–Oct peak season

Fees: Premium RV/tent site with hookups $45, standard RV/tent site with hookups $40, premium walk-in tent site $45, standard walk-in tent site $40, pioneer site $50, yurt $115, 2-bedroom cottage $225, 3-bedroom cottage $275, daily parking fee $5, annual pass $50

Maximum stay: 14 days

Management: Georgia State Parks and Historic Sites Division, 2610 Georgia Highway 155 SW, Stockbridge; (770) 389-7286; www.gastateparks.org

Reservations: (800) 864-7275; www.gastateparks.org/reservations

Pets: Dogs on 6-foot leashes allowed

Quiet hours: 10 p.m.–7 a.m.

Alcohol restrictions: Unlawful in public areas

ADA compliant: Yes

Finding the campground: From I-75 take exit 285 to the east onto Red Top Mountain Road and travel 2.3 miles to the park entrance.

Situated on 12,000-acre Allatoona Lake, the park attracts visitors for its water activities and the 15 miles of hiking trails.

About the campground: Red Top Mountain State Park covers 1,776-acres just west of Cartersville and roughly 35 miles northwest of downtown Atlanta. The park takes its name from the red color of the soil due to concentrations of iron ore. The area was once an important iron mining area.

Red Top Mountain occupies a peninsula at the junction of the Etowah River and Allatoona Creek arms of 12,010-acre Allatoona Lake, which provides fishing and water sports opportunities. Additionally, there are more than 15 miles of hiking trails and the Vaughn Cabin, a re-created pioneer homestead where periodic displays of iron pouring take place.

The campground is located in the southwest section of the park, situated on hilly terrain overlooking the reservoir. Only a few of the tent sites are actually on the shore, with some of the RV sites having lake views, but from up on the hillsides. Virtually all sites are shaded.

48 Sweetwater Creek State Park

Recreation: Hiking, fishing, boating, paddling, birding, playground
Location: 17 miles west of Atlanta; 1750 Mount Vernon Road, Lithia Springs 30122
GPS: N33 75.38' / W84 63.90'

Sweetwater Creek is popular with anglers, kayakers, and those visiting the ruins of the textile mill once located on the scenic waterway.

Facilities and amenities: Flush toilets, showers, grills, tables, picnic shelters, picnic areas, playgrounds, hiking trails, boat ramp, fishing piers, rental boats, bait shop, museum, historic site
Elevation: 883
Road conditions: Paved roads
Hookups: None
Sites: 5 walk-in tent sites, 10 yurts
Maximum RV length: NA
Season: Year-round, Apr–Oct peak season
Fees: Walk-in tent sites $28, yurts $100, daily parking fee $5, annual pass $50
Maximum stay: 14 days
Management: Georgia State Parks and Historic Sites Division, 2610 Georgia Highway 155 SW, Stockbridge; (770) 389-7286; www.gastateparks.org
Reservations: (800) 864-7275; www.gastateparks.org/reservations
Pets: Dogs on 6-foot leashes allowed
Quiet hours: 10 p.m.–7 a.m.
Alcohol restrictions: Unlawful in public areas
ADA compliant: Yes
Finding the campground: From exit 41 on I-20 head south on Lee Road for 1.1 miles. Turn left on Cedar Terrace Road, and at the end of the road turn left on Mount Vernon Road. The entrance drive for the campground is immediately on the left.
About the campground: Located just on the western outskirts of Atlanta, Sweetwater Creek State Park stretches for 2,459 acres along its namesake waterway. Also, within the park, George H. Sparks Reservoir covers 215 acres, offering fishing and boating activities.

The portion of Sweetwater Creek found here runs through Factory Shoals beside the ruins of the Civil War–era New Manchester Manufacturing Company textile mill, which was burned during that conflict. The park visitor center has a museum centered on the mill and the history of the village that once surrounded it. The creek also is open to anglers within the park boundaries.

Although limited in number, the five walk-in tent campsites are just a few hundred feet from the parking area at the yurt village. Restrooms with showers are at this location to serve both the yurts and campsites.

All the sites are shaded, offer privacy, and overlook an arm of the Sparks Reservoir.

49   Bush Head Shoals Access Park

Recreation: Fishing, paddling
Location: 4 miles northeast of Franklin; Bush Head Shoals Road, Franklin 30217
GPS: N33 31.13' / W85 06.88'
Facilities and amenities: Vault toilets, picnic tables, fire rings, canoe/kayak launch
Elevation: 750
Road conditions: Paved roads
Hookups: None
Sites: 6 tent sites
Maximum RV length: NA
Season: Year-round, Apr–Oct peak season

Fees: None

Maximum stay: None

Management: Heard County Parks and Recreation Department, 2020 Thompson Road, Franklin; (706) 675-3778; www.heardrecreation.com

Reservations: No

Pets: Dogs on 6-foot leashes allowed

Quiet hours: None

Alcohol restrictions: Alcohol not allowed

ADA compliant: No

Finding the campground: From exit 47 on I-85 at Newnan, go 0.6 mile west on GA 34 (Bullsboro Boulevard). Turn right on GA 34 Bypass (Millard Farmer Industrial Boulevard) and drive 6 miles to a 4-way stop. Turn right on GA 34 (Franklin Road). At 13.1 miles turn right on Bush Head Shoals Road. Go 1 mile to the end of the road and the campground on the river shore.

About the campground: Bush Head Shoals Access Park is a new facility on the Chattahoochee River in Heard County. Be aware that Google Maps shows it as a state park, but it is not.

The site has very minimal facilities consisting of a few tent pads and a vault toilet. There is no potable water here. This is a location for use by kayak and canoe enthusiasts during overnight trips down the river or as a headquarters for multiple days of paddling these waters.

Presently there is only a kayak/canoe launch. Be aware that the automatic gate opens at 7 a.m. and closes at 10 p.m. and there is no attendant on site.

50 Clark Creek North Campground

Recreation: Fishing

Location: 11 miles southeast of Cartersville; 5983 Glade Road, Acworth 30102

GPS: N34 10.33' / W84 68.18'

Facilities and amenities: Flush toilets, showers, laundry, water, grill, picnic table, lantern post

Elevation: 900

Road conditions: Paved roads

Hookups: Water, electric

Sites: 24 RV/tent sites with hookups

Maximum RV length: 40

Season: Year-round, Apr–Oct peak season

Fees: $34

Maximum stay: 14 days

Management: Bartow County Parks and Recreation Department, 31 Beavers Street, Cartersville; (770) 387-5149; www.bartowcountyga.gov/departments/clark_creek_south.php

Reservations: (770) 387-5149

Pets: Limit of 2 dogs on 6-foot leashes allowed

Quiet hours: 10 p.m.–7 a.m.

Alcohol restrictions: No open containers

ADA compliant: Yes

Finding the campground: From exit 278 on I-75, go north on Glade Road for 1.7 miles. The campground is on the left.

All sites in the Clark Creek North Campground have waterfront views.

About the campground: Clark Creek North Campground, as the name implies, is located on the north shore of the Clark Creek arm of Allatoona Lake. This 12,010-acre reservoir consistently ranks in the top five most heavily visited US Army Corps of Engineers impoundments in the nation. The nearby Clark Creek South Campground provides free access to a boat ramp and swimming beach while you stay at the North Campground.

The campground is located on a single loop road in a wooded area. All sites are at least partially shaded and have waterfront views.

51 Clark Creek South Campground

Recreation: Fishing, boating, paddling
Location: 11 miles southeast of Cartersville; 5976 Glade Road, Acworth 30102
GPS: N34 10.07' / W84 69.23'
Facilities and amenities: Flush toilets, showers, water, laundry, dump station, picnic table, fire ring, lantern post, swimming beach, boat ramp
Elevation: 900

Road conditions: Paved roads

Hookups: Water, electric

Sites: 25 RV/tent sites with hookups, 11 RV/tent sites with no hookups, 1 tent site with water hookup, 3 tent sites with no hookups

Maximum RV length: 40

Season: Mar–Oct

Fees: RV/tent site with hookups $34, tent site with water $22, tent site with no hookups $22

Maximum stay: 14 days

Management: Bartow County Parks and Recreation Department, 31 Beavers Street, Cartersville; (770) 387-5149; www.bartowcountyga.gov/departments/clark_creek_north2.php

Reservations: (770) 387-5149

Pets: Limit of 2 dogs on 6-foot leashes allowed

Quiet hours: 10 p.m.–7 a.m.

Alcohol restrictions: No open containers

ADA compliant: Yes

Finding the campground: From exit 278 on I-75, go north on Glade Road for 1.5 miles. The campground is on the right.

About the campground: Positioned on the south side of the Clark Creek arm of Allatoona Lake, the campground stretches along the shore of two coves, with most sites on the water. Many of the sites are in wooded areas with full shade.

The lake covers 12,010 acres and rates in the top five most visited US Army Corps of Engineers facilities in the nation.

The boat ramp and beach have shared use with campers staying at the nearby Clark Creek North Campground.

52 Gatewood Park

Recreation: Hiking, fishing, boating, paddling, swimming, playground

Location: 7 miles east of Cartersville; 244 Bartow Beach Road, Cartersville 30121

GPS: N34 17.27' / W84 72.06'

Facilities and amenities: Flush toilets, showers, laundry, water, dump station, picnic table, fire ring, picnic shelters, playground, beach, nature trail, boat ramp

Elevation: 900

Road conditions: Paved roads

Hookups: Water, electric

Sites: 58 RV/tent sites with hookups, 12 RV/tent sites no hookups

Maximum RV length: 40

Season: Mar–Oct

Fees: RV/tent site with hookups $30, RV/tent site with no hookups $18

Maximum stay: 14 days

Management: Bartow County Parks and Recreation Department, 31 Beavers Street, Cartersville; (770) 387-5149; www.bartowcountyga.gov/departments/clark_creek_north2.php

Reservations: (770) 387-5149

Pets: Limit of 2 dogs on 6-foot leashes allowed

Located on the north side of Allatoona Lake, the sites are elevated overlooking the water.

Quiet hours: 10 p.m.–7 a.m.
Alcohol restrictions: No open containers
ADA compliant: Yes
Finding the campground: From exit 290 on I-75, go east on GA 20 and immediately turn right on GA 20 South Spur (Allatoona Dam Road). After 1 mile, turn left at the end of the road onto Bartow Beach Road. At 0.9 mile the road ends at the campground.
About the campground: The campground is located on the north side of Allatoona Lake, near the mouth of the McKaskey Creek arm of the impoundment. The 12,010-acre lake rates in the top five in the nation among US Army Corps of Engineers lakes.

Gatewood Park campground is composed of two loops, each on a separate point jutting into the lake, while a third point holds the boat ramp and picnic area. The campsites are elevated on rolling hillsides overlooking the water. They are well spaced, offer privacy, and are fully shaded.

53 John Tanner Park

Recreation: Hiking, fishing, boating, paddling, playground
Location: 7 miles northwest of Carrollton; 354 Tanners Beach Road, Carrollton 30117
GPS: N33 60.23' / W85 16.69'
Facilities and amenities: Flush toilets, showers, laundry, grills, picnic tables, lantern posts, picnic area and pavilions, miniature golf, volleyball, horseshoe pits, swimming beach, two lakes, hiking trails, pedal and fishing boat rentals, boat launch, amphitheater
Elevation: 1,080
Road conditions: Paved roads
Hookups: Water, electric
Sites: 32 RV/tent sites with hookups, 1 pioneer site
Maximum RV length: 40
Season: Year-round, Apr–Oct peak season
Fees: RV $30, tent $27, pioneer site $40, daily parking fee $5, annual pass $40
Maximum stay: 14 days
Management: Carroll County Parks and Recreation Department, 1201 Newnan Road, Carrollton; (770) 830-2222; www.carrollcountyga.com/290/John-Tanner-Park
Reservations: (770) 830-2222
Pets: Dogs on 6-foot leashes allowed
Quiet hours: 10 p.m.–7 a.m.
Alcohol restrictions: Unlawful in public use areas
ADA compliant: Yes
Finding the campground: From exit 11 on I-20, go south on US 27 for 1.8 miles. Turn right on Bowden Junction Road, and at 4.2 miles turn left on Mt. Zion Road. Proceed 1.6 miles and turn right on Tanners Beach Road. The park entrance is at 0.7 mile.
About the campground: This facility was formerly a state park that now is operated by the county. The park offers a wide range of amenities and activities for all ages. There are two lakes on site that offer boating, fishing, and swimming. Each lake has a boat ramp and Upper Lake offers boat rentals.

The campground is rather tightly spaced and offers partial to full shade. Additionally, construction of a second campground on Lower Lake should be complete in 2023, offering full hookups, including sewer.

54 Little Tallapoosa Park

Recreation: Hiking, fishing, biking, playground, horseback riding
Location: 5 miles north of Carrollton; 1939 Highway 113N, Carrollton 30116
GPS: N33 64.52' / W85 05.11'
Facilities and amenities: Flush toilets, showers, laundry, fire rings, water, tables, picnic shelters, picnic areas, playgrounds, hiking / mountain biking / equestrian trails, fishing lakes, geocaching, splash pad

Elevation: 1,050
Road conditions: Paved roads
Hookups: Water, electric, sewer
Sites: 22 RV sites with full hookups, 32 tent sites with electric hookups, 10 equestrian sites with water and electric hookups
Maximum RV length: 50
Season: Year-round, Apr–Oct peak season
Fees: RV sites $30, tent sites $15, equestrian sites (you must have horses) $12
Maximum stay: 14 days
Management: Carroll County Parks and Recreation Department, 1201 Newnan Road, Carrollton; (770) 830-2222; www.carrollcountyga.com/480/Little-Tallapoosa-Park
Reservations: (770) 830-2222
Pets: Dogs on 6-foot leashes allowed
Quiet hours: 10 p.m.–7 a.m.
Alcohol restrictions: Unlawful in public use areas
ADA compliant: Yes
Finding the campground: From the junction of US 27 and GA 113 in Carrollton, go north on GA 113 for 3.8 miles. The park entrance is on the right.
About the campground: Located in west Georgia near the city of Carrollton, Little Tallapoosa Park is a county-managed facility covering 330 acres. This is a family-friendly environment offering numerous activities for all ages. The park features 9 miles of natural trails and 2.5 miles of paved pathways, providing options for walking, cycling, and horseback riding. There are 17 geocaches in the park, along with two ponds for fishing and a seasonal splash pad for the youngsters.

The separate RV, tent, and equestrian camping areas are partially shaded, with the RV section offering four pull-through sites that are reserved for RVs of 38 feet or longer. Pop-up campers are allowed in the tent area.

55 Blanton Creek Campground

Recreation: Fishing, boating, paddling, playground
Location: 22 miles north of Columbus; 6111 Lick Skillet Road, Hamilton 31811
GPS: N32 74.22' / W85 10.85'
Facilities and amenities: Flush toilets, showers, laundry, water, dump station, picnic tables, fire rings, playground, picnic area and pavilion, hiking and biking trails, volleyball court, boat ramp, fishing piers
Elevation: 600
Road conditions: Paved roads
Hookups: Water, electric
Sites: 43 RV/tent sites with hookups, 8 tent-only sites with hookups
Maximum RV length: 42
Season: Mar–Sep
Fees: RV/tent site $30, tent-only site $25
Maximum stay: 14 days
Management: Georgia Power Company; (855) 607-6462; https://reservations.gplakes.com/

Reservations: (706) 643-7737; https://reservations.gplakes.com/FacilityDetails.aspx?facID=1
Pets: Dogs on 6-foot leashes allowed
Quiet hours: 10 p.m.–7 a.m.
Alcohol restrictions: No alcohol allowed
ADA compliant: Yes
Finding the campground: From exit 25 on I-185, go west on GA 116, which quickly goes through the intersection with GA 219 and then becomes GA 103. At 3.7 miles, turn left onto Lick Skillet Road. At 0.7 mile the campground entrance is on the right.
About the campground: This facility sits on the shores of 5,850-acre Lake Harding (also known as Bartletts Ferry Lake) on the Georgia–Alabama border. This well-kept campground is ideal for family groups, with a variety of activities and amenities.

The campsites are well spaced, with a number of the RV sites and all the tent sites on the water. Those waterfront sites have at least partial shade, while the rest get full shade in a forested setting.

56 Holiday Campground

Recreation: Fishing, boating, paddling, playground
Location: 11 miles northwest of LaGrange; 954 Abbotsford Road, LaGrange 30240
GPS: N33 01.34' / W85 10.44'
Facilities and amenities: Flush toilets, showers, laundry, water, dump station, picnic tables, fire rings, playgrounds, basketball and tennis courts, baseball field, hiking trails, swimming beach, boat ramps
Elevation: 654
Road conditions: Paved roads
Hookups: Water, electric
Sites: 99 standard RV/tent sites with hookups, 1 RV/tent site with no hookups, 1 standard double RV/tent site with hookups, 11 tent-only sites with no hookups, 10 group RV/tent sites with hookups, 8 group tent-only sites with no hookups
Maximum RV length: 80
Season: Year-round, Apr–Oct peak season
Fees: Standard RV/tent site with hookups $30, RV/tent site with no hookups $20, standard RV/tent double sites with hookups $60, group tent sites with no hookups $20, tent sites with no hookups $20, group RV sites $230–$250
Maximum stay: 14 days
Management: US Army Corps of Engineers, West Point Lake Project Office, 500 Resource Management Dr., West Point; (706) 6452937; www.sam.usace.army.mil/Missions/Civil-Works/Recreation/West-Point-Lake/
Reservations: (877) 444-6777; www.recreation.gov
Pets: Dogs on 6-foot leashes allowed
Quiet hours: 10 p.m.–6 a.m.
Alcohol restrictions: No alcohol allowed
ADA compliant: Yes

Finding the campground: From the junction of US 27 and US 29 in LaGrange, go west on US 29 (Vernon Street) for 2.5 miles. Go right on Roanoke Road for 7.6 miles. Turn left onto Thompson Road and at 0.6 mile go left on Abbottsford Road. At 2 miles the campground entrance is on the right.

About the campground: Holiday Campground is on a heavily wooded major peninsula jutting out into 25,900-acre West Point Lake. The site offers a wide array of activities and amenities for families and group outings. It also is a great jumping-off point for fishing and water sports on the reservoir.

The camping areas are spread along almost a dozen points off the main peninsula, with full shade and lake views on most sites.

Be aware that credit cards are the only acceptable payment for campsites

57 McKaskey Creek Campground

Recreation: Fishing, boating, paddling, swimming, playground
Location: 6 miles northeast of Cartersville; 358 McKaskey Creek Road, Cartersville 30121
GPS: N34 11.24' / W84 43.50'
Facilities and amenities: Flush toilets, showers, water, dump station, picnic tables, fire rings, lantern posts, playground, swimming beach, boat ramp
Elevation: 850
Road conditions: Paved roads
Hookups: Water, electric
Sites: 31 standard RV/tent sites with hookups, 19 tent-only sites with no hookups
Maximum RV length: 34
Season: Mid-Mar–Sep
Fees: Standard RV/tent site waterfront with hookups $34, standard RV/tent site with hookups $30, tent site $24
Maximum stay: 14 days
Management: US Army Corps of Engineers, Allatoona Lake Project office, 1138 Georgia Highway 20 Spur, Cartersville; (678) 721-6700; www.sam.usace.army.mil/Missions/Civil-Works/Recreation/Allatoona-Lake/
Reservations: (877) 444-6777; www.recreation.gov
Pets: Dogs on 6-foot leashes allowed
Quiet hours: 10 p.m.–6 a.m.
Alcohol restrictions: No alcohol allowed
ADA compliant: Yes
Finding the campground: From exit 290 on I-75, go east on GA 20 and immediately turn right on GA 20 South Spur (Allatoona Dam Road). At 2 miles turn left onto McKaskey Creek Road. At 1 mile the road runs into the campground.

About the campground: McKaskey Creek Campground is on the shore of an arm of the inundated section of its namesake stream. The campground is composed of five separate loops spreading out onto a point in the lake. The sites are on rolling hillsides in a wooded area with plenty of shade. Some of these well-spaced and scenic campsites are on the waterfront, while they all offer a measure of privacy.

58 McKinney Campground

Recreation: Fishing, boating, paddling, swimming, playground
Location: 11 miles southeast of Cartersville; 6659 McKinney Campground Road SE, Acworth 30102
GPS: N34 06.25' / W84 41.44'
Facilities and amenities: Flush toilets, showers, water, fire rings, picnic tables, lantern posts, picnic shelters, picnic areas, playground, swimming beach, boat ramp
Elevation: 900
Road conditions: Paved roads
Hookups: Water, electric
Sites: 149 standard RV/tent sites with hookups
Maximum RV length: 60
Season: Year-round, Apr–Oct peak season
Fees: Lakefront $34, interior $30
Maximum stay: 14 days
Management: US Army Corps of Engineers, Allatoona Lake Project office, 1138 Georgia Highway 20 Spur, Cartersville; (678) 721-6700; www.sam.usace.army.mil/Missions/Civil-Works/Recreation/Allatoona-Lake/
Reservations: (877) 444-6777; www.recreation.gov
Pets: Dogs on 6-foot leashes allowed
Quiet hours: 10 p.m.–6 a.m.
Alcohol restrictions: No alcohol allowed
ADA compliant: Yes
Finding the campground: From exit 278 on I-75, go north on Glade Road for 2.7 miles. Turn left on Kings Camp Road. At 0.7 mile turn left on McKinney Campground Road. At 0.3 mile the campground is on the right.
About the campground: Located just 30 miles northwest of Atlanta, McKinney Campground is on the shore of the US Army Corps of Engineers' 12,010-acre Allatoona Lake. This reservoir is one of the most popular for recreation in the nation, drawing more than 7 million visitors per year.

McKinney is the only Corps campground on the lake that is open year-round. However, campsites 75 to 150 are only open from March to December. The campground is heavily forested, offering shade on all the sites.

59 R. Shaefer Heard Campground

Recreation: Hiking, fishing, paddling, biking, swimming, playground
Location: 15 miles southwest of LaGrange; 101 Shaefer Heard Park Road, West Point 31833
GPS: N32 55.38' / W85 09.50'
Facilities and amenities: Flush toilets, showers, laundry, water, dump station, picnic tables, fire rings, grills, lantern posts, playground, amphitheater, boat ramps, hiking and biking trails, swimming beach
Elevation: 675

Road conditions: Paved roads

Hookups: Water, electric

Sites: 120 standard RV/tent sites with hookups

Maximum RV length: 90

Season: Year-round, Apr–Oct peak season

Fees: Single site $30, double site $60

Maximum stay: 14 days

Management: US Army Corps of Engineers, West Point Lake Project Office, 500 Resource Management Dr., West Point 31833; (706) 6452937; www.sam.usace.army.mil/Missions/Civil-Works/Recreation/West-Point-Lake/

Reservations: (877) 444-6777; www.recreation.gov

Pets: Dogs on 6-foot leashes allowed

Quiet hours: 10 p.m.–6 a.m.

Alcohol restrictions: No alcohol allowed

ADA compliant: Yes

Finding the campground: From exit 2 on I-85 in West Point, go west on GA 18 (East 10th Street) for 1.4 miles. Turn right onto US 29 (West Point Road) and drive 3.4 miles. The campground entrance will be on the left.

About the campground: R. Shaefer Heard Campground sits on the heavily forested southern shore of 25,900-acre West Point Lake. Most of the sites are on the water, with a few set back in the forest. This is a popular destination for anglers and boaters, since it is on one of the few Corps reservoirs in Georgia with a stated purpose of providing recreation.

The campsites are grouped on two adjacent points facing the northwest. All offer shade and are well spaced for privacy. Some of the waterfront sites are limited to RVs only.

60 Sweetwater Campground

Recreation: Fishing, swimming, boating, paddling, playground

Location: 16 miles southwest of Canton; 1400 Fields Chapel Road, Canton 30114

GPS: N34 11.40' / W84 34.44'

Facilities and amenities: Flush toilets, showers, water, dump station, picnic tables, fire rings, lantern posts, picnic area and shelters, playground, swimming beach, canoe rentals, boat ramp

Elevation: 875

Road conditions: Paved roads

Hookups: Water, electric

Sites: 106 standard RV/tent sites with hookups, 1 standard RV/tent double site with hookups, 42 tent-only sites with no hookups, 1 group site with hookups (72 maximum campers)

Maximum RV length: 70

Season: Mid-Mar–Sep

Fees: Standard RV/tent site $34, standard RV/tent double site $60, tent-only site $24, group site $290

Maximum stay: 14 days

Management: US Army Corps of Engineers, Allatoona Lake Project office, 1138 Georgia Highway 20 Spur, Cartersville; (678) 721-6700; www.sam.usace.army.mil/Missions/Civil-Works/Recreation/Allatoona-Lake/

Reservations: (877) 444-6777; www.recreation.gov

Pets: Dogs on 6-foot leashes allowed

Quiet hours: 10 p.m.–6 a.m.

Alcohol restrictions: No alcohol allowed

ADA compliant: Yes

Finding the campground: From exit 290 on I-75, go east on GA 20 for 12 miles. Turn right on Fields Chapel Road. At 2 miles the road enters the campground.

About the campground: Sweetwater Campground is a quite popular destination for campers on the upper end of Allatoona Lake. In fact, it is the most northerly campground on the reservoir. Situated on the western shore of the lake, it also is a favorite for family camping groups.

The campground is arranged along a rolling hillside, with some sites near the water, while others are farther up the slope, overlooking the lake. Although in a forested area, the sites range from full to partial or no shade.

61 Upper Stamp Creek Campground

Recreation: Fishing, boating, paddling, swimming

Location: 10 miles northeast of Cartersville; 80 Chitwood Cemetery Road, White 30184

GPS: N34 12.10' / W84 40.00'

Facilities and amenities: Flush toilets, showers, water, dump station, picnic tables, fire rings, lantern posts, swimming beach, boat ramp

Elevation: 925

Road conditions: Paved roads

Hookups: Water, electric

Sites: 10 lakefront standard RV/tent sites with hookups, 8 standard RV/tent sites with hookups, 2 tent-only sites with no hookups

Maximum RV length: 32

Season: Mid-May–Sep, open Fri–Sun only

Fees: Standard lakefront RV/tent site $34, standard RV/tent site $30, tent-only site $24

Maximum stay: 14 days

Management: US Army Corps of Engineers, Allatoona Lake Project office, 1138 Georgia Highway 20 Spur, Cartersville 30121; (678) 721-6700; www.sam.usace.army.mil/Missions/Civil-Works/Recreation/Allatoona-Lake/

Reservations: (877) 444-6777; www.recreation.gov

Pets: Dogs on 6-foot leashes allowed

Quiet hours: 10 p.m.–6 a.m.

Alcohol restrictions: No alcohol allowed

ADA compliant: Yes

Finding the campground: From exit 290 on I-75, go east on GA 20 for 4 miles. Turn right onto Wilderness Camp Road. At 1 mile, go left on Chitwood Cemetery Road. The road dead-ends in the campground at 0.7 mile.

About the campground: This small campground positioned on the eastern shore of the Stamp Creek arm of Allatoona Lake is not only seasonal but is open only on weekends. Contained within its grounds is the historic Chitwood family cemetery.

The campground is on a point jutting into the creek in a wooded area, with the sites well-spaced for privacy. All sites enjoy at least partial shade.

62 Victoria Campground

Recreation: Fishing, boating, swimming, playground
Location: 11 miles southwest of Canton; 937 Victoria Drive, Woodstock 30189
GPS: N34 09.50' / W84 37.91'
Facilities and amenities: Flush toilets, showers, water, dump station, picnic tables, fire rings, playground, swimming beach, boat ramp
Elevation: 850
Road conditions: Paved roads
Hookups: Water, electric

Located adjacent to the popular Victoria Landing Marina and Beach, the campground is on a heavily used portion of Allatoona Lake.

Sites: 20 standard lakefront RV/tent sites with hookups, 51 standard RV/tent sites with hookups, 1 tent-only site with no hookups
Maximum RV length: 70
Season: Mid-Mar–Oct
Fees: Standard lakefront RV/tent site $34, standard RV/tent site $30, tent-only site $24
Maximum stay: 14 days
Management: US Army Corps of Engineers, Allatoona Lake Project office, 1138 Georgia Highway 20 Spur; (678) 721-6700; www.sam.usace.army.mil/Missions/Civil-Works/Recreation/Allatoona-Lake/
Reservations: (877) 444-6777; www.recreation.gov
Pets: Dogs on 6-foot leashes allowed
Quiet hours: 10 p.m.–6 a.m.
Alcohol restrictions: No alcohol allowed
ADA compliant: Yes
Finding the campground: From exit 11 on I-575, go west on Sixes Road for 2.5 miles. Turn left on Bells Ferry Road and drive 4 miles. Turn left on Victoria Road. At 1.8 miles turn left on Victoria Landing Road. After another 0.9 mile, the campground is on the left.
About the campground: Victoria Campground lies adjacent to the very popular and privately-run Victoria Landing Marina and Beach, to the north. For that reason, this is a heavily used portion of Allatoona Lake.

The campground itself is about halfway up the lake on the south side of the Etowah River arm of the impoundment. It stretches through a wooded area that offers the sites partial to full shade. Roughly a third of the sites are on the waterfront. The campground has two loops, separated by a cove, on which the swimming beach is located.

63 Whitetail Ridge Campground

Recreation: Fishing, boating, paddling
Location: 10 miles west of LaGrange; 565 Abbottsford Road, LaGrange 30240
GPS: N33 01.20' / W85 11.00'
Facilities and amenities: Flush toilets, showers, laundry, water, dump station, picnic tables, fire rings, lantern posts, boat ramps
Elevation: 650
Road conditions: Paved roads
Hookups: Water, electric
Sites: 55 standard RV/tent sites with hookups, 3 standard double RV/tent sites with hookups
Maximum RV length: 75
Season: Mar–Oct
Fees: Standard RV/tent site $30, standard double RV/tent site $60
Maximum stay: 14 days
Management: US Army Corps of Engineers, West Point Lake Project Office, 500 Resource Management Dr., West Point; (706) 6452937; www.sam.usace.army.mil/Missions/Civil-Works/Recreation/West-Point-Lake/
Reservations: (877) 444-6777; www.recreation.gov

Pets: Dogs on 6-foot leashes allowed

Quiet hours: 10 p.m.–6 a.m.

Alcohol restrictions: No alcohol allowed

ADA compliant: Yes

Finding the campground: From the junction of US 27 and US 29 in LaGrange, go west on US 29 (Vernon Street) for 2.5 miles. Go right on Roanoke Road for 7.6 miles. Turn left onto Thompson Road and at 0.6 mile go left on Abbottsford Road. At 1.7 miles the campground entrance is on the left.

About the campground: Whitetail Ridge Campground sits on the heavily forested shore of 25,900-acre West Point Lake. The bulk of the sites are on the water or have at least lake views. This is a popular destination for anglers and boaters.

The campsites are grouped on two adjacent points facing southeast on the lakeshore. All offer at least partial shade beneath a canopy of mixed pine and hardwood trees.

Atlanta to South Carolina

Campgrounds At-A-Glance

#	Name	Total Sites	Group Sites	Hookup Sites	Hookups	Maximum RV Length	Dump Station	Toilets	Showers	Drinking Water	ADA	Fees	Reservations
Georgia State Parks and Historic Sites Division													
64	A.H. Stephens State Park	55	1	54	WE	50	Y	F	Y	Y	Y	$$$$–$$$$$	Y
65	Dames Ferry Campground	30	0	30	WE	50	Y	F	Y	Y	Y	$$$$	Y
66	Don Carter State Park	58	0	44	WE	100	Y	F	Y	Y	Y	$$$–$$$$	Y
67	Elijah Clark State Park	183	1	172	WE	50	Y	F	Y	Y	Y	$$$$–$$$$$	Y
68	Fort Yargo State Park	50	1	38	WE	50	Y	F	Y	Y	Y	$$$–$$$$$	Y
69	Hamburg State Park	30	0	30	WE	40	Y	F	Y	Y	Y	$$$$	Y
70	Hard Labor Creek State Park	43	4	39	WES	45	Y	F	Y	Y	Y	$$$$–$$$$$	Y
71	High Falls State Park	108	2	106	WE	50	Y	F	Y	Y	Y	$$$$–$$$$$	Y
72	Indian Springs State Park	63	1	64	WE	60	Y	F	Y	Y	Y	$$$$–$$$$$	Y
73	Magnolia Springs State Park	28	1	24	WE	40	Y	F	Y	Y	Y	$$$–$$$$$	Y
74	Mistletoe State Park	110	1	90	WES	50	Y	F	Y	Y	Y	$$–$$$$$	Y
75	Panola Mountain State Park	5	0	0	N	NA	N	V	N	N	N	$$$	Y
76	Richard B. Russell State Park	27	0	27	WE	35	Y	F	Y	Y	Y	$$$$–$$$$$	Y
77	Tugaloo State Park	117	1	105	WE	50	Y	F	Y	Y	Y	$$$–$$$$$	Y
78	Victoria Bryant State Park	34	2	24	WE	50	Y	F	Y	Y	Y	$$$–$$$$$	Y
79	Watson Mill Bridge State Park	33	3	30	WE	50	Y	F	Y	Y	Y	$$$–$$$$$	Y
Georgia Wildlife Resources Division													
80	McDuffie Public Fishing Area	6	0	6	WE	30	Y	F	Y	Y	Y	$$–$$$	Y

Campgrounds At-A-Glance

#	Name	Total Sites	Group Sites	Hookup Sites	Hookups	Maximum RV Length	Dump Station	Toilets	Showers	Drinking Water	ADA	Fees	Reservations
County Parks													
81	Big Hart Campground	32	1	31	WE	45	Y	F	Y	Y	Y	$$$-$$$$$	Y
82	Bobby Brown Park	71	1	70	WE	40	Y	F	Y	Y	Y	$$$-$$$$$	Y
83	Factory Shoals Park	9	0	0	N	24	N	F	Y	Y	N	$$	Y
84	Oconee Springs Campground and Marina	41	0	41	WE	75	Y	F	Y	Y	Y	$$$-$$$$$	Y
85	Paynes Creek Campground	44	0	44	WE	55	Y	F	Y	Y	Y	$$$-$$$$	Y
86	Raysville Campground	55	0	55	WE	30	Y	F	Y	Y	Y	$$$	Y
87	River Forks Park and Campground	63	0	63	WE	45	Y	F	Y	Y	Y	$$-$$$	Y
88	Shady Grove Campground	96	2	86	WE	44	Y	F	Y	Y	Y	$$$-$$$$$	Y
89	War Hill Park	14	0	0	N	80	N	F	Y	Y	Y	$$$	Y
90	Wildwood Park	60	1	58	WE	42	Y	F	Y	Y	Y	$$-$$$$$	Y
Georgia Power Company													
91	Lawrence Shoals Recreation Area	63	0	49	WE	45	Y	F	Y	Y	Y	$$$-$$$$$	Y
92	Old Salem Campground	100	0	92	WE	50	Y	F	Y	Y	Y	$$$	Y
US Army Corps of Engineers													
93	Bald Ridge Creek Campground	92	0	92	WE	109	Y	F	Y	Y	Y	$$$-$$$$	Y
94	Bolding Mill Campground	95	0	86	WE	109	Y	F	Y	Y	Y	$$$-$$$$	Y
95	Bussey Point Campground	14	0	0	N	30	N	V	N	Y	N	$	Y
96	Duckett Mill Campground	111	0	97	WE	75	Y	F	Y	Y	Y	$$-$$$$	Y
97	Georgia River Campground	13	0	0	N	NA	N	F	N	Y	Y	$	N
98	Old Federal Campground	83	0	72	WE	160	Y	F	Y	Y	Y	$$-$$$	Y
99	Petersburg Campground	90	0	82	WE	45	Y	F	Y	Y	Y	$$-$$$	Y

Campgrounds At-A-Glance

#	Name	Total Sites	Group Sites	Hookup Sites	Hookups	Maximum RV Length	Dump Station	Toilets	Showers	Drinking Water	ADA	Fees	Reservations
100	Ridge Road Campground	69	0	62	WE	50	Y	F	Y	Y	Y	$$-$$$$$	Y
101	Sawnee Campground	59	0	48	WE	85	Y	F	Y	Y	Y	$$-$$$$$	Y
102	Toto Creek Campground	9	0	0	N	NA	Y	F	N	Y	N	$$	Y
103	Van Pugh South Campground	53	0	35	WE	35	Y	F	Y	Y	Y	$$-$$$	Y
104	Watsadler Campground	51	0	51	WE	50	Y	F	Y	Y	Y	$$$-$$$$$	Y
105	Winfield Campground	80	0	80	WE	65	Y	F	Y	Y	Y	$$$	Y
USDA Forest Service													
106	Lake Russell Campground	41	0	0	N	65	Y	F	Y	Y	Y	$$-$$$$$	Y
107	Lake Sinclair Campground	35	1	6	WE	30	Y	F	Y	Y	Y	$-$$$$$	Y
108	Oconee River Campground	5	0	0	N	NA	N	V	N	N	N	$	N

See Amenities Chart key on page xxi.

64 A. H. Stephens State Park

Recreation: Hiking, fishing, boating, paddling mountain biking, playground, horseback riding

Location: 1 mile north of Crawfordville; 456 Alexander Street NW, Crawfordville 30631

GPS: N33 56.35' / W82 89.72'

Facilities and amenities: Flush toilets, showers, laundry, grills, water, picnic tables, picnic shelters, picnic areas, dump station, playground, nature, biking, and equestrian trails, bike rentals, horse stables, geocaching, volleyball court, horseshoe pits, boat ramp, aquacycle, canoe/kayak/paddleboard/fishing boat rentals, 3 lakes, Civil War museum and historic site

Elevation: 573

Road conditions: Paved roads

Hookups: Water, electric

Sites: 12 premium RV/tent sites with hookups, 13 standard RV/tent sites with hookups, 29 equestrian RV/tent sites with hookups, 1 pioneer site, 4 cottages

Maximum RV length: 50

Season: Year-round, Apr–Oct peak season

Fees: Premium RV/tent site $36, standard RV/tent site $32, equestrian RV/tent site $32, pioneer site $50, 2-bedroom cottage $150, daily parking fee $5, annual pass $50
Maximum stay: 14 days
Management: Georgia State Parks and Historic Sites Division, 2610 Georgia Highway 155 SW, Stockbridge; (770) 389-7286; www.gastateparks.org
Reservations: (800) 864-7275; www.gastateparks.org/reservations
Pets: Dogs on 6-foot leashes allowed
Quiet hours: 10 p.m.–7 a.m.
Alcohol restrictions: Unlawful in public areas
ADA compliant: Yes
Finding the campground: From exit 154 on I-20, go north on GA 22 (Alexander Street / Lexington Road) for 2.3 miles. Turn right, following GA 22. At 0.6 mile go left on Lexington Street. After 0.2 mile turn left on Alexander Street that enters the park.
About the campground: Located in Taliaferro County (oddly enough it is pronounced as Tolliver), the park is named for Georgia politician and Vice President of the Confederate States Alexander H. Stephens. His home, Liberty Hall, is within the park and open for tours. The park also features horse stables and more than 20 miles of equestrian trails.

The campground is a single loop surrounding a restored historic fire tower built by the Depression-era Works Progress Administration in 1935. The campsites are set amid a sparse stand of hardwood and pines on level ground. There is no understory vegetation, leaving the campsites open and offering little privacy.

65 Dames Ferry Campground

Recreation: Fishing, boating, paddling, playground
Location: 16 miles northwest of Macon; 9546 Georgia Highway 87, Juliette 31046
GPS: N33 04.37' / W83 75.82'
Facilities and amenities: Flush toilets, showers, laundry, water, dump station, picnic tables, fire rings, playground, picnic shelter, boat ramp, rental canoes, kayaks, paddleboards, aquacycles
Elevation: 425
Road conditions: Paved roads
Hookups: Water, electric
Sites: 24 premium pull-through RV/tent sites with hookups, 6 standard RV/tent sites with hookups
Maximum RV length: 50
Season: Year-round, Apr–Oct peak season
Fees: Premium RV/tent site $40, standard RV/tent site $36, any site with tent only $33, daily parking fee $5, annual pass $50
Maximum stay: 14 days
Management: Georgia State Parks and Historic Sites Division, 2610 Georgia Highway 155 SW, Stockbridge; (770) 389-7286; www.gastateparks.org
Reservations: (800) 864-7275; www.gastateparks.org/reservations
Pets: Dogs on 6-foot leashes allowed
Quiet hours: 10 p.m.–7 a.m.

On the eastern shore of Lake Juliette, the location allows scenic views of the water.

Alcohol restrictions: Unlawful in public areas
ADA compliant: Yes
Finding the campground: From exit 185 on I-75, go east on GA 18 for 10.4 miles. Turn left on US 23 / GA 87. At 1.7 miles the campground is on the left.
About the campground: Dames Ferry Campground has a rather unusual management scheme. Although owned by the Georgia Power Company, it is managed by the Georgia State Parks and Historic Sites Division and is operated by High Falls State Park.

The campground is located on the shore of 3,600-acre Lake Juliette. Close by is the small tourist attraction town of Juliette and the Whistle Stop Café, both of which were featured in the movie *Fried Green Tomatoes*.

The campground is on the eastern side of the lake, situated on the rolling hills of a peninsula jutting out into the water. This location makes for great scenic views of the water. The area is covered by mostly pine trees, with the individual sites ranging from full shade to partial shade to no shade.

66 Don Carter State Park

Recreation: Hiking, fishing, boating, paddling, biking, swimming, horseback riding
Location: 11 miles northeast of Gainesville; 5000 North Browning Bridge Road, Gainesville 30506
GPS: N34 38.76' / W84 74.65'
Facilities and amenities: Flush toilets, showers, laundry, dump station, cable TV, grills, water, picnic tables, picnic shelters, picnic areas, playgrounds, swimming beach, hiking/biking/equestrian trails, boat ramps, kayak rental, fishing pier, fish cleaning station
Elevation: 1,125
Road conditions: Paved roads
Hookups: Water, electric
Sites: 28 premium RV/tent sites with hookups, 16 standard RV/tent sites with hookups, 14 walk-in primitive tent sites with no hookups, 8 cottages
Maximum RV length: 100
Season: Year-round, Apr–Oct peak season
Fees: Premium RV/tent site $38, standard RV/tent site $34, primitive tent site $25, 2-bedroom cottage $225, daily parking fee $5, annual pass $50
Maximum stay: 14 days
Management: Georgia State Parks and Historic Sites Division, 2610 Georgia Highway 155 SW, Stockbridge; (770) 389-7286; www.gastateparks.org
Reservations: (800) 864-7275; www.gastateparks.org/reservations
Pets: Dogs on 6-foot leashes allowed
Quiet hours: 10 p.m.–7 a.m.
Alcohol restrictions: Unlawful in public areas
ADA compliant: Yes
Finding the campground: From US 129 just north of Lake Lanier, go east on Nopone Road for 3.2 miles. Turn right on Clarks Bridge Road. At 0.4 mile turn left on North Browning Bridge Road, which enters the park at 1.5 miles.
About the campground: Don Carter State Park covers 1,316 acres of land along the shores of 38,000-acre Lake Sidney Lanier on the northern edge of Atlanta's suburbs. The reservoir consistently rates as the nation's most visited Corps of Engineers impoundment. The park was named for real estate executive Don Carter, who served on the Department of Natural Resources board for 29 years and worked to establish this first state park on Lake Lanier. The park is on the Chattahoochee River arm of the lake's northern end.

The campground is located in the southern section of the park, situated in wooded terrain overlooking the reservoir. All RV sites are paved; Don Carter also offers eight rental cottages.

67 Elijah Clark State Park

Recreation: Hiking, fishing, boating, paddling, playground
Location: 7 miles northeast of Lincolnton; 2959 McCormick Highway, Lincolnton 30817
GPS: N33 85.40' / W82 40.95'

Facilities and amenities: Flush toilets, showers, water, dump station, cable TV, picnic tables, fire rings, playground, swimming beach, hiking trails, miniature golf, basketball and volleyball courts, geocaching, picnic areas and shelters, fishing pier, fish cleaning station, boat ramps, canoe and kayak rentals, log cabin museum

Elevation: 375

Road conditions: Paved roads

Hookups: Water, electric

Sites: 117 premium RV/tent sites with hookups, 55 standard RV/sites with hookups, 10 walk-in tent sites with no hookups, 1 pioneer site, 20 cottages

Maximum RV length: 50

Season: Year-round, Apr–Oct peak season

Fees: Premium RV/tent site $40, standard RV/tent site $34, walk-in tent site $22, pioneer site $45, 2-bedroom cottages $175, daily parking fee $5, annual pass $50

Maximum stay: 14 days

Management: Georgia State Parks and Historic Sites Division, 2610 Georgia Highway 155 SW, Stockbridge; (770) 389-7286; www.gastateparks.org

Reservations: (800) 864-7275; www.gastateparks.org/reservations

Pets: Dogs on 6-foot leashes allowed

Quiet hours: 10 p.m.–7 a.m.

Alcohol restrictions: Unlawful in public areas

ADA compliant: Yes

Finding the campground: From the junction of US 378 and GA 47 (Elm Street) in Lincolnton, go north on US 378 for 6.7 miles. The park entrance road is on the left.

About the campground: This 447-acre park sits on the shore of 71,100-acre Clarks Hill Lake. The park is named for Lieutenant Colonel Elijah Clarke, who was one of the few military leaders from Georgia during the Revolutionary War. A replica of his log cabin home in the park serves as a museum containing furniture and more from the 1780s period. The park also has a wide range of amenities and activities for the entire family.

Campground No. 1 is an RV loop, while No. 2 contains the primitive tent camping loop. These occupy separate, adjacent points sticking out into the lake in the western part of the park. Both loops are in wooded terrain with the trees offering partial to full shade. The waterfront tent sites get full sun.

Eighty of the premium RV/tent sites are on the waterfront, with many providing room for beaching your boat. The tent campground is on a hillside overlooking the water.

68 Fort Yargo State Park

Recreation: Hiking, fishing, boating, paddling, biking, swimming, playground

Location: 1 mile southwest of Winder; 210 South Broad Street, Winder 30680

GPS: N33 97.86' / W83 73.16'

Facilities and amenities: Flush toilets, showers, laundry, dump station, grills, water, tables, picnic shelters, picnic areas, playgrounds, swimming beach, hiking and mountain biking trails, boat ramps, fishing piers, rental boats, amphitheater, disc golf, miniature golf

Elevation: 825

Road conditions: Paved roads
Hookups: Water, electric
Sites: 16 premium RV/tent sites with hookups, 22 standard RV/tent sites with hookups, 6 premium waterfront, walk-in tent sites with no hookups, 5 standard walk-in tent sites, 1 pioneer site, 16 cottages, 8 yurts
Maximum RV length: 50
Season: Year-round, Apr–Oct peak season
Fees: Premium RV/tent site with hookups $40, standard RV/tent site with hookups $36, premium walk-in tent site $30, standard walk-in tent site $27, pioneer site $80, 2-bedroom cottage $165, yurt $100, daily parking fee $5, annual pass $50
Maximum stay: 14 days
Management: Georgia State Parks and Historic Sites Division, 2610 Georgia Highway 155 SW, Stockbridge; (770) 389-7286; www.gastateparks.org
Reservations: (800) 864-7275; www.gastateparks.org/reservations
Pets: Dogs on 6-foot leashes allowed
Quiet hours: 10 p.m.–7 a.m.
Alcohol restrictions: Unlawful in public areas
ADA compliant: Yes
Finding the campground: From GA 316 take exit 5 onto GA 81, which becomes South Broad Street at the Winder city limits. The park's main entrance is on the right at 2.6 miles.
About the campground: Located between Atlanta and Athens in the 1,816-acre state park, the two adjacent campgrounds are on the southeast side of 260-acre Marbury Creek Reservoir. The premium campsites are level and on the waterfront, while standard ones are on the forested hillsides. All sites are in wooded areas and have full shade.

The park offers a wide range of activities, as well as being the site of Fort Yargo, a blockhouse built in 1792 to guard the early Georgia frontier from Creek and Cherokee Indian raids.

69 Hamburg State Park

Recreation: Hiking, fishing, boating, boat, paddling, playground
Location: 15 miles southeast of Sparta; 6071 Hamburg State Park Road, Mitchell 30820
GPS: N33 20.70' / W82 77.84'
Facilities and amenities: Flush toilets, showers, laundry, water, dump station, grills, picnic tables, picnic areas and shelters, playgrounds, hiking trails, lake, boat ramp, fishing pier, aquacyle, canoe, kayak and fishing boat rentals, trolling motor rental, trading post, historic site
Elevation: 375
Road conditions: Paved roads
Hookups: Water, electric
Sites: 27 premium RV/tent sites with hookups, 3 standard RV/tent sites with hookups
Maximum RV length: 40
Season: Year-round, Apr–Oct peak season
Fees: Premium RV/tent site $36, standard RV/tent site $32, daily parking fee $5, annual pass $50
Maximum stay: 14 days

Peaceful 225-acre Hamburg Lake is a centerpiece of the park offering fishing and boating.

Management: Georgia State Parks and Historic Sites Division, 2610 Georgia Highway 155 SW, Stockbridge; (770) 389-7286; www.gastateparks.org
Reservations: (800) 864-7275; www.gastateparks.org/reservations
Pets: Dogs on 6-foot leashes allowed
Quiet hours: 10 p.m.–7 a.m.
Alcohol restrictions: Unlawful in public areas
ADA compliant: Yes
Finding the campground: From the village of Mitchell, go south on GA 102 (Main Street) for 2 miles. Turn right on Hamburg-Agricola Road, which quickly becomes Agricola Road. At 3.5 miles turn left on Hamburg State Park Road and the park entrance is on the right.
About the campground: The centerpieces of this park are the Hamburg Grist Mill and dam built on the Little Ogeechee River in 1921 and forming 225-acre Hamburg Lake. However, the first mill at this site dated from 1825 and operated until the early 1900s. The mill pond now offers boating and fishing options to visitors. The grist mill museum is open for tours during special events.

The campground is located on a point midway up the lake on the south shore. The premium campsites are well spaced, open with no understory vegetation and overlooking the water. The standard sites are set back from the water, but all campsites offer at least partial shade.

Be aware that the lake does have a population of alligators.

70 Hard Labor Creek State Park

Recreation: Hiking, fishing, boating, paddling, birding, swimming, playground, horseback riding, golf
Location: 2 miles northeast of Rutledge; 5 Hard Labor Creek Road, Rutledge 30663
GPS: N33 65.50' / W83 59.69'
Facilities and amenities: Flush toilets, showers, laundry, dump station, grills, picnic tables, picnic areas and shelters, playgrounds, hiking/biking/equestrian trails, 2 lakes, swimming beach, boat ramp, kayak rentals, miniature golf, geocaching, golf course, trading post, horse stables, blacksmith shop
Elevation: 600
Road conditions: Paved roads
Hookups: Water, electric, sewer
Sites: 15 premium RV/tent sites with hookups, 1 premium double RV/tent site with hookups, 11 standard RV/tent sites with hookups, 2 premium equestrian RV/tent sites, 10 standard equestrian RV/tent sites, 4 pioneer sites, 21 cottages
Maximum RV length: 45
Season: Year-round, Apr–Oct peak season
Fees: Premium RV/tent site $40, premium double RV/tent site $62, standard RV/tent sites $36, premium equestrian RV/tent site $38, standard equestrian RV/tent site $35, pioneer site $55, 2-bedroom cottage $190, daily parking fee $5, annual pass $50
Maximum stay: 14 days
Management: Georgia State Parks and Historic Sites Division, 2610 Georgia Highway 155 SW, Stockbridge; (770) 389-7286; www.gastateparks.org
Reservations: (800) 864-7275; www.gastateparks.org/reservations

Pets: Dogs on 6-foot leashes allowed

Quiet hours: 10 p.m.–7 a.m.

Alcohol restrictions: Unlawful in public areas

ADA compliant: Yes

Finding the campground: From exit 105 on I-20, go north on Newborn Road for 2.4 miles. Turn left onto East Dixie Highway. At 100 yards turn right on Fairplay Road and drive 2.5 miles. Turn left on Knox Chapel Road. Hard Labor Creek Road is 0.4 mile on the right.

About the campground: Hard Labor Creek State Park is on the National Register of Historic Places and best known for The Creek Golf Course. It also features two lakes: Brantley at 48 acres and 275-acre Lake Rutledge. Laid out and constructed by the Civilian Conservation Corps during the Great Depression, it was originally part of the National Park System, but was turned over to the state of Georgia in 1946. Today the park offers a wide range of activities for the entire family.

The campground is situated on rolling hills alongside Lake Brantley, with some sites overlooking the lake and Hard Labor Creek. The sites are well spaced and shaded in a wooded area. The equestrian camping is provided in a separate area that is more open. Six of the premium RV/tent sites have full hookups, including sewer.

71 High Falls State Park

Recreation: Hiking, fishing, boating, paddling, swimming, playground

Location: 13 miles northwest of Forsyth; 76 High Falls Park Drive, Jackson 30233

GPS: N33 17.83' / W84 02.05'

Facilities and amenities: Flush toilets, showers, laundry, dump station, water, hiking trails, geocaching, playground, miniature golf, swimming pool, picnic areas, fishing, boat ramps

Elevation: 610

Road conditions: Paved roads

Hookups: Water, electric

Sites: 25 premium RV/tent sites with hookups, 81 standard RV/tent sites with hookups, 1 pioneer site, 1 group paddle-in site, 6 yurts

Maximum RV length: 50

Season: Year-round, Apr–Oct peak season

Fees: Premium RV/tent site $40, standard RV/tent site $36, pioneer site $60, group paddle-in site $80, yurt $100, daily parking fee $5, annual pass $50

Maximum stay: 14 days

Management: Georgia State Parks and Historic Sites Division, 2610 Georgia Highway 155 SW, Stockbridge; (770) 389-7286; www.gastateparks.org

Reservations: (800) 864-7275; www.gastateparks.org/reservations

Pets: Dogs on 6-foot leashes allowed

Quiet hours: 10 p.m.–7 a.m.

Alcohol restrictions: Unlawful in public areas

ADA compliant: Yes

Finding the campground: From exit 198 on I-75, go east for 1.6 miles on High Falls Road. Turn left onto High Falls Park Drive, which enters the park.

Yurts are a great option for families who want the camping experience without all the gear.

About the campground: High Falls State Park sits on the shore of 650-acre High Falls Lake that is formed by a dam on the Towaliga River. The 988-acre park contains Towaliga Falls, arguably the most impressive waterfall in Middle Georgia, along with the ruins of a grist mill dating from antebellum times and an 1890s vintage hydro power plant.

The camping areas within the park are divided into the single loop of the Lakeside Camping Area composed of 15 sites next to the yurt village and multiple loops along the Towaliga below the lake in the River Camping Area totaling 86 sites. All of these are at least partially shaded, with an open understory.

72 Indian Springs State Park

Recreation: Hiking, fishing, boating, paddling, playground
Location: 6 miles southeast of Jackson; 678 Lake Clark Road, Flovilla 30216
GPS: N33 24.74' / W83 92.35'
Facilities and amenities: Flush toilets, showers, laundry, water, dump station, hiking and biking trails, geocaching, playground, miniature golf, picnic areas, outdoor fitness equipment, aquacycle, kayak, canoe, fishing boat rentals, boat ramp, museum, event center
Elevation: 564

Road conditions: Paved roads

Hookups: Water, electric

Sites: 62 standard RV/tent sites with hookups, 1 pioneer site, 10 cottages

Maximum RV length: 60

Season: Year-round, Apr–Oct peak season

Fees: Standard RV/tent site with hookups $34, pioneer site $50, cottages $190, daily parking fee $5, annual pass $50

Maximum stay: 14 days

Management: Georgia State Parks and Historic Sites Division, 2610 Georgia Highway 155 SW, Stockbridge; (770) 389-7286; www.gastateparks.org

Reservations: (800) 864-7275; www.gastateparks.org/reservations

Pets: Dogs on 6-foot leashes allowed

Quiet hours: 10 p.m.–7 a.m.

Alcohol restrictions: Unlawful in public areas

ADA compliant: Yes

Finding the campground: From the junction of US 23 and GA 36 in Jackson, go east on US 23 (East Third Street) for 4.1 miles. Bear right onto GA 42 and continue 1.5 miles to the park entrance on the right.

About the campground: Established in 1927, Indian Springs is Georgia's oldest state park and one of the oldest in the nation. It draws its name from the artesian spring located here, the waters of which the Creek Indians used for medicinal purposes. The area later was a thriving resort community up through the early 1920s. Today the springs and 105-acre McIntosh Lake are the park's main attractions.

The campground is composed of three loops at the upper western end of the lake. The area is surprisingly hilly for Middle Georgia. All the sites are shaded and overlook the lake.

73 Magnolia Springs State Park

Recreation: Hiking, fishing, boating, paddling, biking, playground

Location: 5 miles north of Millen; 1053 Magnolia Springs Drive, Millen 30442

GPS: N32 87.33' / W81 96.16'

Facilities and amenities: Flush toilets, showers, laundry, water, dump station, picnic table, fire ring, picnic area and shelter, hiking and biking trails, playground, splash pad, amphitheater, geocaching, lake, fishing dock, boat ramp, canoe/kayak/pedal boat rentals, natural spring and boardwalk, historic site and museum

Elevation: 174

Road conditions: Paved roads

Hookups: Water, electric

Sites: 7 premium RV/tent sites with hookups, 17 standard RV/tent sites with hookups, 3 walk-in tent sites, 1 pioneer site, 9 cottages

Maximum RV length: 40

Season: Year-round, Apr–Oct peak season

Fees: Premium RV/tent site $38, standard RV/tent site $34, walk-in tent site $22, pioneer site $65, 2-bedroom cottage $175, 3-bedroom cottage $200, daily parking fee $5, annual pass $50

A boardwalk borders Magnolia Springs, allowing you to observe turtles, fish, and even alligators.

Maximum stay: 14 days
Management: Georgia State Parks and Historic Sites Division, 2610 Georgia Highway 155 SW, Stockbridge; (770) 389-7286; www.gastateparks.org
Reservations: (800) 864-7275; www.gastateparks.org/reservations
Pets: Dogs on 6-foot leashes allowed
Quiet hours: 10 p.m.–7 a.m.
Alcohol restrictions: Unlawful in public areas
ADA compliant: Yes
Finding the campground: From the junction of US 25 and GA 17 in Millen, go north on US 25 for 5 miles. The entrance to the park is on the right.
About the campground: Magnolia Springs State Park covers 1,070 acres of land surrounding its namesake spring, which flows with 7 million gallons of crystal-clear water daily. A boardwalk borders the water, allowing you to observe fish, turtles, and alligators that inhabit the spring. While no fishing is allowed in the spring, 28-acre Magnolia Lake within the park is open to boating and fishing.

The other attraction in the park is the site of Fort Lawton, a Confederate prison during the Civil War, and its associated Magnolia Springs History Center.

The campground is composed of a single loop just on the east side of Magnolia Lake. The sites are in a mostly open area with some pine trees offering only partial shade. There is no understory of vegetation, resulting in a lack of privacy.

74 Mistletoe State Park

Recreation: Hiking, fishing, boating, paddling, birding, swimming, playground
Location: 15 miles northwest of Thomson; 3725 Mistletoe Road, Appling 30802
GPS: N33 64.33' / W82 38.52'
Facilities and amenities: Flush toilets, showers, laundry, dump station, grills, water, tables, picnic shelters, picnic areas, playgrounds, swimming beach, hiking and mountain biking trails, geocaching, boat ramps, canoe rental, fish cleaning station, amphitheater
Elevation: 388
Road conditions: Paved roads
Hookups: Water, electric
Sites: 4 premium RV/tent sites with full hookups, 62 premium RV/tent sites with water and electric hookups, 24 standard RV/tent sites with water and electric hookups, 15 walk-in tent sites, 3 backcountry tent sites, 1 pioneer site, 1 tent cabin site, 1 fisherman's cabin, 9 cottages
Maximum RV length: 50
Season: Year-round, Apr–Oct peak season
Fees: Premium RV/tent site $38, standard RV/tent site $34, walk-in tent site $18, backcountry tent site $12, pioneer site $80, tent cabin site $60, fisherman's cabin $135, 2-bedroom cottage $175, daily parking fee $5, annual pass $50

Situated on the shore of Clarks Hill Lake, Mistletoe State Park is a family-friendly destination.

Maximum stay: 14 days
Management: Georgia State Parks and Historic Sites Division, 2610 Georgia Highway 155 SW, Stockbridge; (770) 389-7286; www.gastateparks.org
Reservations: (800) 864-7275; www.gastateparks.org/reservations
Pets: Dogs on 6-foot leashes allowed
Quiet hours: 10 p.m.–7 a.m.
Alcohol restrictions: Unlawful in public areas
ADA compliant: Yes
Finding the campground: From exit 183 on I-20, go north on US 221 for 3.4 miles. Turn left on Shucraft Road. At 1.6 miles cross White Oak Road onto Dozier Road and continue 5.6 miles. Turn left on Cobbham Road (GA 150) and drive 0.5 mile. Turn right on Mistletoe Road and at 2.9 miles the road enters the park.
About the campground: Situated on the shores of 71,100-acre Clarks Hill Lake, Mistletoe State Park is a family-friendly vacation destination offering a wide variety of activities. This 1,921-acre facility offers woodland trails and water sports, but it is best known for providing outstanding bass fishing on the reservoir.

The campground is positioned on three points in the northern part of the park. Some of the premium sites are on the water, while many more offer lake views. The sites range from partially to fully shaded.

75 Panola Mountain State Park

Recreation: Hiking, fishing, biking, birding, rock climbing, playground
Location: 9 miles northeast of Stockbridge; 2620 Georgia Highway 155 SW, Stockbridge 30281
GPS: N33 62.34' / W84 17.28'
Facilities and amenities: Vault toilet, picnic tables, fire rings, lantern posts, hiking and biking trails, archery range, playground, 2 lakes, nature center
Elevation: 790
Road conditions: Paved roads
Hookups: None
Sites: 5 walk-in tent sites
Maximum RV length: NA
Season: Year-round, Apr–Oct peak season
Fees: Walk-in tent sites $25, daily parking fee $5, annual pass $50
Maximum stay: 14 days
Management: Georgia State Parks and Historic Sites Division, 2610 Georgia Highway 155 SW, Stockbridge; (770) 389-7286; www.gastateparks.org
Reservations: (800) 864-7275; www.gastateparks.org/reservations
Pets: Dogs on 6-foot leashes allowed
Quiet hours: 10 p.m.–7 a.m.
Alcohol restrictions: Unlawful in public areas
ADA compliant: Yes
Finding the campground: From exit 68 on I-20, go south on Wesley Chapel Road for 0.3 mile. Turn left on Snapfinger Road (GA 155). At 6.9 miles the park entrance is on the left.

About the campground: Panola Mountain State Park is basically a nature preserve centered around a 100-acre granite rock outcropping. That feature, along with Panola Mountain itself, is open only to ranger-guided tours, while the rest of the park offers Upper and Lower Alexander Lakes for fishing or paddling and a myriad of hiking/biking trails.

The primitive camping area provides a backpacking destination but is not in close proximity to the park's other amenities.

76 Richard B. Russell State Park

Recreation: Hiking, fishing, boating, paddling, biking, swimming, playground, golf
Location: 9 miles northeast of Elberton; 2650 Russell State Park Drive, Elberton 30635
GPS: N34 16.72' / W82 75.04'
Facilities and amenities: Flush toilets, showers, laundry, water, dump station, picnic tables, fire rings, cable TV, swimming beach, playground, picnic area and shelters, geocaching, hiking and biking trails, bike rentals, canoe/kayak/pontoon boat rentals, fishing pier, disc golf, golf course, historic site
Elevation: 562
Road conditions: Paved roads
Hookups: Water, electric
Sites: 20 premium RV/tent sites with hookups, 7 standard RV/tent sites with hookups, 20 cottages
Maximum RV length: 35
Season: Year-round, Apr–Oct peak season
Fees: Premium RV/tent site $38, standard RV/tent site $34, 2-bedroom cottage $185, daily parking fee $5, annual pass $50
Maximum stay: 14 days
Management: Georgia State Parks and Historic Sites Division, 2610 Georgia Highway 155 SW, Stockbridge; (770) 389-7286; www.gastateparks.org
Reservations: (800) 864-7275; www.gastateparks.org/reservations
Pets: Dogs on 6-foot leashes allowed
Quiet hours: 10 p.m.–7 a.m.
Alcohol restrictions: Unlawful in public areas
ADA compliant: Yes
Finding the campground: From the junction of GA 72 (College Avenue) and GA 77 (North Oliver Street, which becomes Hartwell Highway), go north on GA 77 for 1.2 miles. Turn right on Martin Luther King Jr. Boulevard and continue for 0.2 mile. Turn left onto Willie Black Road and drive 0.6 mile to the end of the road. Turn right onto Ruckersville Road. At 7.1 miles the park entrance is on the right.
About the campground: The park and the 26,500-acre reservoir on the shore of which it is located were both named in honor of Sen. Richard B. Russell, who represented Georgia in Washington from 1931 to 1971. The park has a wide range of activities and amenities for the entire family, as well as having the historic Blackwell Bridge on one of the hiking trails. This steel truss bridge was constructed in 1917 over Beaverdam Creek but was moved to its present location in 1984, rather than have it inundated in the newly built lake.

The campground is centrally located in the park near the beach and concession area. The campsites are spread along a hillside overlooking the lake. They are fairly well separated for privacy and in a wooded section that provides lots of shade.

77 Tugaloo State Park

Recreation: Hiking, fishing, boating, paddling, swimming, playground
Location: 8 miles northeast of Lavonia; 1763 Tugaloo State Park Road, Lavonia 30553
GPS: N34 49.91' / W83 07.81'
Facilities and amenities: Flush toilets, showers, laundry, dump station, fire rings, picnic tables, grills, lantern posts, picnic shelters, playgrounds, swimming beach, hiking trails, miniature golf, tennis and volleyball courts, horseshoes, nature hut, canoe rentals, boat ramps, camp store, gift shop
Elevation: 725
Road conditions: Paved roads
Hookups: Water, electric
Sites: 60 premium RV/tent sites with hookups, 45 standard RV/tent sites with hookups, 11 walk-in tent sites, 1 pioneer site, 6 yurts, 20 cottages

Tugaloo State Park, on Hartwell Lake, offers yurts, cottages, and a generous number of camp-sites for you to take advantage of a wide variety of activities.

Maximum RV length: 50

Season: Year-round, Apr–Oct peak season

Fees: Premium RV/tent site $40, standard RV/tent site $36, walk-in tent site $27, pioneer site $40, yurt $100, 2-bedroom premier cottage $175, 2-bedroom standard cottage $160, 3-bedroom premier cottage $200

Maximum stay: 14 days

Management: Georgia State Parks and Historic Sites Division, 2610 Georgia Highway 155 SW, Stockbridge; (770) 389-7286; www.gastateparks.org

Reservations: (800) 864-7275; www.gastateparks.org/reservations

Pets: Dogs on 6-foot leashes allowed

Quiet hours: 10 p.m.–7 a.m.

Alcohol restrictions: Unlawful in public areas

ADA compliant: Yes

Finding the campground: From exit 173 on I-85, go north on GA 17 for 0.4 mile. Turn right on Pleasant Hill Road and immediately right on Gerrard Road. At 1.9 miles, go left on Gumlog Road for 3.2 miles. Turn right onto Tugaloo State Park Road. At 1.6 miles the road enters the park.

About the campground: Tugaloo State Park is a 393-acre facility located on a peninsula jutting out into the upper reaches of 56,000-acre Hartwell Lake. The park offers a wide variety of activities and amenities for the entire family. In addition to the campground, the park has rental cabins and a yurt village.

The RV campground is situated in the northeast corner of the park, while the walk-in tent sites are near the yurt village in the southwest portion of the peninsula. Most of the campsites are up on the hillside overlooking the lake, but there are 38 waterfront sites offered. All sites are well spaced, providing some privacy, and the wooded terrain offers full shade to most of the back-in and pull-through sites.

78 Victoria Bryant State Park

Recreation: Hiking, fishing, biking, swimming, playground, golf

Location: 4 miles west of Royston; 1105 Bryant Park Road, Royston 30662

GPS: N34 23.67' / W83 16.07'

Facilities and amenities: Flush toilets, showers, laundry, water, dump station, picnic tables, fire rings, picnic areas and shelters, playground, hiking and biking trails, horseshoe pits, volleyball court, swimming pool, archery range, fishing ponds, fishing piers, golf course, pro shop, nature center, gift shop

Elevation: 621

Road conditions: Paved roads

Hookups: Water, electric

Sites: 8 premium RV/tent sites with hookups, 15 standard RV/tent sites with hookups, 1 double RV/tent site with hookups, 8 platform tent sites, 2 pioneer sites, 1 cottage

Maximum RV length: 50

Season: Year-round, Apr–Oct peak season

Fees: Premium RV/tent site $38, standard RV/tent site $34, combo RV/tent site $44, platform tent site $30, pioneer site $80, 4-bedroom cottage $175, daily parking fee $5, annual pass $50

In addition to traditional campsites, Victoria Bryant State Park offers platform sites for added comfort and protection from the elements.

Maximum stay: 14 days
Management: Georgia State Parks and Historic Sites Division, 2610 Georgia Highway 155 SW, Stockbridge; (770) 389-7286; www.gastateparks.org
Reservations: (800) 864-7275; www.gastateparks.org/reservations
Pets: Dogs on 6-foot leashes allowed
Quiet hours: 10 p.m.–7 a.m.
Alcohol restrictions: Unlawful in public areas
ADA compliant: Yes
Finding the campground: From exit 160 on I-85, go east on GA 51 for 9.9 miles. Turn right onto GA 145 (Toccoa Carnesville Road). At 1.2 miles go left on US 29 for 0.1 mile and turn left onto Bryant Park Road. The park is on the left at 0.9 mile.
About the campground: This 502-acre park is named for Victoria Bryant, the mother of Paul Bryant, who donated the land to the state in 1950. The park lies on rolling Piedmont Plateau terrain, with the southern portion along the banks of Rice Creek and the northern section dominated by the Highland Walk Golf Course and the park's hiking and biking trails.

The campground is situated in the center of the southern portion in an area of hardwood forest. The individual sites range from very little shade to heavily covered. There is no understory, so the sites offer little in the way of privacy.

79 Watson Mill Bridge State Park

Recreation: Hiking, fishing, paddling, biking, playground, horseback riding
Location: 19 miles northeast of Athens; 650 Watson Mill Road, Comer 30620
GPS: N34 02.50' / W83 07.50'
Facilities and amenities: Flush toilets, showers, laundry, water, dump station, grills, tables, picnic shelters, picnic areas, playground, hiking, mountain biking and equestrian trails, lake, canoe and kayak rentals, geocaching, historic sites
Elevation: 561
Road conditions: Paved roads
Hookups: Water, electric
Sites: 18 premium RV/tent sites with hookups, 3 standard RV/tent sites with hookups, 3 premium equestrian RV/tent sites with hookups, 5 standard equestrian RV/tent sites with hookups, 1 standard double equestrian RV/tent site with hookups, 3 pioneer sites, 3 log bunkhouses
Maximum RV length: 50
Season: Year-round, Apr–Oct peak season
Fees: Premium RV/tent site $36, standard RV/tent site $32, premium equestrian RV/tent site $34, standard equestrian RV/tent site $30, standard double equestrian RV/tent site $60, pioneer site $40, log bunkhouse $85, daily parking fee $5, annual pass $50

Watson Mill Bridge, spanning the South Fork of the Broad River, is the longest covered bridge still in use in Georgia.

Maximum stay: 14 days
Management: Georgia State Parks and Historic Sites Division, 2610 Georgia Highway 155 SW, Stockbridge; (770) 389-7286; www.gastateparks.org
Reservations: (800) 864-7275; www.gastateparks.org/reservations
Pets: Dogs on 6-foot leashes allowed
Quiet hours: 10 p.m.–7 a.m.
Alcohol restrictions: Unlawful in public areas
ADA compliant: Yes
Finding the campground: (For RV campers) From the junction of GA 72 (Sunset Avenue) and GA 22 (Main Street) in Comer, go south on GA 22 for 3 miles. Turn left onto Watson Mill Road and continue another 3 miles to the park entrance.

(For equestrian campers) From the junction of GA 72 and GA 22, go east on GA 72 for 2.7 miles. Turn right onto Old Fork Cemetery Road and drive 1.5 miles. The equestrian camping area is on the right.
About the campground: Watson Mill Bridge State Park contains Georgia's longest covered bridge still in use, as the 229-foot span dating from 1885 crosses the South Fork River (actually the South Fork of the Broad River). The site is considered one of the state's most picturesque parks. Also, on-site are an old mill pond and mill ruins. Additionally, the park is a popular destination for horse camping and riding.

The campground is situated on a level portion of high ground in the southern part of the park. The sites are well spaced and shaded by mixed stands of pines and hardwoods.

Other facilities on-site are three log bunkhouses and horse stables for equestrians.

Be aware that due to height and weight limits for crossing Watson Mill Bridge, RV campers should approach the park from the west, while equestrian campers should arrive from the east.

80 McDuffie Public Fishing Area

Recreation: Hiking, fishing, boating
Location: 10 miles southeast of Thomson; 4695 Fish Hatchery Road SE, Dearing 30808
GPS: N33 37.85' / W82 42.35'
Facilities and amenities: Flush toilets, showers, water, dump station, fire rings, picnic tables, picnic shelters, nature trails, lakes, fishing, fishing piers, boat ramps, fish cleaning station, archery range, dove and waterfowl hunts, environmental education center
Elevation: 494
Road conditions: Gravel roads throughout the area
Hookups: Water, electric
Sites: 1 premium RV/tent site with hookups, 5 standard RV/tent sites with hookups
Maximum RV length: 30
Season: Year-round, Mar–Nov peak season
Fees: Premium RV/tent site $30, standard RV/tent site $20
Maximum stay: 14 days
Management: Georgia Wildlife Resources Division, 2067 US Highway 278 SE, Social Circle; (706) 557-3333; www.georgiawildlife.com
Reservations: (800) 336-2661; www.gooutdoorsgeorgia.com

Pets: Dogs on 6-foot leashes allowed

Quiet hours: 10 p.m.–7 a.m.

Alcohol restrictions: Alcohol allowed only in the campground

ADA compliant: Yes

Finding the campground: From US 78 in Dearing, go south on Main Street, which becomes Iron Hill Road, for 2.2 miles. Turn right on Ellington Airline Road and drive 0.1 mile. Turn left on Fish Hatchery Road. At 1.4 miles the road dead-ends in the public fishing area.

About the campground: McDuffie Public Fishing Area is a 570-acre tract containing seven lakes ranging in size from 5 to 37 acres. While angling is the main attraction, visitors can also hunt in season, walk the nature trails, practice their archery skills, have a picnic, or visit the environmental education facility.

The camping area has gravel drives and parking pads. The sites are very open but well-spaced. The few trees in the campground provide only partial to no shade for the individual sites.

Anyone using the PFA facilities must have a hunting or fishing license or a land-use permit from the WRD. All reservations for camping must be made online using a credit card.

81 Big Hart Campground

Recreation: Fishing, boating, paddling, swimming, playground

Location: 12 miles north of Thomson; 5258 Washington Road NE, Thomson 30824

GPS: N33 61.47' / W82 50.85'

Facilities and amenities: Flush toilets, showers, water, dump station, picnic tables, fire rings, pavilion, picnic area, swimming beach, playground, boat ramp

Elevation: 360

Road conditions: Paved roads

Hookups: Water, electric

Sites: 31 standard RV/tent sites, 1 group site

Maximum RV length: 45

Season: Year-round, Apr–Oct peak season

Fees: Standard RV/tent site $30, group site $150

Maximum stay: 14 days

Management: McDuffie County and City of Thomson, 210 Railroad Street, Thomson; (706) 595-1781; thomson-mcduffie.gov

Reservations: https://betabookings10.rmscloud.com/Search/Index/13026/90/?Y=1

Pets: Dogs on leashes allowed

Quiet hours: 10 p.m.–7 a.m.

Alcohol restrictions: Alcohol not allowed

ADA compliant: Yes

Finding the campground: From the intersection of US 78 and Gordon Street in downtown Thomson, go north on US 78 (Main Street, which becomes Washington Road) for 9 miles. Turn right onto Russell's Landing Road. At 2.8 miles the entrance to the campground is on the right.

About the campground: Big Hart Campground is a McDuffie County–owned and –managed facility on the shore of Clarks Hill Lake (officially J. Strom Thurmond Reservoir). The lake is a 71,100-acre US Army Corps of Engineers project on the Savannah River.

The campground stretches out onto a peninsula in the lake. The sites are well spaced for privacy, with most of them on the lakefront. The group site can host seven RVs with hookups.

82 Bobby Brown Park

Recreation: Hiking, fishing, boating, paddling, playground
Location: 21 miles southeast of Elberton; 2509 Bobby Brown Park Road, Elberton 30635
GPS: N33 58.70' / W82 35.30'
Facilities and amenities: Flush toilets, showers, laundry, water, dump station, picnic tables, fire rings, hiking trail, archery range, disc golf, playground, picnic area, fishing pier, fish cleaning station, boat ramp
Elevation: 409
Road conditions: Paved roads; yurt village is on a gravel drive
Hookups: Water, electric
Sites: 18 premium RV/tent sites with hookups, 52 standard RV/tent sites with hookups, 1 pioneer site, 5 yurts, 1 cabin
Maximum RV length: 40
Season: Year-round, Apr–Oct peak season

A former state park, Bobby Brown Park sits on the shore of Clarks Hill Lake.

Fees: Premium RV/tent site $26, standard RV/tent site $24, pioneer site $30, yurts $85, cabin $100, park pass $3
Maximum stay: 14 days
Management: Elbert County, 45 Forest Avenue, Elberton; (706)-283-2000; www.elbertga.us/index.html
Reservations: (706) 283-5500; www.bobbybrownpark.com/index.html
Pets: Dogs allowed on 6-foot leashes
Quiet hours: 10 p.m.–7 a.m.
Alcohol restrictions: Alcohol allowed only in campsites
ADA compliant: Yes
Finding the campground: From the junction of GA 72 and GA 17 just east of Elberton, go east on GA 17 (Calhoun Falls Highway) for 12.2 miles. Turn right onto Bobby Brown State Park Road. At 7.6 miles the road ends in the park.
About the campground: Bobby Brown Park is a former state park that now is operated by Elbert County. It is on the shore of 71,100-acre Clarks Hill Lake (J. Strom Thurmond Reservoir), on the point at the junction of the Broad and Savannah River arms of the impoundment. The park is named for former Georgia congressman Paul Brown's son, Navy Lt. Robert T. Brown, who lost his life during World War II.

The campground is composed of Broad Side and Savannah Side Loops, facing their respective namesake rivers. The loops have matching bathhouses and other facilities. The sites in both are spread along rolling hillsides overlooking the water, with most having at least partial shade.

83 Factory Shoals Park

Recreation: Hiking, fishing, paddling, swimming
Location: 11 miles south of Covington; 450 Newton Factory Bridge Road, Covington 30014
GPS: N33 27.02' / W83 49.90'
Facilities and amenities: Flush toilets, showers, water, picnic tables, fire rings, lantern posts, hiking trails, river swimming, picnic area
Elevation: 650
Road conditions: Rough approach road and drive within the campground are gravel and dirt tracks
Hookups: None
Sites: 9 RV/tent sites with no hookups
Maximum RV length: 24
Season: Mar–Nov
Fees: $15
Maximum stay: 14 days
Management: Newton County, 1124 Clark Street, Covington; (770) 784-2000; www.co.newton.ga.us/236/Factory-Shoals
Reservations: (678) 699-2809
Pets: Dogs on 6-foot leashes allowed
Quiet hours: 10 p.m.–7 a.m.
Alcohol restrictions: No alcohol allowed

ADA compliant: No

Finding the campground: From exit 90 on I-20, go south on Turner Lake Road for 1.1 miles. Go right on GA 81 for 1.5 miles and turn left onto Flat Shoals Road. After 4.9 miles turn right onto GA 36 and continue for 5.6 miles. Turn left onto Newton Factory Bridge Road. At 0.7 mile the drive to the campground is on the left.

About the campground: This primitive campground is set within a 450-acre nature park at the point that the Alcovy River dashes through Factory Shoals to empty into Jackson Lake. The park offers hiking trails along the river, kayaking and rafting through the shoals, and a natural beach and swimming hole where the river meets the lake.

The campground is across the road and upstream of the park's picnic area. The entrance drive to the campground passes the historic Factory Shoals Cemetery that dates from the 19th century, when a mill town occupied the area.

The campsites are upstream of the shoals and aligned along the river in a heavily wooded section that provides full shade. They also are separated to provide privacy.

84 Oconee Springs Campground and Marina

Recreation: Fishing, boating, paddling, swimming, playground

Location: 13 miles east of Eatonton; 109 South Spring Road, Eatonton 31024

GPS: N33 17.34' / W83 11.97'

Facilities and amenities: Flush toilets, showers, laundry, water, dump station, cable TV, picnic table, fire ring, swimming beach, water park, event center, volleyball court, dog park, boat ramp, marina

Elevation: 372

Road conditions: Paved roads

Hookups: Water, electric

Sites: 20 RV/tent sites with 50-amp electric hookups, 21 RV/tent sites with 30-amp electric hookups, 8 cabins

Maximum RV length: 75

Season: Year-round, Apr-Oct peak season

Fees: RV/tent site with 50-amp electric $40, RV/tent sites with 30 amp-electric $30, cabins $145, daily pass $3

Maximum stay: 14 days

Management: Putnam County, 109 South Spring Road, Eatonton; (706) 485-8423; www.putnamcountyga.us/oconee-park

Reservations: (706) 485-8423; www.oconeespringspark.com

Pets: Dogs allowed on leashes

Quiet hours: 10 p.m.–7 a.m.

Alcohol restrictions: No alcohol in public areas

ADA compliant: Yes

Finding the campground: From the junction of US 129 BUS and GA 44 in Eatonton, go east on GA 44 for 500 feet and turn right on Oconee Street (which turns into Oconee Springs Road). At 10.3 miles, turn right on Rockville Road and continue for 1.8 miles. Bear to the right onto Spring Road and drive 1.5 miles to the park entrance on the left.

About the campground: Oconee Springs Park is more than just a campground. It is a full-service vacation destination with a wide range of activities and amenities for the entire family. All of those attractions center around water, particularly so regarding 15,300-acre Lake Sinclair on which the park is located.

The campground, however, resembles a suburban trailer park, with its Beach and Lake sections made up of tightly grouped sites in wide open areas. There is minimal privacy in this communal setting.

85 Paynes Creek Campground

Recreation: Fishing, boating, paddling, swimming, playground
Location: 10 miles north of Hartwell; 518 Ramp Road, Hartwell 30643
GPS: N34 47.42' / W82 97.11'
Facilities and amenities: Flush toilets, showers, dump station, fire ring, picnic tables, boat ramp, playground, swimming beaches
Elevation: 660
Road conditions: Paved roads

Located on the Tugaloo River arm of Hartwell Lake, most of the campsites are on or overlook the water.

Hookups: Water, electric
Sites: 43 RV/tent sites with hookups, 1 double RV/tent site with hookups
Maximum RV length: 55
Season: May 1–Sep 30
Fees: RV/tent site Sun–Wed $30, Thu–Sat $35; RV/tent double site $37
Maximum stay: 14 days
Management: Hart County Parks and Recreation Department, 200 Clay Street, Hartwell; www.hartcountyga.gov/recreation.html
Reservations: (706) 377-3456; https://pc.bookmysites.com/reservations/checkout-availability?
Pets: Dogs on 6-foot leashes allowed
Quiet hours: 10 p.m.–6 a.m.
Alcohol restrictions: No alcohol allowed
ADA compliant: Yes
Finding the campground: From US 29 in Hartwell, take GA 51 (Chandler Street, then Reed Creek Highway) north for 7.1 miles. Turn left onto Boleman Hill Road and continue 3.7 miles to the campground entrance.
About the campground: Paynes Creek Campground is on the Tugaloo River arm of Hartwell Lake in northeast Georgia. All but seven of the campsites are on the lakeshore, offering scenic views of the water. The others are up on the hillside overlooking the lake. All the sites are in a wooded setting, providing partial to full shade. Additionally, they are well spaced, with thick vegetation providing privacy.

A boat ramp and two swimming areas provide access to the lake.

86 Raysville Campground

Recreation: Fishing, boating, paddling
Location: 12 miles north of Thomson; 6489 Lincolnton Road, Thomson 30824
GPS: N33 38.14' / W82 28.33'
Facilities and amenities: Flush toilets, showers, water, dump station, picnic tables, fire rings, grills, lantern posts, boat ramp, dock, kayak/paddleboard rentals
Elevation: 333
Road conditions: Paved roads
Hookups: Water, electric
Sites: 55 RV/tent sites with hookups
Maximum RV length: 30
Season: Year-round, Apr–Oct peak season
Fees: $30
Maximum stay: 14 days
Management: McDuffie County and City of Thomson, 210 Railroad Street, Thomson; (706) 595-1781; www.thomson-mcduffie.gov
Reservations: https://betabookings10.rmscloud.com/Search/Index/10257/90/?Y=1
Pets: Dogs on leashes allowed
Quiet hours: 10 p.m.–7 a.m.
Alcohol restrictions: Alcohol not allowed

ADA compliant: Yes

Finding the campground: From exit 172 on I-20, go north on US 78 (Washington Road) for 2.7 miles. Turn right onto Lincolnton Highway and at 6.5 miles the campground is on the left.

About the campground: The family-oriented, county-managed campground is situated on Georgia's Little River section of Clarks Hill Lake, the largest US Corps of Engineers lake east of the Mississippi River. The 71,100-acre impoundment has 1,000-plus miles of shoreline.

The campsites are set back from the shoreline in heavily wooded terrain. This provides full shade to the spacious sites with plenty of privacy.

87 River Forks Park and Campground

Recreation: Hiking, fishing, boating, paddling, swimming, playground
Location: 6 miles northwest of Gainesville; 3500 Keith Bridge Road, Gainesville 30504
GPS: N34 17.54' / W83 54.44'
Facilities and amenities: Flush toilets, showers, water, dump station, picnic tables, fire rings, swimming beach, picnic areas and pavilions, playgrounds, hiking trail, boat ramp
Elevation: 1,085
Road conditions: Paved roads
Hookups: Water, electric
Sites: 47 RV sites with hookups, 16 tent sites with hookups
Maximum RV length: 45
Season: Year-round, Apr–Oct peak season
Fees: RV site $30, tent site $20, daily entry fee $5
Maximum stay: 14 days
Management: Hall County Parks and Leisure Services, 4175 Nopone Road, Gainesville; (770) 535-8280; www.hallcounty.org/308/Parks-Leisure
Reservations: (770) 534-3952; https://secure.itinio.com/hallcounty/
Pets: Dogs on 6-foot leashes allowed
Quiet hours: 10 p.m.–7 a.m.
Alcohol restrictions: No alcohol allowed
ADA compliant: Yes
Finding the campground: From exit 16 on I-985, go west on Munday Mill Road (GA 53) for 2.3 miles. Turn right to follow GA 53 for 2.5 miles. Then turn left onto Browns Bridge Road (GA 369). After 1.1 miles, go right on Keith Bridge Road. The road enters the park at 0.5 mile.

About the campground: This 112-acre park takes its name from its location at the junction of the Chattahoochee and Chestatee River arms of 38,000-acre Lake Sidney Lanier. This reservoir draws 11 million visitors annually, often ranking as the most heavily used US Army Corps of Engineers lake in the nation.

The campground sprawls across a hilly peninsula on the lake's eastern shore, providing the campsites with views of the water. Though the area is wooded, the sites range from full sun to full shade.

88 Shady Grove Campground

Recreation: Hiking, fishing, boating, paddling, swimming, playground
Location: 9 miles northeast of Cumming; 7800 Allyn Lane Memorial Way, Cumming 30041
GPS: N34 12.34' / W84 02.17'
Facilities and amenities: Flush toilets, showers, water, dump station, picnic tables, fire rings, lantern posts, picnic area and shelters, playground, volleyball court, swimming beach, hiking trails, boat ramp and dock
Elevation: 1,128
Road conditions: Paved roads
Hookups: Water, electric
Sites: 83 standard RV/tent sites with hookups, 1 tent-only site with hookups, 10 tent-only sites with no hookups, 2 RV group sites
Maximum RV length: 44
Season: Mar–Nov
Fees: Standard RV/tent site $28, tent-only site with hookups $28, tent-only site with no hookups $25, group RV site $240
Maximum stay: 14 days

Shady Grove Campground is a popular destination for those visiting Lake Lanier.

Management: Forsyth County Parks and Recreation Department, 2300 Keith Bridge Road, Cumming; (770) 781- 2215; https://parks.forsythco.com
Reservations: www.reserveamerica.com/explore/shady-grove-campground/PRCG/1070700/overview
Pets: Dogs allowed on 10-foot leashes
Quiet hours: 10 p.m.–6 a.m.
Alcohol restrictions: No alcohol allowed
ADA compliant: Yes
Finding the campground: From exit 16 on US 19 / GA 400, go east on Pilgrim Mill Road for 0.9 mile. Turn left onto Holtzclaw Road, and in 0.2 mile go right on Chattahoochee Road. After 2.1 miles turn right on Shady Grove Road. After 2.1 miles turn left onto Shadburn Ferry Road. At 0.7 miles turn right into the campground onto Allyn Lane Memorial Way.
About the campground: Shady Grove Campground sits on a peninsula on the lower portion of 38,000-acre Lake Sidney Lanier. The lake draws around 11 million visitors per year, which results in Shady Grove being a popular destination.

The park is located on land owned by the US Army Corps of Engineers but is leased by Forsyth County for recreational purposes. The campground is heavily forested, offering shade for virtually all the sites. One unique feature is the presence of two group RV sites. These sites have electric and water hookups and can handle up to 18 to 24 vehicles and 48 to 64 people.

89 War Hill Park

Recreation: Fishing, boating, paddling, swimming
Location: 12 miles southeast of Dawsonville; 4081 War Hill Park Road, Dawsonville 30534
GPS: N34 19.88' / W83 57.72'
Facilities and amenities: Flush toilets, showers, water, picnic tables, grills, fire rings, lantern posts, swimming beach, boat ramps
Elevation: 1,150
Road conditions: Paved roads
Hookups: None
Sites: 14 RV/tent sites with no hookups
Maximum RV length: 80
Season: Mar–Oct
Fees: $25, daily user fee $3, annual pass $30
Maximum stay: 14 days
Management: Dawson County Parks and Recreation Department, 445 Martin Road, Dawsonville; (706) 344-3646
Reservations: www.dawsoncountyga.gov/parksrec/page/war-hill-park
Pets: Dogs on 6-foot leashes allowed
Quiet hours: 10 p.m.–6 a.m.
Alcohol restrictions: No alcohol allowed
ADA compliant: Yes

Finding the campground: From the intersection of US 19 and GA 53 southeast of Dawsonville, drive southeast on GA 53 for 1.8 miles. Turn left onto War Hill Park Road. At 7.8 miles the road ends at the park.

About the campground: While War Hill Park's day-use areas are open year-round, the county managed campground is seasonal. It sits on what was an island in 38,000-acre Lake Sidney Lanier, but a causeway now connects it to the shore.

The campsites are spread around the fringe of the old island, with most well shaded by a mix of hardwoods and pines. The park also features a four-lane boat ramp that is open all year.

90 Wildwood Park

Recreation: Hiking, fishing, boating, paddling, biking, swimming, playground, horseback riding
Location: 27 miles northeast of Thomson; 3780 Dogwood Lane, Appling 30802
GPS: N33 38.95' / W82 16.95
Facilities and amenities: Flush toilets, showers, water, dump station, picnic tables, fire rings, grills, lantern posts, picnic area and shelters, playground, hiking/biking/equestrian trails, disc golf, boat ramps, fish cleaning and weigh-in stations
Elevation: 355
Road conditions: Paved roads
Hookups: Water, electric
Sites: 52 RV/tent sites with hookups, 6 glamping sites with hookups, 2 primitive tent areas
Maximum RV length: 42
Season: Year-round, Apr–Oct peak season
Fees: RV/tent site $25, glamping site $25, primitive tent site $15, daily pass $3, annual pass $30
Maximum stay: 30 days
Management: Columbia County Parks and Recreation, 630 Ronald Reagan Drive, Evans; (706) 868-3375; www.columbiacountyga.gov/community/parks-the-environment
Reservations: (706) 541-0586; www.columbiacountyga.gov/Home/Components/FacilityDirectory/FacilityDirectory/42/4823?npage=2
Pets: Dogs on leashes allowed
Quiet hours: 10 p.m.–7 a.m.
Alcohol restrictions: No alcohol allowed
ADA compliant: Yes
Finding the campground: From exit 183 on I-20, take US 221 north for 12.1 miles. Turn left onto GA 47 and at 2 miles the entrance to the park is on the right.
About the campground: Positioned on the shore of 71,100-acre Clarks Hill Lake, Wildwood Park is a major draw for a variety of enthusiasts. Its 6-lane mega boat ramp and weigh-in facility has hosted a number of major regional and national bass-fishing tournaments, while it also is home to three professional-quality disc golf courses. Additionally, the International Disc Golf Center and Hall of Fame are located within its grounds.

The park's 12-mile system of hiking, biking, and equestrian trails includes a portion of the 115-mile Bartram Trail, which crosses the property. This pathway follows the course of naturalist William Bartram's travels through the area in the 1790s.

The campground consists of four sections, three of which offer RV hookups. These are located on three adjacent north-facing points sticking out into the lake. Camping Area 3 shares its point with the two primitive tent areas. The primitive areas do not have marked sites but rather allow you to pitch a tent anywhere within them. The camping areas all are in wooded terrain, with the sites getting at least partial shade.

91 Lawrence Shoals Recreation Area

Recreation: Hiking, fishing, boating, paddling, biking, birding, swimming, playground
Location: 15 miles east of Eatonton; 123 Lawrence Shoals Road, Eatonton 31024
GPS: N33 21/31' / W83 10.25'
Facilities and amenities: Flush toilets, showers, laundry, water, dump station, picnic tables, fire rings, grills, playground, hiking and biking trails, picnic area, swimming beach, boat ramp
Elevation: 470
Road conditions: Paved roads
Hookups: Water, electric
Sites: 49 RV/tent sites with hookups, 14 tent-only sites with no hookups
Maximum length: 50
Season: Mar–Nov
Fees: RV/tent site $30, tent-only sites $25, one-time registration fee $5, daily parking fee $5, annual pass $50, debit or credit card only
Maximum stay: 14 days
Management: Georgia Power Company; Lake Resources Office, 125 Wallace Dam Road; 706-484-7500; www.georgiapower.com/gplake
Reservations: https://reservations.gplakes.com/default.aspx
Pets: Dogs on leashes allowed
Quiet hours: 10 p.m.–7 a.m.
Alcohol restrictions: No alcohol allowed
ADA compliant: Yes
Maximum RV length: 45
Finding the campground: From the courthouse square in Eatonton, head northeast on GA 44 (East Sumter Street) for 1.2 miles. Bear right onto GA 16 (Sparta Highway) and continue for 12.1 miles. Turn left on Wallace Dam Road, then at 0.2 mile turn left onto Lawrence Shoals Road, which leads into the campground.
About the campground: The two major attractions for this campground are 19,000-acre Lake Oconee on which it is located and the presence of Rock Hawk in the adjacent recreation area. The latter feature is a Native American effigy formed from rocks laid on the ground in the shape of a bird. It is called Rock Hawk because it is smaller than another effigy that is located in the same general area and called Rock Eagle. A viewing tower allows you to climb up for a better view of Rock Hawk.

Lake Oconee offers campers access to water sports, including swimming, boating, and fishing. The Rock Hawk area has a system of hiking and mountain biking trails that are connected to the campground. Those trails are also good places for birding.

The camping area is in a wooded area, offering shade to most sites. On the other hand, there is little in the way of understory vegetation, and the sites are rather tightly spaced, which gives it more of a communal feel.

92 Old Salem Campground

Recreation: Fishing, boating, paddling, swimming, playground
Location: 13 miles southwest of Greensboro; 1530 Old Salem Road, Greensboro 30642
GPS: N33 26.17' / W83 14.79'
Facilities and amenities: Flush toilets, showers, laundry, water, dump station, picnic tables, fire rings, grills, lantern posts, swimming beach, playground, picnic pavilions, fishing docks, boat ramp
Elevation: 472
Road conditions: Paved roads
Hookups: Water, electric
Sites: 92 RV/tent sites with hookups, 8 tent-only sites with no hookups
Maximum RV length: 50
Season: Mar–Nov
Fees: RV/tent site $30, tent-only site $25, one-time registration fee $5, daily parking fee $5, annual pass $50, debit or credit card only
Maximum stay: 14 days
Management: Georgia Power Company; Lake Resources Office, 125 Wallace Dam Road, Eatonton; 706-484-7500; www.georgiapower.com/gplake
Reservations: https://reservations.gplakes.com/default.aspx
Pets: Dogs on leashes allowed
Quiet hours: 10 p.m.–7 a.m.
Alcohol restrictions: No alcohol allowed
ADA compliant: Yes
Finding the campground: From exit 130 on I-20, head south on GA 44 (Lake Oconee Highway) for 7.1 miles. Turn left onto Linger Longer Road and at 0.7 mile go right on Old Salem Road. At 1.8 miles the road ends in the campground.
About the campground: Old Salem Campground sits on the eastern shore of the Oconee River arm of Lake Oconee. Its boat ramp and beach provide access to the 19,000-acre lake's swimming, paddling, boating, and fishing options.

The RV campground sits on the eastern side of the south-facing point. The tent sites are located on the other side of the point near the boat ramp. All the spaces are rather close together, with all having either partial or full shade.

93 Bald Ridge Creek Campground

Recreation: Fishing, boating, paddling, biking, swimming
Location: 5 miles northeast of Cumming; 4055 Chestatee Road, Cumming 30041
GPS: N34 12.23' / W84 05.16'

Facilities and amenities: Flush toilets, showers, laundry, water, dump station, picnic tables, fire rings, grills, swimming beach, boat ramp, fishing pier
Elevation: 1,073
Road conditions: Paved roads
Hookups: Water, electric
Sites: 92 standard RV/tent sites with hookups
Maximum RV length: 109
Season: Mid-Mar–mid-Oct
Fees: Standard RV/tent site $26, weekends $36
Maximum stay: 14 days
Management: US Army Corps of Engineers, Lake Sidney Lanier Project Management Office, 1050 Buford Dam Road, Buford; (770) 904-3290; www.sam.usace.army.mil/Missions/Civil-Works/Recreation/Lake-Sidney-Lanier/
Reservations: (877) 444-6777; www.recreation.gov
Pets: Dogs on 6-foot leashes allowed
Quiet hours: 10 p.m.–6 a.m.
Alcohol restrictions: No alcohol allowed
ADA compliant: Yes

This popular campground on Lake Lanier offers a lake view from virtually all of the campsites.

Finding the campground: From the junction of US 19 / GA 400 and Pilgrim Mill Road, go east on Pilgrim Mill Road for 2 miles. Turn right onto Sinclair Shores Road and continue for 0.6 mile. Turn left onto Bald Ridge Park Road. At 0.2 mile the road enters the campground.

About the campground: Bald Ridge Creek Campground is one of the most popular on 38,000-acre Lake Sidney Lanier. This reservoir draws 11 million visitors annually, often ranking as the most heavily used US Army Corps of Engineers lake in the nation. Both this campground and the lake owe their popularity to their proximity to and easy access from metro Atlanta.

The campground occupies a south-facing point protruding into its namesake arm of the lake. This provides lake views from virtually all of the campsites. Those sites are well spaced in a forested area, offering partial to full shade on all of them.

94 Bolding Mill Campground

Recreation: Fishing, boating, paddling, biking, swimming, playground
Location: 11 miles northwest of Gainesville; 4055 Chestatee Road, Gainesville 30506
GPS: N34 20.23' / W83 57.01'
Facilities and amenities: Flush toilets, showers, laundry, water, dump station, picnic tables, grills, fire rings, picnic shelters, playgrounds, basketball and volleyball courts, horseshoe pits, swimming beach, fishing pier, boat ramp
Elevation: 1,083
Road conditions: Paved roads
Hookups: Water, electric
Sites: 86 standard RV/tent sites with hookups, 9 tent sites with no hookups
Maximum RV length: 109
Season: Mid-Mar–mid-Oct
Fees: Standard RV/tent site $26, weekends $36, tent-only site $20
Maximum stay: 14 days
Management: US Army Corps of Engineers, Lake Sidney Lanier Project Management Office, 1050 Buford Dam Road, Buford; (770) 904-3290; www.sam.usace.army.mil/Missions/Civil-Works/Recreation/Lake-Sidney-Lanier/
Reservations: (877) 444-6777; www.recreation.gov
Pets: Dogs on 6-foot leashes allowed
Quiet hours: 10 p.m.–6 a.m.
Alcohol restrictions: No alcohol allowed
ADA compliant: Yes
Finding the campground: From exit 22 on I-985, go northeast on US 129 BUS for 1.3 miles. Turn left onto Jesse Jewell Parkway, and at 0.5 mile take a right onto John W. Morrow Jr. Parkway (which becomes Dawsonville Highway). Drive 5.7 miles and turn right onto Sardis Road. At 0.6 mile turn left on Chestatee Road and proceed 4.2 miles to the campground at the end of the road.

About the campground: Bolding Mill Campground is positioned on the Chestatee River arm in the upper reaches of 38,000-acre Lake Sidney Lanier. This reservoir draws 11 million visitors annually, often ranking as the most heavily used US Army Corps of Engineers lake in the nation.

The campground has a wide range of amenities and activities for the whole family, with playgrounds, volleyball, basketball, fishing, and boating.

The RV camping area spreads over three parallel points reaching into the lake, with the tip of the center point holding the primitive tent campsites. All the campsites are set back from the water, but some offer views of the lake. The tent sites are in a shaded, wooded area, but the rest of the sites are spaced out in more open terrain with sparse shade.

95 Bussey Point Campground

Recreation: Hiking, fishing, boating, horseback riding
Location: 12 miles southeast of Lincolnton; Reece Price Road, Lincolnton 30817
GPS: N33 43.38' / W82 18.19'
Facilities and amenities: Vault toilets, water hand-pump, picnic table, fire ring, grill, lantern post, boat ramp, hiking and equestrian trails, hitching post
Elevation: 348
Road conditions: From Reece Price Road to camping areas are gravel and dirt roads, as are the loops in the campground
Hookups: None
Sites: 14 RV/tent sites with no hookups
Maximum RV length: 30
Season: Year-round, Apr–Oct peak season
Fees: $10
Maximum stay: 14 days
Management: US Army Corps of Engineers, J. Strom Thurmond Dam and Lake, 510 Clarks Hill Highway, Clarks Hill, SC; (864) 333-1100; www.sas.usace.army.mil/About/Divisions-and-Offices/Operations-Division/J-Strom-Thurmond-Dam-and-Lake/
Reservations: (877) 444-6777; www.recreation.gov
Pets: Dogs on 6-foot leashes allowed
Quiet hours: 10 p.m.–6 a.m.
Alcohol restrictions: No alcohol allowed
ADA compliant: No
Finding the campground: From the intersection of US 378 and GA 47 (Elm Street) in Lincolnton, go east on GA 47 for 4.3 miles. Turn left onto Double Branches Road for 7.8 miles. Make a left turn at this point, where the road name changes to Reece Price Road. The turn puts you on dirt and gravel Mosley Camp Road. Osprey Camp Road runs off to the right to Camping Loop A at 0.2 mile. Going straight past this intersection takes you 0.4 mile to Camp Loop B.
About the campground: Bussey Point Campground is for those who like their camping on the primitive side. The camp is divided into two loops with A having ten sites, while B has four. Loop B also has a boat ramp. All sites are well shaded.

The appeal of this area is the location of 12.5 miles of marked hiking, mountain biking and, especially, equestrian trails. Those meander through a wilderness area on the shore of 71,100-acre Clarks Hill Lake. There also is a plethora of old roads and unmarked trails to explore.

96 Duckett Mill Campground

Recreation: Fishing, boating, paddling, swimming, playground
Location: 9 miles northwest of Gainesville; 3720 Duckett Mill Road, Gainesville 30506
GPS: N34 18.38' / W83 55.85'
Facilities and amenities: Flush toilets, showers, laundry, water, dump station, picnic table, fire ring, grill, swimming beach, playground, boat ramp, fishing piers
Elevation: 1,074
Road conditions: Paved roads
Hookups: Water, electric
Sites: 97 standard RV/tent sites with hookups, 14 primitive tent sites with no hookups
Maximum RV length: 75
Season: Late Mar–mid-Sep
Fees: Standard RV/tent site $26, weekends $36, primitive tent site $20, weekends $30
Maximum stay: 14 days
Management: US Army Corps of Engineers, Lake Sidney Lanier Project Management Office, 1050 Buford Dam Road, Buford; (770) 904-3290; www.sam.usace.army.mil/Missions/Civil-Works/Recreation/Lake-Sidney-Lanier/
Reservations: (877) 444-6777; www.recreation.gov
Pets: Dogs on 6-foot leashes allowed
Quiet hours: 10 p.m.–6 a.m.
Alcohol restrictions: No alcohol allowed
ADA compliant: Yes
Finding the campground: From the intersection of US 19 / GA 400 and GA 53 in Dawsonville, go east on GA 53 for 10.2 miles. Turn right on Duckett Mill Road and go 2 miles to the end of the road into the campground.
About the campground: The Duckett Mill facility sits on a point on the north side of the Chestatee River arm of 38,000-acre Lake Sidney Lanier. This reservoir draws 11 million visitors annually, often ranking as the most heavily used US Army Corps of Engineers lake in the nation. The large campground sprawls across almost a dozen smaller protrusions sticking out in all directions into the lake. That shape means that virtually all the campsites have lake views.

The terrain on these secondary points is quite hilly. The campsites range from full sun to partial and fully shaded.

97 Georgia River Campground

Recreation: Fishing
Location: 8 miles east of Hartwell; US Highway 29, Hartwell 30643
GPS: N34 35.41' / W82 81.84'
Facilities and amenities: Flush toilets, picnic tables, fire rings, trash cans, fishing pier
Elevation: 600
Road conditions: Paved roads
Hookups: None

Sites: 13 tent sites
Maximum RV length: NA
Season: May–Sep
Fees: $6
Maximum stay: 14 days
Management: US Army Corps of Engineers, 5625 Anderson Highway, Hartwell; (706) 856-0678; www.recreation.gov/camping/campgrounds/232735
Reservations: No
Pets: Dogs on 6-foot leash
Quiet hours: 10 p.m.–6 a.m.
Alcohol restrictions: No alcohol allowed
ADA compliant: Yes
Finding the campground: From the intersection of US 29 and GA 51 (Chandler Street) in Hartwell, go east on US 29 for 7.6 miles. Turn left into the Georgia River Recreation Area drive.
About the campground: This campground is within the Georgia River Recreation Area, positioned on the Savannah River immediately downstream of Hartwell Dam. The attraction of the area is fishing in the river, which is stocked spring through fall with trout by both Georgia and South Carolina. A long boardwalk-style fishing pier lines the shore near the dam. Other warm water species of fish can also be caught in this area.

The campground offers only sparse amenities in the sites that are in a shaded forest setting.

98 Old Federal Campground

Recreation: Fishing, boating, paddling, swimming, playground
Location: 13 miles southwest of Gainesville; 6219 Old Federal Road, Gainesville 30542
GPS: N34 13.35' / W83 56.96'
Facilities and amenities: Flush toilets, showers, laundry, water, dump station, picnic tables, fire rings, grills, picnic shelters, playground, beach, boat ramp
Elevation: 1,094
Road conditions: Paved roads
Hookups: Water, electric
Sites: 6 RV-only sites with hookups, 56 RV/tent sites with hookups, 10 tent-only sites with hookups, 4 tent-only sites with no hookups, 7 walk-in tent sites with no hookups
Maximum RV length:160
Season: Late Mar–mid-Oct
Fees: RV-only site $26, weekend $36; RV/tent site $26, weekend $36; tent-only site with hookups $22, weekend $36; tent-only site with no hookups or walk-in tent site $20, weekend $30
Maximum stay: 14 days
Management: US Army Corps of Engineers, Lake Sidney Lanier Project Management Office, 1050 Buford Dam Road, Buford; (770) 904-3290; www.sam.usace.army.mil/Missions/Civil-Works/Recreation/Lake-Sidney-Lanier/
Reservations: (877) 444-6777; www.recreation.gov
Pets: Dogs on 6-foot leashes allowed
Quiet hours: 10 p.m.–6 a.m.

On the eastern shore of Lake Lanier, Old Federal Campground offers some of the longest RV sites in the state.

Alcohol restrictions: No alcohol allowed
ADA compliant: Yes
Finding the campground: From exit 120 on I-985, go west on Phil Niekro Boulevard for 0.7 mile. Continue straight onto Snelling Avenue, and after 1.2 miles turn right onto McEver Road. At 0.8 mile, turn left on C. G. Crow Road. After 1.9 miles bear left onto Old Federal Road. At 0.6 mile the campground is on the left.
About the campground: Old Federal Campground is located midway up the eastern shore of 38,000-acre Lake Sidney Lanier. This reservoir draws 11 million visitors annually, often ranking as the most heavily used US Army Corps of Engineers lake in the nation.

The campground has several of the longest RV sites in the state. The RV sections are mostly on peninsulas jutting out into the water. These areas are void of understory vegetation and have sparse overstory providing little shade. On the other hand, some of the tent camping areas are heavily wooded with plenty of full shade. The entire campground is on rolling, hilly terrain.

99 Petersburg Campground

Recreation: Hiking, fishing, boating, paddling, swimming
Location: 23 miles northwest of Augusta; 3998 Petersburg Road, Appling 30802
GPS: N33 39.42' / W82 15.39'

Facilities and amenities: Flush toilets, showers, laundry, water, dump station, picnic tables, fire rings, grills, lantern posts, hiking trail, swimming beach, boat ramp, fishing dock, fish cleaning station

Elevation: 353

Road conditions: Paved roads

Hookups: Water, electric

Sites: 82 RV/tent sites with hookups, 8 RV/tent sites with no hookups

Maximum RV length: 45

Season: Year-round, Apr–Nov peak season

Fees: RV/tent site with hookups $28, non-peak $26, RV/tent site with no hookups $18

Maximum stay: 14 days

Management: US Army Corps of Engineers, J. Strom Thurmond Dam and Lake, 510 Clarks Hill Highway, Clarks Hill, SC; (864) 333-1100; www.sas.usace.army.mil/About/Divisions-and-Offices/Operations-Division/J-Strom-Thurmond-Dam-and-Lake/

Reservations: (877) 444-6777; www.recreation.gov

Pets: Dogs on 6-foot leashes allowed

Quiet hours: 10 p.m.–6 a.m.

Alcohol restrictions: No alcohol allowed

ADA compliant: Yes

Finding the campground: From exit 196 on I-20, go north on I-520 (Bobby Jones Expressway) for 1.4 miles. Turn left onto Washington Road for 13.3 miles. Take a right onto US 221 and drive 2.2 miles to Petersburg Road. Turn left and it is 1 mile to the campground at the end of the road.

About the campground: The campground is named for the 19th-century village of Petersburg that now lies beneath the waters of 71,100-acre Clarks Hill Lake. The campground sits on a peninsula roughly 4 miles from the reservoir's dam.

The Petersburg Trailhead and a section of the 115-mile Bartram Trail are within the campground. This pathway follows the course of naturalist William Bartram's travels through North Carolina and Georgia in the 1790s.

The camping area is beneath a canopy of mixed pine and hardwood trees, with a sparse understory. Many of the campsites are on the water with minimal shade, while others get partial to full cover.

There are signs in the campground warning of the presence of alligators. Sightings of these animals in Clarks Hill are extremely rare, and there is not thought to be a permanent resident population of the reptiles in the lake.

100 Ridge Road Campground

Recreation: Fishing, boating, paddling, swimming, playground

Location: 25 miles northwest of Augusta; 5886 Ridge Road, Appling 30802

GPS: N33 40.76' / W82 15.58'

Facilities and amenities: Flush toilets, showers, laundry, water, dump station, picnic tables, fire rings, grills, lantern posts, playground, swimming beach, fish cleaning station, boat ramp

Elevation: 360

Road conditions: Paved roads

Hookups: Water, electric

Sites: 58 RV/tent sites with hookups, 4 RV/tent double sites with hookups, 7 RV/tent sites with no hookups

Maximum RV length: 50

Season: Late Mar–mid-Oct

Fees: RV/tent sites with hookups $28, double RV/tent sites with hookups $54, RV/tent sites without hookups $18

Maximum stay: 14 days

Management: US Army Corps of Engineers, J. Strom Thurmond Dam and Lake, 510 Clarks Hill Highway, Clarks Hill, SC; (864) 333-1100; www.sas.usace.army.mil/About/Divisions-and-Offices/Operations-Division/J-Strom-Thurmond-Dam-and-Lake/

Reservations: (877) 444-6777; www.recreation.gov

Pets: Dogs on 6-foot leashes allowed

Quiet hours: 10 p.m.–6 a.m.

Alcohol restrictions: No alcohol allowed

ADA compliant: Yes

Finding the campground: From exit 183 on I-20, go north on US 221 (Ray Owens Road) for 11.8 miles. Turn right onto Ridge Road and at 4.9 miles the road ends in the campground.

About the campground: Located on the lower end of 71,100-acre Clarks Hill Lake, the campground is on an island connected to the shore by a short causeway a bit to the west of the reservoir's dam.

The RV sites with hookups are on this main island, which has a forested canopy shading them. However, the understory of plants has been cleared, leaving the area open. The sites without hookups are on a second smaller isle connected to the north by another causeway.

101 Sawnee Campground

Recreation: Fishing, boating, paddling, swimming, playground

Location: 5 miles southeast of Cumming; 3200 Buford Dam Road, Cumming 30041

GPS: N34 10.64' / W84 04.47'

Facilities and amenities: Flush toilets, showers, laundry, water, dump station, picnic tables, fire rings, grills, lantern posts, playground, swimming beach, boat ramp

Elevation: 1,072

Road conditions: Paved roads

Hookups: Water, electric

Sites: 43 RV/tent sites with hookups, 5 tent sites with hookups, 10 tent sites without hookups, 1 double tent site with no hookups

Maximum RV length: 85

Season: Late Mar–early Sep

Fees: RV/tent site with hookups $26, tent site with hookups $22, tent sites without hookups $20, double tent site without hookups $36, add $10 extra for all sites on weekends

Maximum stay: 14 days

Management: US Army Corps of Engineers, Lake Sidney Lanier Project Management Office, 1050 Buford Dam Road, Buford; (770) 904-3290; www.sam.usace.army.mil/Missions/Civil-Works/ Recreation/Lake-Sidney-Lanier/
Reservations: (877) 444-6777; www.recreation.gov
Pets: Dogs on 6-foot leashes allowed
Quiet hours: 10 p.m.–6 a.m.
Alcohol restrictions: No alcohol allowed
ADA compliant: Yes
Finding the campground: From exit 14 on US 19/GA 400, go east on GA 20 for 0.7 mile. Turn left onto Sanders Road and continue for 0.9 mile. Turn right on Buford Dam Road, and at 2.5 miles the campground entrance is on the left.
About the campground: Sawnee Campground is located just to the northwest of Buford Dam on 38,000-acre Lake Sidney Lanier. This reservoir draws 11 million visitors annually, often ranking as the most heavily used US Army Corps of Engineers lake in the nation. Sawnee gets many of those visitors due to its location close to GA 400, which is the main thoroughfare for campers coming from metro Atlanta.

The campground is on hilly terrain, with some sites on the lakefront. Many of the others have at least lake views. The majority of sites get full to partial shade, while the understory is open with little vegetation.

102 Toto Creek Campground

Recreation: Fishing, boating, paddling
Location: 10 miles east of Dawsonville; 154 Toto Creek Park Road, Dawsonville 30506
GPS: N34 23.71' / W83 58.84'
Facilities and amenities: Flush toilets, water, picnic tables, fire rings, grills, lantern posts, picnic area, boat ramp
Elevation: 1,090
Road conditions: Paved roads
Hookups: None
Sites: 9 primitive tent sites
Maximum RV length: NA
Season: Apr–Sep
Fees: $16
Maximum stay: 14 days
Management: US Army Corps of Engineers, Lake Sidney Lanier Project Management Office, 1050 Buford Dam Road, Buford; (770) 904-3290; www.sam.usace.army.mil/Missions/Civil-Works/ Recreation/Lake-Sidney-Lanier/
Reservations: (877) 444-6777; www.recreation.gov
Pets: Dogs on 6-foot leashes allowed
Quiet hours: 10 p.m.–6 a.m.
Alcohol restrictions: No alcohol allowed
ADA compliant: Yes

Finding the campground: From the junction of US 19 / GA 400 and Henry Grady Highway at Dawsonvillle, go east on Henry Grady Highway for 1.1 miles. As the road crosses GA 136, it becomes Toto Creek Park Road. Continue for 0.2 mile to where Toto Creek Park Road turns right into the park.

About the campground: This small primitive campground is in the upper reaches of 38,000-acre Lake Sidney Lanier's Chestatee River arm of the impoundment. Toto Creek offers minimal amenities, including a central water spigot and restrooms in the adjacent day-use area.

The campsites are in a heavily wooded area with full shade. There also is a short walking path with picnic tables and grills along it.

103 Van Pugh South Campground

Recreation: Fishing, boating, paddling, playground
Location: 16 miles southwest of Gainesville; 6749 Gaines Ferry Road, Flowery Branch 30542
GPS: N34 11.05' / W83 59.45'
Facilities and amenities: Flush toilets, showers, laundry, water, dump station, picnic tables, fire rings, grills, lantern posts, playground, boat ramp
Elevation: 1,115
Road conditions: Paved roads
Hookups: Water, electric

On the southeastern section of Lake Lanier, the campground is on hilly terrain overlooking the lake.

Sites: 35 standard RV/tent sites with hookups, 18 tent sites with no hookups
Maximum RV length: 35
Season: Late Mar–mid-Sep
Fees: Standard RV/tent site $22, tent site $18
Maximum stay: 14 days
Management: US Army Corps of Engineers, Lake Sidney Lanier Project Management Office, 1050 Buford Dam Road, Buford; (770) 904-3290; www.sam.usace.army.mil/Missions/Civil-Works/Recreation/Lake-Sidney-Lanier/
Reservations: (877) 444-6777; www.recreation.gov
Pets: Dogs on 6-foot leashes allowed
Quiet hours: 10 p.m.–6 a.m.
Alcohol restrictions: No alcohol allowed
ADA compliant: Yes
Finding the campground: From exit 12 on I-985, go west on Phil Niekro Boulevard for 0.7 mile. Turn left onto Atlanta Highway, and at 1.5 miles go right onto Gaines Ferry Road. After 2.8 miles, turn left into the park.
About the campground: Van Pugh South Campground is situated on a long point thrusting out into the southeastern section of 38,000-acre Lake Sidney Lanier. This reservoir was named for famed 19th-century Georgia poet Sidney Lanier.

The campground is on very hilly terrain overlooking the lake, but the sites are set back from the water up on the hillsides. The entire area is heavily forested, providing shade to all the campsites.

104 **Watsadler Campground**

Recreation: Fishing, boating, playground
Location: 6 miles east of Hartwell; 286 Watsadler Road, Hartwell 30643
GPS: N34 20.38' / W82 29.00'
Facilities and amenities: Flush toilets, showers, water, dump station, fire rings, picnic tables, grills, lantern posts, playgrounds, boat ramp
Elevation: 660
Road conditions: Paved roads
Hookups: Water, electric
Sites: 49 RV/tent sites with hookups, 2 double RV/tent sites with hookups
Maximum RV length: 50
Season: Year-round, Apr–Nov peak season
Fees: RV/tent site $28, double RV/tent site $56
Maximum stay: 14 days
Management: US Army Corps of Engineers, 5625 Anderson Highway, Hartwell; (706) 856-0678; www.recreation.gov/camping/campgrounds/232735
Reservations: (877) 444-6777; www.recreation.gov
Pets: Dogs on 6-foot leashes allowed
Quiet hours: 10 p.m.–6 a.m.
Alcohol restrictions: No alcohol allowed

Watsadler Campground is very popular with boaters and anglers on Hartwell Lake with all sites on or very close to the water.

ADA compliant: Yes

Finding the campground: From exit 177 on I-85, take GA 77 south for 10.3 miles. Merge left onto GA 51. At 1.9 miles turn left on US 29. Proceed 5.7 miles and turn left on Watsadler Road. The campground entrance is 0.3 mile on the right.

About the campground: Watsadler Campground sits on the shore of 56,000-acre Hartwell Lake. The reservoir is an Army Corps of Engineers impoundment that lies on the border with South Carolina in northeast Georgia.

The campground is popular with anglers and boaters accessing the lake at the on-site boat ramp. It is also one of the most popular and heavily visited campgrounds on the lake.

All campsites are either on or very close to the lakeshore, with most offering some measure of privacy. The thick pine and hardwood stands provide at least partial shade to the sites. Accessible, double, and pull-through sites are available.

105 Winfield Campground

Recreation: Fishing, boating, paddling, swimming, playground

Location: 15 miles northeast of Thomson; 7701 Winfield Road, Appling 30802

GPS: N33 38.65' / W82 25.26'

Facilities and amenities: Flush toilets, showers, water, dump station, picnic tables, fire rings, grills, lantern posts, playground, swimming beach, boat ramp

Elevation: 333

Road conditions: Paved roads

Hookups: Water, electric

Sites: 80 standard RV/tent sites with hookups

Maximum RV length: 65

Season: Late Mar–Sep

Fees: $28

Maximum stay: 14 days

Management: US Army Corps of Engineers, J. Strom Thurmond Dam and Lake, 510 Clarks Hill Highway, Clarks Hill, SC; (864) 333-1100; www.sas.usace.army.mil/About/Divisions-and-Offices/Operations-Division/J-Strom-Thurmond-Dam-and-Lake/

Reservations: (877) 444-6777; www.recreation.gov

Pets: Dogs on 6-foot leashes allowed

Quiet hours: 10 p.m.–6 a.m.

Alcohol restrictions: No alcohol allowed

ADA compliant: Yes

Finding the campground: From exit 175 on I-20, go north on Cobbham Road (GA 150) for 7.7 miles. Turn left onto Mistletoe Road. After another 1.9 miles, turn left onto Winfield Road. The road enters the campground at 1.4 miles.

About the campground: The Winfield Campground is on a peninsula jutting out into 71,100-acre Clarks Hill Lake on the eastern side of the entrance to the Rousseau Creek arm of the reservoir, where it joins the larger Little River arm.

The campsites offer plenty of views of the water due to the lack of understory vegetation. The openness is despite the thick stands of pine trees that shade the camping area. Some of the sites are right on the waterfront.

106 Lake Russell Campground

Recreation: Hiking, fishing, boating, paddling, swimming,

Location: 3 miles south of Mount Airy; 3059 Lake Russell Road, Mount Airy 30563

GPS: N34 29.35' / W84 29.42'

Facilities and amenities: Flush toilets, showers, water, dump station, fire rings, picnic tables, lantern posts, picnic shelters, grass beach swimming area, hiking trails, fishing dock, boat ramp

Elevation: 1,050

Road conditions: Paved roads

Hookups: None

Sites: 32 RV/tent sites, 9 tent-only sites

Maximum RV length: 65

Season: Year-round, mid-Apr–Oct peak season

Fees: Single site peak season $24, non-peak $18; double site peak season $48, non-peak $36

Maximum stay: 14 days

Management: USDA Forest Service, Chattooga River Ranger District, 9975 US Highway 441, Lakemont; (706) 754-6221; www.fs.usda.gov/Internet/FSE_DOCUMENTS/fseprd496058.pdf

Reservations: (877) 444-6777; www.recreation.gov

Pets: Dogs on 6-foot leashes allowed
Quiet hours: 10 p.m.–6 a.m.
Alcohol restrictions: Alcohol allowed in campground only
ADA compliant: Yes
Finding the campground: From the junction of US 441 BUS and Wyly Street in Cornelia, go east on Wyly Street (which changes names to Dicks Hill Parkway) for 1.9 miles. Turn right onto Lake Russell Road and drive 2.6 miles to the campground entrance.
About the campground: The centerpiece of the Lake Russell Recreation Area is 100-acre Lake Russell. The campground sits adjacent to this man-made impoundment. The lake is open to boating and fishing, while the area has hiking and biking trails available.

The campground is composed of two loops. Loop A contains 17 sites that are open seasonally from mid-April through October. Loop B has 24 sites that are open year-round. Both loops are on heavily wooded hillsides with a mixed pine and hardwood overstory providing full shade. Only a few of the campsites offer lake views. Reservations can be made, but some sites are available on a first-come, first-served basis.

107 Lake Sinclair Campground

Recreation: Hiking, fishing, boating, paddling, swimming
Location: 10 miles south of Eatonton; 100 Putnam Beach Road, Eatonton 31024
GPS: N33 12.58' / W83 23.83'
Facilities and amenities: Flush toilets, showers, water, dump station, picnic tables, grills, lantern posts, swimming beach, boat ramp
Elevation: 349
Road conditions: Loop drives are dirt and gravel
Hookups: Water, electric
Sites: 6 RV/tent sites with hookups, 28 RV/tent sites with no hookups, 1 group site
Maximum RV length: 30
Season: Year-round, Apr–Oct peak season
Fees: RV/tent site with hookups $15, RV/tent sites without hookups $9, group site $80
Maximum stay: 14 days
Management: USDA Forest Service, Oconee Ranger District, 1199 Madison Road, Eatonton; (706) 485-3180; www.fs.usda.gov/Internet/FSE_DOCUMENTS/stelprd3830911.pdf
Reservations: No
Pets: Dogs on 6-foot leashes allowed
Quiet hours: 10 p.m.–6 a.m.
Alcohol restrictions: No alcohol allowed
ADA compliant: Yes
Finding the campground: From the intersection of US 129 and US 441 in Eatonton, go south on US 129 for 7.8 miles. Turn left onto Kinderhook Road (GA 212) and proceed 0.9 mile. Turn left onto Twin Bridges Road and go 1.1 miles to Putnam Beach Road. Turn left and at 0.8 mile the road ends in the recreation area.

About the campground: The campground in the recreation area is situated on the fringe of 15,330-acre Lake Sinclair that is owned by Georgia Power Company. However, the shore on which it is located is on USDA Forest Service land within the Chattahoochee-Oconee National Forest.

The campground itself is an old one that could use a bit of maintenance. It is in a rustic setting, surrounded by thick woodlands. A few of the sites overlook the lake, but for the most part they are back in the forest. The campground originally was composed of four loops labeled A through D. Loop A has the sites with hookups, B holds sites 6 to 15, Loop C is now permanently closed, and Loop D has sites 27 to 44.

The trailhead for the Twin Bridges Trail also is found in the campground. That path offers a 3.6-mile, out-and-back hike along the shore of the lake.

108 Oconee River Campground

Recreation: Hiking, fishing, boating, paddling
Location: 13 miles northwest of Greensboro; FS 204, Oconee National Forest, Greensboro 30642
GPS: N33 43.27' / W83 17.40'
Facilities and amenities: Vault toilet, picnic tables, fire rings, lantern posts, picnic area, boat ramp
Elevation: 454
Road conditions: Paved roads
Hookups: None
Sites: 5 tent sites
Maximum RV length: NA
Season: Year-round, Apr–Oct peak season
Fees: $5
Maximum stay: 14 days
Management: USDA Forest Service, Oconee Ranger District, 1199 Madison Road, Eatonton; (706) 485-3180; www.fs.usda.gov/Internet/FSE_DOCUMENTS/stelprd3830911.pdf
Reservations: No
Pets: Dogs on 6-foot leashes allowed
Quiet hours: 10 p.m.–6 a.m.
Alcohol restrictions: No alcohol allowed
ADA compliant: No
Finding the campground: From the intersection of US 278 and GA 15 (North Laurel Street) in Greensboro, go north on GA 15 (which becomes Athens Highway) for 11.7 miles. Bear right onto FS 264. The campground is at the end of the road at 0.7 mile.
About the campground: The Oconee River Campground is in the Scull Shoals Experimental Forest section of the Oconee National Forest. The site has the trailhead for the Scull Shoals Foot Trail, which runs along the Oconee River shore for 1 mile to the ruins of the old mill town of Scull Shoals. The site also has a boat ramp for access to the river.

The campsites are set back on the hillside in the forest. The thick ground-cover vegetation provides privacy as it separates the sites, all of which are shaded. Be aware that during inclement weather this area can experience flash flooding.

Upper Coastal Plain

Georgia's Upper Coastal Plain stretches from the Chattahoochee River along the Alabama border across to the Savannah River at the South Carolina line. North to south it takes in the region from the Fall Line from Columbus to Macon and Augusta, down to the Florida border. The only part of South Georgia not in this region are the counties along the Atlantic Coast that form the Lower Coastal Plain.

The first thing you notice about these regional boundaries is that they don't touch any portion of an actual coast. Rather, the region derives its name from having been on the bottom of an ancient seacoast that had its beaches along the Fall Line. As you might expect from a place that was part of the ocean floor of the continental shelf, most of this area is quite flat.

Although not as fertile as the Piedmont, today the region is the agricultural heartland of the Peach State. Much of that agrarian activity centers on vast fields of cotton, corn, and soybeans, along with stands of commercially grown pine trees.

While the western edge of the region features several large reservoirs along the Chattahoochee–Flint River drainage that provide recreational options, the eastern portion is dependent on flowing rivers and small man-made ponds for water sports. In both these sections the areas around those water resources most often are where you find the campgrounds.

This region also has traditionally been the least populated portion of Georgia. Despite that drawback, it has some interesting historical background. The entire area was steeped in antebellum plantation lore, as well as the much more recent plantation system of long-leaf pine, wiregrass, and quail hunting that is found in the corridor from Albany down to Thomasville. In the late 1800s up through the 1940s, northern industrialists and financiers bought up large parcels of land to create hunting preserves. Many of these remain in the same families today.

Some of Georgia's earliest inhabitants left behind clues to their Woodland Period lifestyle in the Kolomoki Indian Mounds near Blakely. Today they are the centerpiece of a state park.

Also in the region, the area around the small town of Plains has two notable sites. The Jimmy Carter National Historical Park features tours of structures related to the

early years of the 39th president. Not far down the road at its namesake town is the Andersonville National Historic Site. This venue features the National Prisoner of War Museum, along with the site of Camp Sumter. The camp is better known simply as Andersonville Prison, where more than 40,000 Union prisoners of war were held during the latter stages of the Civil War.

Up near Warner Robins, the Museum of Aviation houses the US Air Force's second largest collection of historic aircraft. Included are 85 airplanes and many associated exhibits. The Georgia Aviation Hall of Fame also is located at this site.

◀ *The cypress tree–studded Parrish Mill Pond is a draw for anglers to George L. Smith State Park.*

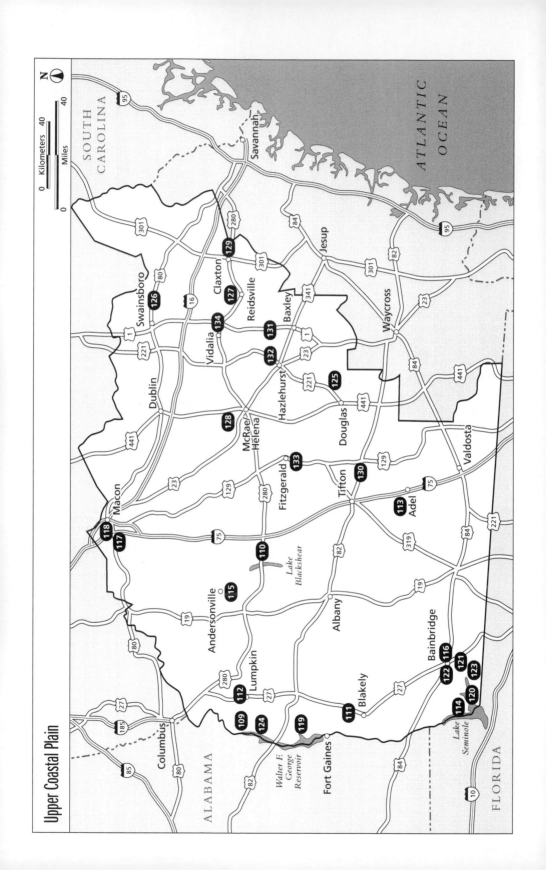

Upper Coastal Plain

Columbus to Macon

Campgrounds At-A-Glance

#	Name	Total Sites	Group Sites	Hookup Sites	Hookups	Maximum RV Length	Dump Station	Toilets	Showers	Drinking Water	ADA	Fees	Reservations
Georgia State Parks and Historic Sites Division													
109	Florence Marina State Park	41	0	41	WE	180	Y	F	Y	Y	Y	$$$$-$$$$$	Y
110	Georgia Veterans Memorial State Park	89	2	82	WE	50	Y	F	Y	Y	Y	$$-$$$$$	Y
111	Kolomoki Mounds State Park	27	3	24	WE	135	Y	F	Y	Y	Y	$$$$	Y
112	Providence Canyon State Park	9	3	0	N	NA	N	N	N	N	Y	$$-$$$$$	Y
113	Reed Bingham State Park	46	3	49	WES	50	Y	F	Y	Y	Y	$$$$-$$$$$	Y
114	Seminole State Park	54	4	50	WE	50	Y	F	Y	Y	Y	$$$$-$$$$$	Y
City Parks													
115	Andersonville RV Park	23	0	20	WES	40	Y	F	Y	Y	Y	$$-$$$	Y
116	Earle May Boat Basin Recreation Area	10	0	10	WES	30	Y	F	Y	Y	N	$$	N
County Parks													
117	Arrowhead Campground	58	0	58	WES	60	Y	F	Y	Y	Y	$$$	Y
118	Claystone Park	45	0	45	WES	80	Y	F	Y	Y	Y	$$$-$$$$	Y
US Army Corps of Engineers													
119	Cotton Hill Campground	101	0	101	WE	45	Y	F	Y	Y	Y	$$$	Y
120	East Bank Campground	62	2	60	WE	60	Y	F	Y	Y	Y	$$-$$$	Y
121	Faceville Landing Campground	7	0	0	N	NA	N	V	N	N	N	$	N
122	Hales Landing Campground	24	0	24	WE	40	Y	F	Y	Y	Y	$$	Y
123	River Junction Campground	11	0	11	WE	50	Y	F	Y	Y	Y	$$	N
124	Rood Creek Park	18	0	0	N	24	N	V	N	N	N	N	N

See Amenities Chart key on page xxi.

109 Florence Marina State Park

Recreation: Fishing, boating, paddling, birding, playground
Location: 16 miles west of Lumpkin; 218 Florence Road, Omaha 31821
GPS: N32 05.46' / W85 02.59'
Facilities and amenities: Flush toilets, showers, laundry, water, dump station, picnic area and shelter, playgrounds, miniature golf, geocaching, lighted fishing dock, fish cleaning station, marina, boat ramp and dock, Kirbo Interpretive Center
Elevation: 201
Road conditions: Paved roads
Hookups: Water, electric
Sites: 41 RV/tent sites with hookups, 14 cottages
Maximum RV length: 180
Season: Year-round, Apr–Oct peak season
Fees: RV/tent site $38, premium 2-bedroom cottage $190, standard 2-bedroom cottage $175, efficiency cottage $85, daily parking fee $5, annual pass $50
Maximum stay: 14 days
Management: Georgia State Parks and Historic Sites Division, 2610 Georgia Highway 155 SW, Stockbridge; (770) 389-7286; www.gastateparks.org
Reservations: (800) 864-7275; www.gastateparks.org/reservations
Pets: Dogs on 6-foot leashes allowed
Quiet hours: 10 p.m.–7 a.m.
Alcohol restrictions: Unlawful in public areas
ADA compliant: Yes
Finding the campground: From US 27 in Lumpkin, go west on GA 39C (Canyon Road) for 15.2 miles. At the end of the road, the entrance to the park is straight ahead.
About the campground: Florence Marina State Park sits on the shore of 45,000-acre Walter F. George Reservoir on the border with Alabama. The impoundment is usually known as Lake Eufaula for the Alabama town that is on the opposite side.

The park holds one of the Georgia State Park System's only two full-service marinas, providing everything you need for access to the reservoir. As you might expect this is a very popular destination for boaters and anglers.

The Kirbo Interpretive Center focuses on local wildlife and plants, history, and Native American artifacts.

The campground consists of four connected loops, with half the sites pull-throughs. A pine and hardwood canopy provides full shade throughout. The sites are rather closely spaced, with no ground vegetation separating them, thus providing minimal privacy.

110 Georgia Veterans Memorial State Park

Recreation: Hiking, fishing, boating, paddling, biking, swimming, playground, golf
Location: 8 miles west of Cordele; 2459-A US Highway 280 West, Cordele 31015
GPS: N31 57.47' / W83 54.22'
Facilities and amenities: Flush toilets, showers, laundry, water, dump station, picnic tables, fire rings, picnic areas and shelters, playgrounds, hiking and biking trails, geocaching, swimming beach, archery and air gun ranges, disc golf, outdoor fitness center, SAM Shortline Excursion Train, military museum, airplane and armaments displays, model airplane flying field, golf course, fishing pier, fishing gear rentals, canoe and kayak rentals, boat ramps, marina, Cordelia's Restaurant, Cypress Grill, 88's Lakeside Bar
Elevation: 139
Road conditions: Paved roads
Hookups: Water, electric
Sites: 23 premium RV/tent sites with 50-amp hookups, 4 premium RV/tent sites with 30-amp hookups, 7 standard RV/tent sites with 50-amp hookups, 48 standard RV/tent sites with 30-amp hookups, 5 primitive tent sites with no hookups, 14 lodge rooms, 64 villa rooms, 10 cottages, 1 pioneer site with full bathroom facilities, 1 pioneer site
Maximum RV length: 50
Season: Year-round, Apr–Oct peak season
Fees: Premium RV/tent site with 50-amp hookups $65, premium RV/tent site with 30-amp hookups $65, standard RV/tent site with 50-amp hookups $60, standard RV/tent site with 30-amp hookups $55, tent site $18, lodge room $162, villa room $162, 2-bedroom cottage $199, pioneer site with bathroom facilities $85, pioneer site $50, daily parking fee $5, annual pass $50
Maximum stay: 14 days
Management: Georgia State Parks and Historic Sites Division, 2610 Georgia Highway 155 SW, Stockbridge; (770) 389-7286; www.gastateparks.org
Reservations: (800) 864-7275; www.gastateparks.org/reservations
Pets: Dogs on 6-foot leashes allowed
Quiet hours: 10 p.m.–7 a.m.
Alcohol restrictions: Unlawful in public areas
ADA compliant: Yes
Finding the campground: From exit 101 on I-75, go west on US 280 for 10 miles. The park entrance is on the left.
About the campground: Georgia Veterans State Park is operated on behalf of the state by Coral Hospitality and truly is a first-rate vacation destination. The range of activities and amenities is remarkable, and all are well maintained.

Besides the usual state park features, Georgia Veterans is the railhead for short-line excursion trains to the historic Plains area and Jimmy Carter National Historical Park, a four-star 18-hole championship golf course, a military museum and displays that include a B-29 bomber, a full-service marina with access to 8,500-acre Lake Blackshear, and a host of other unique offerings.

The campgrounds consist of two areas, with the premium sites on the lakeshore, while the standard ones are split between just off the lake and a separate inland loop. All sites are partially shaded by stands of mostly pine trees. They also are relatively close together, with a cleared understory offering little privacy.

It is worth noting that Lake Blackshear has a resident population of alligators.

111 Kolomoki Mounds State Park

Recreation: Hiking, fishing, boating, paddling, swimming, playground
Location: 7 miles north of Blakely; 295 Indian Mounds Road, Blakely 39823
GPS: N31 28.30' / W84 55.52
Facilities and amenities: Flush toilets, showers, laundry, water, dump station, picnic tables, fire rings, grills, lantern posts, picnic areas and shelters, playgrounds, miniature golf, geocaching, amphitheater, hiking trails, swimming beach, 2 lakes, fishing docks, canoe, kayak and pedal boat rentals, boat ramp, Indian mounds, museum, gift shop
Elevation: 301
Road conditions: Paved roads
Hookups: Water, electric
Sites: 18 premium RV/tent sites with hookups, 6 standard RV/tent sites with hookups, 3 pioneer sites
Maximum RV length: 135
Season: Year-round, Apr–Oct peak season
Fees: Premium RV/tent site with hookups $36, standard RV/tent site with hookups $32, pioneer site $40, daily parking fee $5, annual pass $50
Maximum stay: 14 days
Management: Georgia State Parks and Historic Sites Division, 2610 Georgia Highway 155 SW, Stockbridge; (770) 389-7286; www.gastateparks.org
Reservations: (800) 864-7275; www.gastateparks.org/reservations
Pets: Dogs on 6-foot leashes allowed
Quiet hours: 10 p.m.–7 a.m.
Alcohol restrictions: Unlawful in public areas
ADA compliant: Yes
Finding the campground: From the intersection of US 27 and GA 62 (Martin Luther King Jr. Boulevard) in Blakely, go north on US 27 for 1.3 miles. Turn left onto North Main Street and at 0.3 mile take a right onto 1st Kolomoki Road (you will pass 2nd Kolomoki Road before reaching your turn). At 4.5 miles the park entrance is on the right.
About the campground: The centerpiece of this park is the eight Indian mounds that date from the Woodland Period of 350 to 750 AD and their associated museum. However, Kolomoki also provides a host of activities and amenities for the family. These center around Lakes Kolomoki and Yahola, which offer water sports and fishing.

The campground is located on the north shore of Lake Kolomoki, with half the sites right on the water. These sites are relatively close together and receive only partial shade.

112 Providence Canyon State Park

Recreation: Hiking, playground
Location: 8 miles west of Lumpkin; 8930 Canyon Road, Lumpkin 31815
GPS: N32 03.94' / W84 55.25'
Facilities and amenities: Fire ring, playground, picnic area and shelters
Elevation: 399
Road conditions: Paved roads
Hookups: None
Sites: 6 backcountry tent sites, 3 pioneer sites
Maximum RV length: NA
Season: Year-round, Apr-Oct peak season
Fees: Backcountry site $12, pioneer site $45–$85, daily parking fee $5, annual pass $50
Maximum stay: 14 days
Management: Georgia State Parks and Historic Sites Division, 2610 Georgia Highway 155 SW, Stockbridge; (770) 389-7286; www.gastateparks.org

Even with limited camping options, the draw to Providence Canyon State Park is the spectacular gorge.

Reservations: (800) 864-7275; www.gastateparks.org/reservations
Pets: Dogs on 6-foot leashes allowed
Quiet hours: 10 p.m.–7 a.m.
Alcohol restrictions: Unlawful in public areas
ADA compliant: Yes
Finding the campground: From US 27 in Lumpkin, go west on GA 39C (Canyon Road) for 6.8 miles. The park entrance is on the left.
About the campground: The attraction that draws visitors to this park is its canyon. In fact, the canyon is just a gigantic erosion ditch that has formed due to poor early farming techniques. On the other hand, it is a spectacular ditch that has been called "Georgia's Grand Canyon." The clay soils of the region paint a tableau of pink, orange, red, and purple layers of clay on the canyon walls, drawing photographers from all of the state to capture their beauty.

The camping options are quite limited, with just six primitive backcountry tent sites and three pioneer group sites available. These are scattered along the hiking trails in and around the gorge, offering fire rings as their only amenity. But they are placed to provide you with great views of the canyon that otherwise cannot be enjoyed.

One of the pioneer sites offers the only ADA-accessible camping in the park.

113 Reed Bingham State Park

Recreation: Hiking, fishing, boating, paddling, biking, birding, swimming, playground
Location: 7 miles west of Adel; 542 Reed Bingham Road, Adel 31620
GPS: N31 10.01' / W83 32.88'
Facilities and amenities: Flush toilets, showers, laundry, water, dump station, picnic table, fire ring, grill, picnic areas and shelters, playground, miniature golf, swimming beach, hiking and biking trails, bike rentals, lake, canoe and kayak trail, canoe and kayak rentals, boat ramp, wildlife viewing areas
Elevation: 198
Road conditions: Paved roads
Hookups: Water, electric, sewer
Sites: 20 premium RV/sites with full hookups, 12 premium pull-through RV/tent sites with water and electric hookups, 14 standard RV/tent sites with water and electric hookups, pioneer site
Maximum RV length: 50
Season: Year-round, Apr–Oct peak season
Fees: Premium RV site with full hookups $40, premium pull-through RV/tent site with water and electric hookups $40, standard RV/tent site with hookups $32, pioneer site $40–$50, daily parking fee $5, annual pass $50
Maximum stay: 14 days
Management: Georgia State Parks and Historic Sites Division, 2610 Georgia Highway 155 SW, Stockbridge; (770) 389-7286; www.gastateparks.org
Reservations: (800) 864-7275; www.gastateparks.org/reservations
Pets: Dogs on 6-foot leashes allowed
Quiet hours: 10 p.m.–7 a.m.

With Reed Bingham in a part of the state without many public waters, its 375-acre lake is a popular draw.

Alcohol restrictions: Unlawful in public areas
ADA compliant: Yes
Finding the campground: From exit 39 on I-75, go west on GA 37 (Fourth Street) for 5.5 miles. Turn right onto Evergreen Church Road, then at 0.3 mile go left on Reed Bingham Road. At 0.4 mile the road enters the park.
About the campground: Reed Bingham State Park covers 1,613 acres, including a 375-acre lake. It is positioned in a portion of the state that does not have a lot of access to public waters, thus it is a regional attraction. The park is also noted for its variety of wildlife and birds that also attracts visitors. Endangered gopher tortoises and indigo snakes are present. Bald eagles nest here, and the lake draws lots of wading birds, but the most unusual avian attraction is the summertime appearance of large flocks of buzzards. Literally thousands of black and turkey vultures can be seen in the trees and floating on the air currents.

The campground is located in thin stands of pine trees that offer anything from no shade to full shade, depending on the site chosen and the time of day. The understory also is quite open, so there is little privacy.

114 Seminole State Park

Recreation: Hiking, fishing, boating, paddling, birding, swimming, playground
Location: 21 miles southwest of Bainbridge; 7870 State Park Drive, Donalsonville 39846
GPS: N30 48.34' / W84 52.53'
Facilities and amenities: Flush toilets, showers, laundry, water, dump station, picnic table, fire ring, grill, picnic areas and shelters, playground, miniature golf, geocaching, swimming beach, hiking trails, canoe/kayak/pontoon boat rentals, boat ramp, fishing dock, gift shop
Elevation: 84
Road conditions: Paved roads
Hookups: Water, electric
Sites: 43 premium RV/tent sites with hookups, 7 standard RV/tent sites with hookups, 1 pioneer site in main park, 3 pioneer sites in Cummings Landing, 14 cottages
Maximum RV length: 50
Season: Year-round, Apr–Oct peak season
Fees: Premium RV/tent site $38, standard RV/tent site $34, pioneer site in main park $35, pioneer site at Cummings Landing $20, 2-bedroom cottage $185, daily parking fee $5, annual pass $50
Maximum stay: 14 days

You cross this boardwalk while walking the Gopher Tortoise Trail at Seminole State Park.

Management: Georgia State Parks and Historic Sites Division, 2610 Georgia Highway 155 SW, Stockbridge; (770) 389-7286; www.gastateparks.org

Reservations: (800) 864-7275; www.gastateparks.org/reservations

Pets: Dogs on 6-foot leashes allowed

Quiet hours: 10 p.m.–7 a.m.

Alcohol restrictions: Unlawful in public areas

ADA compliant: Yes

Finding the campground: From the junction of US 84 and GA 253 in Bainbridge, go southwest on GA 253 (Spring Creek Road) for 19.6 miles. The park entrance is on the left.

About the campground: Seminole State Park is located in the extreme southwest corner of the Peach State on the shore of its namesake reservoir. The 37,500 acres of water in Lake Seminole provide a venue for watersports. The park surrounds a large cove off the Spring Creek arm of the reservoir.

There's a swimming beach and multiple boat ramps for accessing the lake. There also are hiking trails through a long-leaf pine and wiregrass forest, playgrounds for the kids, and fishing docks for all ages.

The campground is positioned on the point at the south side of the mouth of the cove, where it joins the main lake. There are some pine trees spread through the campsites that provide partial shade.

Lake Seminole is another place where you are likely to see some alligators.

115 Andersonville RV Park

Recreation: None

Location: In the village of Andersonville; 209 West Church Street, Andersonville 31711

GPS: N32 11.66' / W84 08.43'

Facilities and amenities: Restrooms, water, showers, dump station, fire pit, historic sites

Elevation: 400

Road conditions: Gravel drive within the campground

Hookups: Water, electric, sewer

Sites: 20 RV/tent sites with full hookups, 3 RV/tent sites with no hookups

Maximum RV length: 40

Season: Year-round, Apr–Dec peak season

Fees: RV/tent site with full hookups $26, RV/tent site with no hookups $16

Maximum stay: 14 days

Management: City of Andersonville, PO Box 35, Andersonville 31711; (229) 924-2064

Reservations: (229) 924-2558; www.andersonvillegeorgia.info/accommodations.html

Pets: Dogs allowed on 6-foot leashes

Quiet hours: 10 p.m.–7 a.m.

Alcohol restrictions: No alcohol allowed

ADA compliant: Yes

Finding the campground: From GA 49 in Andersonville, go west on Church Street for 0.4 mile. The campground entrance is on the left.

About the campground: The campground is situated in the midst of the historic Civil War town and used mainly by tourists. The town contains museums, antique shops, and restaurants, while the Andersonville National Historic Site is less than a mile away. That facility has a museum and exhibits about Camp Sumter and the Andersonville Civil War prison, as well as the National Prisoner of War Museum.

The campground has a gravel loop drive with partial shade on all the sites. There are four pull-through and seven back-in sites that have concrete pads.

116 Earle May Boat Basin Recreation Area

Recreation: Hiking, fishing, boating, paddling, playground
Location: In the city of Bainbridge; 100 Boat Basin Circle, Bainbridge 39817
GPS: N30 89.78' / W84 59.83'
Facilities and amenities: Flush toilet, showers, dump station, picnic area and shelters, boat ramps, playground, nature trails
Elevation: 79
Road conditions: Gravel and dirt campground loop drive
Hookups: Water, electric, sewer
Sites: 10 RV/tent sites with hookups
Maximum RV length: 30
Season: Year-round, Apr–Dec peak season
Fees: $20
Maximum stay: 14 days
Management: City of Bainbridge, 101 S. Broad Street, Bainbridge; (229) 248-2000; www.bainbridgecity.com
Reservations: No
Pets: Dogs allowed on 6-foot leashes
Quiet hours: 10 p.m.–7 a.m.
Alcohol restrictions: No alcohol allowed
ADA compliant: No
Finding the campground: Heading south on US 84 at Bainbridge, take the exit for Shotwell Street and stay in the left lane at the fork. Go straight across GA 97 onto Boat Basin Circle. Turn left at the first intersection. At 0.6 mile the campground entrance is on the left.
About the campground: Earle May Boat Basin Recreation Area has a wide range of facilities and activities for all ages. But the focus of the site is the mega boat ramp featuring 10 lanes that provide access to the Flint River arm of 37,500-acre Lake Seminole.

The campground is in a secluded, forested area, with half the sites, including one pull-through site, on the lakefront fees are collected on the honor system at a station near the entrance, which is monitored daily.

Be aware, however, that the campground does not measure up to the other facilities in the recreation area. The campsites, restroom, and showers are in very poor condition and badly in need of replacement. This is a site suitable for only the hardiest and most adventurous of hard-core anglers.

117 Arrowhead Campground

Recreation: Hiking, fishing, boating, paddling, biking, swimming, playground
Location: 12 miles west of Macon; 2800 Arrowhead Drive, Lizella 31062
GPS: N32 49.22' / W83 48.08'
Facilities and amenities: Flush toilets, showers, laundry, water, dump station, picnic tables, grills, picnic area, playground, hiking and biking trails, boat ramp
Elevation: 394
Road conditions: Paved roads
Hookups: Water, electric, sewer
Sites: 17 RV-only sites with full hookups, 11 RV/tent waterfront sites with water and electric hookups, 24 RV/tent sites with water and electric hookups, 6 tent-only sites with water and electric hookups
Maximum RV length: 60
Season: Year-round, Apr–Oct peak season
Fees: RV site with full hookups $30, RV/tent waterfront site with water and electric hookups $30, RV/tent site with water and electric hookups $27, tent-only site $23
Maximum stay: 14 days
Management: Macon/Bibb County, 700 Poplar Street, Macon; (478) 751-7400; www. maconbibb.us
Reservations: https://laketobo.maconbibb.us/camping/
Pets: Dogs on leashes allowed
Quiet hours: 10 p.m.–8 a.m.
Alcohol restrictions: No alcohol allowed
ADA compliant: Yes
Finding the campground: From exit 3 on I-475, go west on Eisenhower Parkway (GA 22) for 4.2 miles. Turn right onto Tidwell Road and drive 0.4 mile to the end of the road. Turn left on GA 22 CON. At 0.1 mile, turn right onto Arrowhead Road and follow it for 0.6 mile where it enters the park.
About the campground: This county-managed park is exceptionally well maintained, offering a number of outdoor activities on the shore of 1,800-acre Lake Tobesofkee. The reservoir provides options for boating, fishing, swimming, and paddling. Nearby Macon is the home to both the Georgia Music Hall of Fame and the Georgia Sports Hall of Fame, which are well worth a visit.

The campground, which is on the south side of the impoundment, is quite open with the sparse tree canopy providing partial to no shade. The campsites are close together, creating a communal situation.

118 Claystone Park

Recreation: Fishing, boating, paddling, swimming, playground
Location: 12 miles west of Macon; 6600 Moseley Dixon Road, Macon 31220
GPS: N32 49.73' / W83 46.58'

Facilities and amenities: Flush toilets, showers, laundry, water, dump station, picnic tables, fire rings, grills, picnic shelters, butterfly garden, playground, disc golf course, swimming beach, boat ramp

Elevation: 395

Road conditions: Paved roads

Hookups: Water, electric, sewer

Sites: 6 RV-only waterfront sites with full hookups, 30 RV/tent sites with water and electric hookups, 9 tent-only sites with water and electric hookups

Maximum RV length: 80

Season: Year-round, Apr–Oct peak season

Fees: RV-only site with full hookups $35, RV/tent site with water and electric hookups $27, tent-only site with water and electric hookups $23

Maximum stay: 14 days

Management: Macon/Bibb County, 700 Poplar Street, Macon; (478) 751-7400; www.maconbibb.us

Reservations: https://laketobo.maconbibb.us/camping/

Pets: Dogs on leashes allowed

Quiet hours: 10 p.m.–8 a.m.

Alcohol restrictions: No alcohol allowed

ADA compliant: Yes

Finding the campground: From exit 5 on I-475, go west on GA 74 for 0.7 mile. Turn left onto Moseley Dixon Road and at 1.9 miles turn left into the park.

About the campground: Claystone Campground is positioned on the north side of Lake Tobesofkee, not far from the dining and entertainment options in Macon. At the same time, the 1,800 acres of water in Lake Tobesofkee provide plenty of opportunities for water sports fun and action.

The campground is located at the west end of the park, set up on rolling hills overlooking the water. An overstory of pines and hardwoods delivers partial shade to the campsites, with the grassy, open understory making for a communal setting.

119 Cotton Hill Campground

Recreation: Hiking, fishing, boating, paddling, swimming, playground

Location: 7 miles north of Fort Gaines; 177A Campground Drive, Fort Gaines 39851

GPS: N31 40.28' / W85 03.51'

Facilities and amenities: Flush toilets, showers, laundry, water, dump station, picnic tables, picnic shelter, playground, hiking trails, swimming beach, dog park, boat ramp, courtesy dock, fish cleaning station

Elevation: 210

Road conditions: Paved roads

Hookups: Water, electric

Sites: 91 RV/tent sites with electric and water hookups, 10 tent sites with electric hookups and group water

Maximum RV length: 45

Season: Year-round, Apr–Oct peak season

Fees: RV/tent site with hookups $28, tent site with hookups $24
Maximum stay: 14 days
Management: US Army Corps of Engineers, Walter F. George / George Andrews Lakes, 427 Eufaula Road, Fort Gaines 39851; (229) 768-2916; www.sam.usace.army.mil/Missions/Civil-Works/Recreation/Walter-F-George-Lake-Lake-George-W-Andrews/
Reservations: (877) 444-6777; www.recreation.gov
Pets: Dogs on 6-foot leashes allowed
Quiet hours: 10 p.m.–6 a.m.
Alcohol restrictions: No alcohol allowed
ADA compliant: Yes
Finding the campground: From the junction of GA 266 (Coleman Road) and GA 39 (Eufaula Highway) in Fort Gaines, travel north on GA 39 for 4.7 miles. Turn left onto Sandy Branch Road. At 0.2 mile turn left on Campground Drive (County Road 85) and continue 0.9 mile to the park entrance.
About the campground: Cotton Hill Campground is located on 45,000-acre Walter F. George Reservoir on the Georgia/Alabama border. The impoundment was named for a longtime US senator from the Peach State, but it is more commonly referred to as Lake Eufaula for the nearby Alabama town.

The campground is composed of two sections on a point in the lake. The Old Mill Road section faces the Sandy Creek arm of the lake, while the Pine Island section is across the point on the main lake.

All RV/tent sites are on rolling terrain overlooking the water, wellspaced, and shaded. A few of the tent sites are right at the water's edge and get only partial shade.

120 East Bank Campground

Recreation: Fishing, boating, paddling
Location: 27 miles southwest of Bainbridge; 153 East Bank Road, Bainbridge 39819
GPS: N30 43.03' / W84 50.98'
Facilities and amenities: Flush toilets, showers, laundry, water, dump station, picnic tables, grills, lantern posts, picnic area and shelter, horseshoe pits, volleyball court, fish cleaning station, boat ramp, courtesy dock
Elevation: 120
Road conditions: Paved roads
Hookups: Water, electric
Sites: 60 RV/tent sites with electric and water hookups, 2 primitive tent sites
Maximum RV length: 60
Season: Year-round, Apr–Oct peak season
Fees: RV/tent site $24, tent slte $14
Maximum stay: 14 days
Management: US Army Corps of Engineers, 1 Jim Woodruff Dam Access Road, Chattahoochee, FL; (850) 663-4692; sam.usace.army.mil/Missions/Civil-Works/Recreation/Lake-Seminole/Camping/
Reservations: (877) 444-6777; www.recreation.gov
Pets: Dogs on 6-foot leashes allowed

Quiet hours: 10 p.m.–6 a.m.

Alcohol restrictions: No alcohol allowed

ADA compliant: Yes

Finding the campground: From US 84 in Bainbridge, take GA 97 south for 22.6 miles, crossing the border into Florida. Turn right on US 90 and drive 3.5 miles into Chattahoochee, Florida. Turn right on North Bolivar Street and continue for 1.4 miles. Turn left onto East Bank Road. The campground is 0.6 mile at the end of the road.

About the campground: East Bank Campground is situated on the east side of the main body of 37,500-acre Lake Seminole, just north of the Jim Woodruff Lock and Dam.

The 60 campsites with hookups are positioned in three loops, with A and C along the lakeshore, while B is farther back. The sites are very open offering little privacy, with only some shaded. The two primitive tent sites are on the lake beside the boat ramp, with no shade.

121 Faceville Landing Campground

Recreation: Fishing, boating, paddling

Location: 15 miles southwest of Bainbridge; Faceville Landing Road, Bainbridge 39819

GPS: N30 47.87' / W84 39.56'

Facilities and amenities: Vault toilet, picnic shelter, boat ramp, fishing pier

Elevation: 115

Road conditions: Dirt and gravel in campground

Hookups: None

Sites: 7 tent sites

Maximum RV length: NA

Season: Year-round, Apr–Oct peak season

Fees: $7

Maximum stay: 14 days

Management: US Army Corps of Engineers, 1 Jim Woodruff Dam Access Road, Chattahoochee, FL; (850) 663-4692; sam.usace.army.mil/Missions/Civil-Works/Recreation/Lake-Seminole/Camping/

Reservations: No

Pets: Dogs on 6-foot leashes allowed

Quiet hours: 10 p.m.–6 a.m.

Alcohol restrictions: No alcohol allowed

ADA compliant: No

Finding the campground: From US 84 in Bainbridge, travel south on GA 97 (Faceville Highway) for 13 miles. Turn right onto Faceville Landing Road. The road dead ends in the park at 3.2 miles.

About the campground: Faceville Landing is located on the south side of the Flint River arm of 37,500-acre Lake Seminole in the southwest corner of Georgia. The camping area is mostly used by anglers who are accessing the reservoir from the boat ramp that is on-site. Additionally, a picnic shelter, fishing pier, and pit toilet are also provided. Water is available at the shelter.

The campground consists of seven tent sites, each having a tent pad, picnic table, grill, and lantern pole. These sites are situated around a dirt loop drive near the shore of the lake, with little to no shade.

122 Hales Landing Campground

Recreation: Fishing, boating, paddling
Location: 7 miles southwest of Bainbridge; Hales Landing Road, Bainbridge 39817
GPS: N30 84.74' / W84 66.12'
Facilities and amenities: Flush toilets, showers, water, dump station, picnic tables, picnic shelter, boat ramp, courtesy dock
Elevation: 85
Road conditions: Paved roads
Hookups: Water, electric
Sites: 24 RV/tent sites with electric and water hookups
Maximum RV length: 40
Season: Year-round, Apr–Oct peak season
Fees: $20
Maximum stay: 14 days

Some of the waterfront sites at Hales Landing have places for tying up boats.

Management: US Army Corps of Engineers, 1 Jim Woodruff Dam Access Road, Chattahoochee, FL; (850) 663-4692; sam.usace.army.mil/Missions/Civil-Works/Recreation/Lake-Seminole/Camping/
Reservations: (877) 444-6777; www.recreation.gov
Pets: Dogs on 6-foot leashes allowed
Quiet hours: 10 p.m.–6 a.m.
Alcohol restrictions: No alcohol allowed
ADA compliant: Yes
Finding the campground: From US 84 in Bainbridge, take GA 253 west for 3.8 miles. Bear to the left onto 10 Mile Still Road and continue for 2 miles. Turn left onto Hales Landing Road. The campground is at the end of the road.
About the campground: Hales Landing Campground is located on the north shore of the Flint River arm of 37,500-acre Lake Seminole in extreme southwest Georgia. The campground has one site that is ADA-accessible and seven on the water, but it does not have any pull-through sites. Campground attendants are on-site March to July.

The sites are partially shaded, with those on the waterfront having cypress trees with Spanish moss over them. A couple have on-site access for tying up boats. A boat ramp with courtesy dock is located adjacent to the campground.

123 River Junction Campground

Recreation: Fishing, boating, paddling
Location: 25 miles southwest of Bainbridge; River Junction Landing Road, Bainbridge 39819
GPS: N30 74.96' / W84 83.975'
Facilities and amenities: Flush toilets, showers, water, dump station, picnic tables, grills, lantern posts, boat ramp, courtesy dock
Elevation: 95
Road conditions: Paved roads
Hookups: Water, electric
Sites: 11 RV sites with electric and water hookups
Maximum RV length: 50
Season: Year-round, Apr–Oct peak season
Fees: $20
Maximum stay: 14 days
Management: US Army Corps of Engineers, 1 Jim Woodruff Dam Access Road, Chattahoochee, FL; (850) 663-4692; sam.usace.army.mil/Missions/Civil-Works/Recreation/Lake-Seminole/Camping/
Reservations: No
Pets: Dogs on 6-foot leashes allowed
Quiet hours: 10 p.m.–6 a.m.
Alcohol restrictions: No alcohol allowed
ADA compliant: Yes

Finding the campground: From US 84 in Bainbridge, drive west on GA 97 for 15.5 miles. Turn right on Booster Club Road and proceed 9.7 miles. Turn right on River Junction Landing Road. At 1 mile the campground is at the end of the road.

About the campground: As the name implies, River Junction Campground is located near the confluence of the Chattahoochee and Flint River arms of 37,500-acre Lake Seminole.

The campsites are well spaced and mostly shaded. Only one of the sites is a pull-through. All sites are first come, first served with a pay station on-site.

The boat ramp and courtesy dock are at the end of a canal leading out to the main lake. That area also offers some room for fishing from the shore.

124 Rood Creek Park

Recreation: Fishing, boating, paddling
Location: 20 miles southwest of Lumpkin; 1337 Rood Creek Landing Road, Omaha 31821
GPS: N32 02.63' / W85 03.68'
Facilities and amenities: Vault toilet, picnic tables, grills, picnic area, boat ramp
Elevation: 194
Road conditions: Very rough dirt track approach road
Hookups: None
Sites: 18 RV/tent sites with no hookups
Maximum RV length: 24
Season: Year-round, Apr–Oct peak season
Fees: None
Maximum stay: 14 days
Management: US Army Corps of Engineers, Walter F. George / George Andrews Lakes, 427 Eufaula Road, Fort Gaines; (229) 768-2916; www.sam.usace.army.mil/Missions/Civil-Works/Recreation/Walter-F-George-Lake-Lake-George-W-Andrews/
Reservations: No
Pets: Dogs on 6-foot leashes allowed
Quiet hours: 10 p.m.–6 a.m.
Alcohol restrictions: No alcohol allowed
ADA compliant: No
Finding the campground: From Omaha, drive 7.9 miles south on GA 39. Turn right onto Rood Creek Landing Road. The campground entrance is at 1.3 miles.
About the campground: Rood Creek is a quite primitive camping area offering minimal amenities. Though the sites appear to be mainly for tent camping, there is room for smaller RVs. There is a good boat ramp, providing access to Walter F. George Reservoir. This is a site mainly for anglers. Be aware that the Rood Creek Landing Road is a rough dirt track.

Macon to Augusta

Campgrounds At-A-Glance

#	Name	Total Sites	Group Sites	Hookup Sites	Hookups	Maximum RV Length	Dump Station	Toilets	Showers	Drinking Water	ADA	Fees	Reservations
Georgia State Parks and Historic Sites Division													
125	General Coffee State Park	60	2	54	WE	50	Y	F	Y	Y	Y	$$-$$$$$	Y
126	George L. Smith State Park	29	1	24	WE	40	Y	F	Y	Y	Y	$-$$$$$	Y
127	Jack Hill State Park	26	0	25	WES	60	Y	F	Y	Y	Y	$$$-$$$$$	Y
128	Little Ocmulgee State Park	52	0	52	WE	40	Y	F	Y	Y	Y	$$$$$	Y
Georgia Wildlife Resources Division													
129	Evans County Public Fishing Area	22	0	22	WES	60	Y	F	Y	Y	Y	$$-$$$$	Y
130	Paradise Public Fishing Area	8	1	0	N	NA	N	F	N	Y	Y	$	Y
County Parks													
131	Falling Rocks Campground and RV Park	22	0	14	WE	50	Y	F	Y	Y	Y	$$-$$$	Y
132	Towns Bluff Park and Heritage Center	24	0	24	WE	60	Y	F	Y	Y	Y	$$$$-$$$$$	Y
City Parks													
133	Paulk Park RV and Tent Campground	59	0	24	WES	50	Y	F	Y	Y	Y	$-$$$	Y
134	Sweet Onion RV Park	12	0	12	WES	80	Y	N	N	Y	Y	$$	N

See Amenities Chart key on page xxi.

125 General Coffee State Park

Recreation: Fishing, paddling, biking, birding, playground, horseback riding
Location: 6 miles east of Douglas; 46 John Coffee Road, Nichols 31554
GPS: N31 50.93' / W82 75.51'
Facilities and amenities: Flush toilets, showers, laundry, water, dump station, hiking and equestrian trails, playground, picnic areas, amphitheater, bike rentals, canoe/kayak/pedal boat rentals, Heritage Farm
Elevation: 165
Road conditions: Paved roads
Hookups: Water, electric
Sites: 44 premium RV/tent sites with hookups, 6 standard RV/tent sites with hookups, 4 equestrian sites with hookups, 4 backcountry tent sites, 2 pioneer sites, 4 cottages
Maximum RV length: 50
Season: Year-round, Apr–Oct peak season
Fees: Premium RV/tent site $36, standard RV/tent site $32, equestrian site $23, backcountry tent site $12, pioneer site $40, 2-bedroom cottage $155, daily parking fee $5, annual pass $50
Maximum stay: 14 days
Management: Georgia State Parks and Historic Sites Division, 2610 Georgia Highway 155 SW, Stockbridge; (770) 389-7286; www.gastateparks.org
Reservations: (800) 864-7275; www.gastateparks.org/reservations
Pets: Dogs on 6-foot leashes allowed
Quiet hours: 10 p.m.–7 a.m.
Alcohol restrictions: Unlawful in public areas
ADA compliant: Yes
Finding the campground: From the junction of US 221 and GA 32 in Douglas, go east on GA 32 for 4.6 miles. Turn left onto John Coffee Road to enter the park.
About the campground: General Coffee State Park covers 1,511 acres and is named for local planter, US congressman, and military leader General John Coffee. The park's centerpieces are the interpretative 19th-century Heritage Farm and 4-acre fishing pond. Other facilities offer a wide range of family activities, including equestrian trails. The park is home to endangered gopher tortoises and indigo snakes.

The campground consists of two loops, both of which are well shaded by moss-draped water oaks and long-leaf pine trees. The surrounding substrata of plants are dominated by palmetto fans. The sites, most of which are pull-throughs, are well spaced for privacy, particularly in Loop 1, which has a gravel driveway. Loop 2 has a paved drive.

126 George L. Smith State Park

Recreation: Hiking, fishing, boating, paddling, mountain biking, birding, playground
Location: 14 miles east of Swainsboro; 471 George L. Smith State Park Road, Twin City 30471
GPS: N32 55.86' / W82 11.94'

Facilities and amenities: Flush toilets, showers, laundry, dump station, grills, tables, picnic shelters, picnic areas, playgrounds, hiking and biking trails, geocaching, fishing pier, fish cleaning station, boat ramp, aquacycle, canoe/kayak/fishing boat rentals, canoe and kayak trails, historic site
Elevation: 220
Road conditions: Paved roads
Hookups: Water, electric
Sites: 5 premium pull-through RV-only sites with hookups, 19 standard RV/tent sites with hookups, 4 walk-in tent sites, 1 pioneer site, 6 cottages
Maximum RV length: 40
Season: Year-round, Apr–Oct peak season
Fees: Premium RV-only site $38, standard RV/tent site $35, walk-in tent site $10, pioneer site $50, 2-bedroom cottage $200, daily parking fee $5, annual pass $50
Maximum stay: 14 days
Management: Georgia State Parks and Historic Sites Division, 2610 Georgia Highway 155 SW, Stockbridge; (770) 389-7286; www.gastateparks.org
Reservations: (800) 864-7275; www.gastateparks.org/reservations
Pets: Dogs on 6-foot leashes allowed
Quiet hours: 10 p.m.–7 a.m.

A highlight of George L. Smith State Park is the old covered bridge/mill works of the Parrish Mill.

Alcohol restrictions: Unlawful in public areas

ADA compliant: Yes

Finding the campground: From US 80 in Twin City, go south on GA 23 (5th Avenue) for 3.5 miles. Turn left onto George L. Smith State Park Road. At 1.9 miles the road ends at the park office.

About the campground: The highlights of George L. Smith State Park are 412-acre Parrish Mill Pond and the combination covered bridge / mill works of the Parrish Mill that forms the dam creating the lake. The cypress tree–studded lake offers an array of water sports for visitors, while surrounding lands provide several hiking trails.

The campground is composed of a single loop on a point protruding into the lake. While most sites face the water, the thick stands of cypress trees prevent open lake views. The park's four walk-in sites are along the 2.7 Mile Trail on the west side of Bear Branch that runs into the mill pond from the west on the upper end of the impoundment.

This is another of Georgia's state parks where alligators are present.

127 Jack Hill State Park

Recreation: Hiking, fishing, boating, paddling, playground, golf

Location: In the town of Reidsville; 162 Park Lane, Reidsville 30453

GPS: N32 08.23' / W82 12.27'

Facilities and amenities: Flush toilets, showers, laundry, water, dump station, hiking trail, geocaching, playground, splash pad, picnic areas, footgolf, outdoor fitness equipment, fishing pier, boat ramp, aquacycle, pedal boat / paddle board / fishing boat rentals, golf course, gift/ souvenir shop

Elevation: 172

Road conditions: Paved roads

Hookups: Water, electric, sewer

Sites: 13 premium RV sites with full hookups, 12 RV/tent sites with electric and water hookups, 1 walk-in tent site, 10 cottages

Maximum RV length: 60

Season: Year-round, Apr–Oct peak season

Fees: Premium RV site with full hookups $40, standard RV/tent site with water and electric hook-ups $36, walk-in tent site $22, 2-bedroom cottage $200, 3-bedroom cottage $300, daily parking fee $5, annual pass $50

Maximum stay: 14 days

Management: Georgia State Parks and Historic Sites Division, 2610 Georgia Highway 155 SW, Stockbridge; (770) 389-7286; www.gastateparks.org

Reservations: (800) 864-7275; www.gastateparks.org/reservations

Pets: Dogs on 6-foot leashes allowed

Quiet hours: 10 p.m.–7 a.m.

Alcohol restrictions: Unlawful in public areas

ADA compliant: Yes

Finding the campground: From the junction of US 280 and GA 97 in downtown Reidsville, go 1.2 miles west on US 280. Turn right on Park Lane to enter the park.

About the campground: Renamed in 2020 in honor of State Senator Jack Hill, this park covers 662 acres, including a 12-acre lake and the Brazell's Creek Golf Course. The park is a favorite with golfers, as well as for family reunions and day-use picnicking. To fulfill those latter two roles, the park has a number of family-oriented amenities. One that is a bit unusual is a footgolf course, for a game that is a combination of soccer and golf!

The campground is located on the west side of the small lake, consisting of a single loop. Two premium sites are on the water. Private boats are allowed on the lake.

128 Little Ocmulgee State Park

Recreation: Hiking, fishing, boating, paddling, playground
Location: 3 miles north of McRae; 80 Live Oak Trail, Helena 31037
GPS: N32 09.29' / W82 89.59'
Facilities and amenities: Flush toilets, showers, laundry, water, dump station, hiking trails, fishing pier, boat ramp, playgrounds, splash pad, swimming beach, rental canoes, picnic areas and shelters, volleyball and tennis courts, miniature golf, golf course, observation deck, amphitheater, restaurant
Elevation: 168
Road conditions: Paved roads
Hookups: Water, electric
Sites: 13 premium RV sites with full hookups, 39 standard RV/tent sites with electric and water hookups, 60 lodge rooms, 10 cottages
Maximum RV length: 40
Season: Year-round, Apr–Oct peak season
Fees: Premium RV site $50, standard RV/tent site $45, lodge room $129, efficiency cottage $135, 1-bedroom cottage $135, 2-bedroom cottage $195, daily parking fee $5, annual pass $50
Maximum stay: 14 days
Management: Georgia State Parks and Historic Sites Division, 2610 Georgia Highway 155 SW, Stockbridge; (770) 389-7286; www.gastateparks.org
Reservations: (800) 864-7275; www.gastateparks.org/reservations
Pets: Dogs on 6-foot leashes allowed
Quiet hours: 10 p.m.–7 a.m.
Alcohol restrictions: Unlawful in public areas
ADA compliant: Yes
Finding the campground: From the junction of US 341 and US 280 in McRae, go east on US 280 for 1.7 miles. Turn left on US 441 and go 0.6 mile. Turn left on Spanish Moss Drive and follow the road to the visitor center.
About the campground: The park was established in 1940 through the efforts of the local citizenry and the Civilian Conservation Corps. Today the main attractions are 265-acre Little Ocmulgee Lake on the river from which it derives its name, the Wallace Adams Memorial Golf Course, and the Pete Phillips Lodge & Restaurant.

The campground is situated on two loops in the middle of the park and convenient to most of the amenities. The campsites are in close proximity to each other, but all are shaded. A dozen of the sites are pull-throughs.

129 Evans County Public Fishing Area

Recreation: Hiking, fishing, boating, paddling
Location: 8 miles southeast of Claxton; 4757 Area Line Road, Claxton 30417
GPS: N32 12.71' / W81 80.01'
Facilities and amenities: Flush toilets, showers, water, dump station, picnic area, hiking trails, archery range, event center, three lakes, fishing docks, boat ramps, canoe and kayak launches
Elevation: 92
Road conditions: Gravel drive through the camping area
Hookups: Water, electric, sewer
Sites: 5 premium RV sites with full hookups, 9 standard RV/tent sites with water and electric hookups, 8 tent-only sites with water and electric hookups
Maximum RV length: 60
Season: Year-round, Apr–Oct peak season
Fees: Premium RV site $40, standard RV/tent site $35, tent-only site $20
Maximum stay: 14 days
Management: Georgia Wildlife Resources Division, 2067 US Highway 278 SE, Social Circle; (706) 557-3333; www.georgiawildlife.com
Reservations: (800) 336-2661; www.gooutdoorsgeorgia.com
Pets: Dogs allowed on leashes
Quiet hours: 10 p.m.–7 a.m.
Alcohol restrictions: Alcohol allowed only in campsites
ADA compliant: Yes
Finding the campground: From the junction of US 301 and US 280 in Claxton, go east for 6.7 miles on US 280. Turn right on Sunbury Road (County Road 204). At 1.7 miles the public fishing area entrance is on the left.
About the campground: This campground is used exclusively by anglers fishing in lakes Longleaf, Bidd Sand, and Wood on the 372-acre tract. The campground overlooks the largest of those bodies of water, and some of the sites are right on the shore.

The campsites are located in a stand of mixed pine and hardwoods. All sites have at least partial shade.

Be aware that special quota and youth waterfowl hunts are held in the area during the fall and winter months.

130 Paradise Public Fishing Area

Recreation: Hiking, fishing, boating, paddling
Location: 9 miles southeast of Tifton; 536 Paradise Drive, Enigma 31749
GPS: N31 40.03' / W83 35.99'
Facilities and amenities: Flush toilets, water, picnic table, fire ring, lantern post, picnic area and shelter, nature trails, archery range, geocaching, hunting, fishing lakes, fishing docks, boat ramps, canoe and kayak launches
Elevation: 289

Road conditions: Gravel drive through the camping area
Hookups: None
Sites: 7 tent sites, 1 group site
Maximum RV length: NA
Season: Year-round, Apr–Oct peak season
Fees: $10
Maximum stay: 14 days
Management: Georgia Wildlife Resources Division, 2067 US Highway 278 SE, Social Circle; (706) 557-3333; www.georgiawildlife.com
Reservations: (800) 336-2661; www.gooutdoorsgeorgia.com
Pets: Dogs allowed on leashes
Quiet hours: 10 p.m.–7 a.m.
Alcohol restrictions: Alcohol allowed only in campsites
ADA compliant: Yes
Finding the campground: From exit 62 on I-75 in Tifton, travel east on US 82 / GA 520 for 9.1 miles. Turn right onto Hall Whitley Road. At 0.1 mile, go left on Brookfield Nashville Road. Paradise Drive and the entrance to the public fishing area are on the left at 1.5 miles.
About the campground: Paradise Public Fishing Area consists of a 1,351-acre tract with 68 lakes and ponds totaling 525 acres of water. The obvious attraction of this area is angling, though it does host some other activities.

The campground is primitive, offering minimal amenities, including a non-flush toilet. Restrooms near the area entrance do have flush facilities. The campsites are level, offering partial shade on some. This is a site used exclusively by anglers or by hunters during managed hunt dates in the fall and winter.

131 Falling Rocks Campground and RV Park

Recreation: Hiking, fishing, boating, paddling
Location: 12 miles north of Baxley; 483 Deen's Landing Road, Baxley 31513
GPS: N31 94.30' / W82 37.17'
Facilities and amenities: Flush toilets, showers, water, laundry, dump station, fire rings, picnic tables, lantern posts, picnic shelters, nature trail
Elevation: 83
Road conditions: Paved roads
Hookups: Water, electric
Sites: 14 RV/tent site with hookups, 8 tent-only sites with no hookups
Maximum RV length: 50
Season: Year-round, Apr–Oct peak season
Fees: RV/tent sites $21, tent-only site $10.50
Maximum stay: 14 days
Management: Appling County, 69 Tippens Street, Baxley; (912) 367-8300; www.baxley.org/appling-county/
Reservations: (912) 367-8100; www.baxley.org/falling-rocks-campground/
Pets: Dogs on leashes allowed

Quiet hours: 10 p.m.–7 a.m.

Alcohol restrictions: No alcohol allowed

ADA compliant: Yes

Finding the campground: From the junction of US 1 and US 341 in Baxley, go north on US 1 for 10.7 miles. Turn left on West River Road. At 0.9 mile turn right on Deen's Landing Road. At 0.5 mile the campground entrance is on the left.

About the campground: The main attraction of this 20-acre facility is its close proximity to Deen's Landing on the Altamaha River. That location offers a boat launch and parking area on Georgia's largest river and is a popular spot with boaters and paddlers.

The Falling Rocks Campground (identified on some maps as Deen's RV Park and close to a privately operated facility named Deen's Campground) is positioned on a wooded hillside in a single loop. Sites 1 and 14 are in the open, with the remaining sites having full shade.

There are three picnic shelters in the campground, but only one of those has a single table in it. Overall, the grounds are in poor shape and in need of repairs and updating.

132 Towns Bluff Park and Heritage Center

Recreation: Hiking, fishing, boating, paddling, biking, playground, horseback riding

Location: 8 miles northeast of Hazlehurst; 45 Riverwood Trail, Hazlehurst 31539

GPS: N31 94.87' / W82 50.87'

Facilities and amenities: Flush toilets, shower, laundry, dump station, picnic area, playground, fire pits, hiking, fitness and equestrian trails, archery range, boat ramps, hunting, geocaching, heritage center, museum, gift shop

Elevation: 85

Road conditions: Gravel drive through the campground

Hookups: Water, electric

Sites: 24 RV/tent sites with hookups, 2 yurts

Maximum RV length: 60

Season: Year-round, Apr–Oct peak season

Fees: RV/tent site $32, yurt $65

Maximum stay: 14 days

Management: Georgia Wildlife Resources Division, 2067 US Highway 278 SE, Social Circle; (706) 557-3333; www.georgiawildlife.com; www.facebook.com/townsbluffpark

Reservations: (912) 379-9303

Pets: Dogs allowed on leashes

Quiet hours: 10 p.m.–7 a.m.

Alcohol restrictions: Allowed only in designated campsites

ADA compliant: Yes

Finding the campground: From the junction of US 341 and US 221 in Hazlehurst, go 7.3 miles north on US 221 (North Tallahassee Street). Turn right on Uvalda Landing Road and follow it around to the left for 0.1 mile. Turn right on Riverwood Trail. At 0.5 mile the campground is on the right.

About the campground: Towns Bluff Campground is located on the shore of the Altamaha, Georgia's largest river. It also is positioned in the midst of the state's Bullard Creek Wildlife

Management Area. The Georgia Wildlife Resources Division manages the land and most of the activities. The campground and its amenities are operated as a separate entity.

The campground offers access to a wide range of family activities, including the river fishing and boating, along with hunting on the WMA and an archery range for sportsmen.

The campsites are on a single loop on level ground offering partial shade. Half of the sites are pull-throughs.

133 Paulk Park RV and Tent Campground

Recreation: Hiking, fishing, boating, paddling
Location: In the city of Fitzgerald; 146 Paulk Park Lane, Fitzgerald 31750
GPS: N31 68.55' / W83 26.57'
Facilities and amenities: Flush toilets, showers, laundry, water, dump station, picnic shelters, nature trail, fishing lake, boat ramp
Elevation: 335
Road conditions: Gravel drive in the park and the camping area
Hookups: Water, electric, sewer
Sites: 24 RV sites with full hookups, 35 tent-only sites with no hookups
Maximum RV length: 50
Season: Year-round, Apr–Oct peak season
Fees: RV sites $30, tent sites $10
Maximum stay: 14 days
Management: Fitzgerald-Ben Hill Department of Leisure Services, 816 North Main Street, Fitzgerald; (229) 426-5050; www.fitzgeraldga.org/parks.htm
Reservations: www.hipcamp.com/en-US/discover/georgia/paulk-park-s-peaceful-pond?pic=%7B%3Alocale%3D>%3A"en-US"%7D
Pets: Dogs allowed on leashes
Quiet hours: 10 p.m.–7 a.m.
Alcohol restrictions: No alcohol allowed
ADA compliant: Yes
Finding the campground: From the junction of US 319 and GA 107 (Benjamin H. Hill Drive), go west on GA 107 for 1.4 miles. Turn left onto Paulk Park Lane (shown on some maps as Paulk Park Road), which runs into the campground.
About the campground: This campground is an open field with some trees in the RV section, but tent camping offers no shade. It sits on the shore of a 5-acre lake that provides fishing and boating access.

The campground is mostly used in connection with events at the nearby Agricultural Center and event fields.

134 Sweet Onion RV Park

Recreation: Hiking
Location: 3 miles east of Vidalia; 514 Pete Phillips Drive, Vidalia 30474
GPS: N32 20.04' / W82 37.17'
Facilities and amenities: Picnic tables, fire rings, lighted walking trail, dump station
Elevation: 268
Road conditions: Paved roads
Hookups: Water, electric, sewer
Sites: 12 RV sites with full hookups
Maximum RV length: 80
Season: Year-round, Mar–Dec peak season
Fees: $20, $350 monthly
Maximum stay: No limit but intended for temporary stays only
Management: Vidalia City Marshal Office; (912) 537-7661; www.vidaliaga.gov/cm/page/sweet-onion-rv-park
Reservations: No
Pets: Dogs on leashes allowed
Quiet hours: 10 p.m.–8 a.m.
Alcohol restrictions: No alcohol allowed
ADA compliant: Yes
Finding the campground: From US 280 in Vidalia, go south on Pete Phillips Drive for 0.7 mile. The campground entrance is on the right.
About the campground: The campground takes its name from the famed Vidalia sweet onions that are farmed in the area. It is situated within walking distance of the downtown, the Vidalia Onion Museum, and the Vidalia Onion Festival Arts and Crafts grounds. The facility is most often used during festivals or for visiting the downtown attractions.

The campground is first-come, first served on a self-check-in system. There are no restrooms in the campground.

The sites are positioned on a single loop with all of them pull-throughs. The area is wooded, with full shade on the sites.

Lower Coastal Plain

The Lower Coastal Plain is often referred to as Georgia's Colonial Coast. Georgians have been drawn to this strip of land that meets the Atlantic Ocean ever since Gen. James Oglethorpe came ashore in 1733 to found Savannah. Eventually the new colony stretched southward, down to the quaint 19th-century seaport of Saint Marys at the Florida border.

A string of 14 major barrier islands separates the mainland from the ocean along this coast. Tybee Island fronts Savannah, anchoring the northern tip of the chain of isles. Cumberland Island and its fabulous national seashore are at the other end. A mixture of historic settlements and wilderness areas line the coast in between.

Miles of sand beaches harboring myriad numbers of seabirds and providing nesting areas for endangered sea turtles are on the ocean side of the barrier isles. Stately live oaks, festooned with Spanish moss and limbs drooping to the ground, offer a subtropical tableau of beauty in the interior of these islands.

Thousands of acres of spartina grass fringe tidal creeks and sounds on the shoreward side of the islands. These "prairies" of grass offer ever-changing vistas of varied colors, as the sea breezes sweep across them. Just such panoramas inspired the verses of Sidney Lanier's epic poem *The Marshes of Glynn*.

The mysterious landscape of the Okefenokee Swamp lies just inland as you move up the Saint Marys River in the south. This "Land of the Trembling Earth" covers almost half a million acres of wilderness, filled with exotic vistas and abundant wildlife.

Plenty of human history also spans this region. Savannah is filled with picturesque squares surrounded by mansions, some of which predate the Revolutionary War. The waterfront on the Savannah River is now a thriving entertainment district.

Guarding the seaward river entrances to the city are Fort Jackson that dates from the War of 1812, along with Forts Pulaski and McAllister from Civil War times. You can spend a day touring each of these landmarks.

The ruins of the Carnegie family mansion Dungeness are a popular site on Cumberland Island.

Fort Frederica is located farther south on Saint Simons Island. This colonial-era, fortified town—another of General Oglethorpe's legacies—was established in the 1740s to protect against Spanish invasions from Florida. The site now is open to the public as a National Monument.

The island also is home to one of the region's most historic churches. Here you can walk the cemetery grounds of Christ Church that has been continuously active since 1808, as well as visiting the associated garden dedicated to John and Charles Wesley. Those brothers both ministered on the island in colonial times and are considered mainstays of the founding of Methodism.

The other historic structure mentioned is Midway Church in Liberty County. This structure dates from 1792. The Midway Society now maintains the building, its cemetery, and an associated museum, all of which are open to the public.

The Jekyll Island Club was a private retreat founded in 1886 by a group of northern businessmen that continued in existence until 1942. Club members through the years bore names like Rockefeller, Vanderbilt, Pulitzer, and Morgan, the titans of the Robber Baron period of American finance. A state authority now manages this Historic District as the Millionaires Village. The restored "cottages," which to most of us would be mansions, now are open to the public, along with the clubhouse that operates as a resort hotel.

It is a short hop by ferry from Saint Marys to the Cumberland Island National Seashore at the southern end of the Georgia coast. Here you find the ruins of the Carnegie family mansion Dungeness, along with the still standing Plum Orchard mansion. You can also expect to see some of the island's herd of wild horses while walking to reach the 17.5 miles of unspoiled beaches.

Best of all, the Lower Coastal Plain Region features a number of camping opportunities to provide access to all these features.

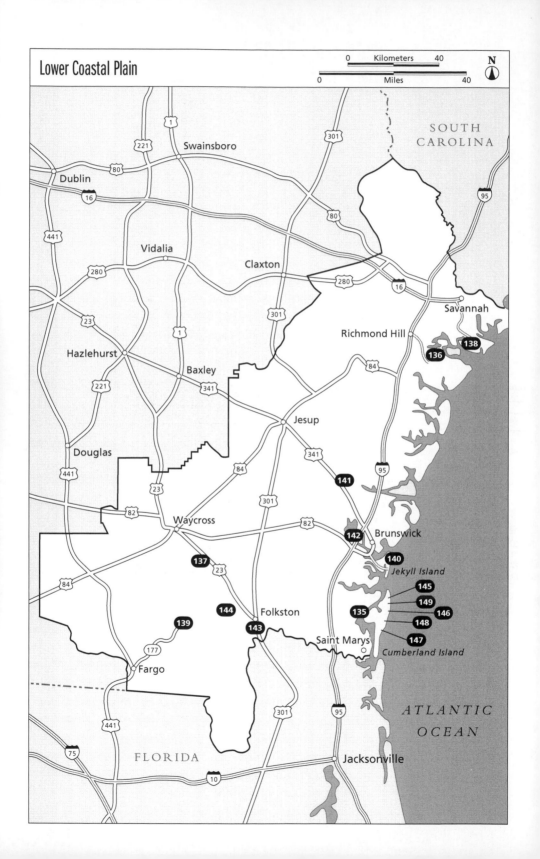

Lower Coastal Plain

Campgrounds At-A-Glance

#	Name	Total Sites	Group Sites	Hookup Sites	Hookups	Maximum RV Length	Dump Station	Toilets	Showers	Drinking Water	ADA	Fees	Reservations
Georgia State Parks and Historic Sites Division													
135	Crooked River State Park	53	1	52	WES	130	Y	F	Y	Y	Y	$$$$-$$$$$	Y
136	Fort McAllister State Park	69	2	65	WES	50	Y	F	Y	Y	Y	$$-$$$$$	Y
137	Laura S. Walker State Park	44	1	43	WES	40	Y	F	Y	Y	Y	$$$$-$$$$$	Y
138	Skidaway Island State Park	92	0	92	WES	70	Y	F	Y	Y	Y	$$$$$	Y
139	Stephen C. Foster State Park	63	1	62	WE	50	Y	F	Y	Y	Y	$$$$-$$$$$	Y
Georgia State Authority													
140	Jekyll Island Campground	179	0	167	WES	60	N	F	Y	Y	Y	$$$$-$$$$$	Y
County Parks													
141	Altamaha Regional Park	56	0	56	WES	50	Y	F	Y	Y	Y	$$-$$$$$	Y
142	Blythe Island Regional Park	121	0	97	WES	50	Y	F	Y	Y	Y	$$-$$$$$	Y
143	Traders Hill Recreation Area and Campground	47	1	46	WES	60	Y	F	Y	Y	Y	$-$$	Y
US Fish and Wildlife Service													
144	Okefenokee National Wildlife Refuge	9	9	0	N	NA	N	V	N	N	N	$$	Y
National Park Service													
145	Brickhill Bluff Wilderness Campsite	4	0	0	N	NA	N	N	N	Y	N	$	Y
146	Hickory Hill Wilderness Campsite	4	0	0	N	NA	N	N	N	Y	N	$	Y
147	Sea Camp Campground	20	2	0	N	NA	N	F	Y	Y	N	$$$-$$$$	Y
148	Stafford Beach Campground	10	0	0	N	NA	N	F	Y	Y	N	$$	Y
149	Yankee Paradise Wilderness Campsite	4	0	0	N	NA	N	N	N	Y	N	$	Y

See Amenities Chart key on page xxi.

135 Crooked River State Park

Recreation: Hiking, fishing, boating, paddling, biking, birding, playground
Location: 8 miles north of Saint Marys; 6222 Charlie Smith Sr. Highway, Saint Marys 31558
GPS: N30 84.22' / W81 55.25'
Facilities and amenities: Flush toilets, showers, laundry, water, dump station, grills, tables, picnic shelters, picnic areas, playgrounds, hiking trails, boat ramp, fishing pier, bait shop, bike rentals, miniature golf, geocaching, bird watching, nature center
Elevation: 20
Road conditions: Paved roads
Hookups: Water, electric, sewer
Sites: 20 premium RV sites with full hookups, 7 premium RV/tent sites with water and electric hookups, 25 standard RV/tent sites with water and electric hookups, 1 pioneer site, 11 cottages
Maximum RV length: 130
Season: Year-round, Apr–Dec peak season
Fees: Premium RV site $44, premium RV/tent site $44, standard RV/tent site $38, pioneer site $75, premium 2-bedroom cottage $225, standard 2-bedroom cottage $175, premium 3-bedroom cottage $250, daily parking fee $5, annual pass $50
Maximum stay: 14 days
Management: Georgia State Parks and Historic Sites Division, 2610 Georgia Highway 155 SW, Stockbridge; (770) 389-7286; www.gastateparks.org
Reservations: (800) 864-7275; www.gastateparks.org/reservations
Pets: Dogs on 6-foot leashes allowed
Quiet hours: 10 p.m.–7 a.m.
Alcohol restrictions: Unlawful in public areas
ADA compliant: Yes
Finding the campground: From exit 2 on I-95, turn east on GA 40 (East King Avenue). Drive 2.5 miles and turn left onto Kings Bay Road. At 3.1 miles turn left on GA 40 (Charlie Smith Sr. Highway). Continue for 3.5 miles; the park entrance is on the right.
About the campground: Crooked River is the southernmost state park on the Georgia Coast. It covers 500 acres on a bluff overlooking its namesake river, just north of the town of Saint Marys. The park provides a wide range of activities and amenities for entire families, as well as being a popular jumping-off point for boating anglers and kayakers.

The campground is on very flat terrain amid a pine forest. The well-spaced sites mostly have partial shade. The lack of understory vegetation makes the camping area rather open, not affording much privacy.

136 Fort McAllister State Park

Recreation: Hiking, fishing, boating, paddling, birding, playground
Location: 8 miles southeast of Richmond Hill; 3894 Fort McAllister Road, Richmond Hill 31324
GPS: N31 88.86' / W81 20.09'

Facilities and amenities: Flush toilets, showers, laundry, water, dump station, picnic tables, fire rings, playground, picnic area and pavilion, geocaching, hiking and biking trails, canoe, kayak and paddleboard rentals, fishing pier, boating, boat ramp, bike rentals, museum, historic site
Elevation: 9
Road conditions: Paved roads
Hookups: Water, electric, sewer
Sites: 16 premium RV sites with full hookups, 37 standard RV/tent sites with water and electric hookups, 12 tent-only sites with water and electric hookups, 2 backcountry tent sites, 2 pioneer sites, 4 premium 2-bedroom cottages, 3 standard 2-bedroom cottages
Maximum RV length: 50
Season: Year-round, Apr–Oct peak season
Fees: Premium RV site with full hookups $42, standard RV/tent site with water and electric hookups $36, tent-only site with water and electric hookups $36, backcountry tent site $12, pioneer site $55, premium 2-bedroom cottage $230, standard 2-bedroom cottage $210, daily parking fee $5, annual pass $50
Maximum stay: 14 days
Management: Georgia State Parks and Historic Sites Division, 2610 Georgia Highway 155 SW, Stockbridge; (770) 389-7286; www.gastateparks.org
Reservations: (800) 864-7275; www.gastateparks.org/reservations
Pets: Dogs on 6-foot leashes allowed
Quiet hours: 10 p.m.–7 a.m.
Alcohol restrictions: Unlawful in public areas
ADA compliant: Yes
Finding the campground: From exit 90 on I-95, go east on GA 144 for 6.7 miles. Turn left on GA 144 Spur and continue 3.7 miles to where the road enters the park.
About the campground: Situated on the banks of the Ogeechee River, the centerpiece of the park is the historic fortifications of Fort McAllister that guarded the southern approach to Savannah during the Civil War, along with a museum explaining that period.

The campground is located on Savage Island in the western area of the park, with frontage on Redbird Creek. The sites are arranged in four sections: Savage Loop, Raccoon Way, Possum Trot, and Deer Run. The latter of these has the 12 tent-only sites.

The sites are somewhat spaced, with Spanish moss-draped trees providing partial to full shade.

137 Laura S. Walker State Park

Recreation: Hiking, fishing, boating, paddling, biking, birding, swimming, playground, golf
Location: 10 miles southeast of Waycross; 5653 Laura Walker Road, Waycross 31503
GPS: N31 14.35' / W82 21.45'
Facilities and amenities: Flush toilets, showers, laundry, water, dump station, picnic tables, fire rings, playground, picnic area and pavilion, amphitheater, dog park, volleyball court, horseshoe pits, hiking trails, swimming beach, kayak rentals, boat ramp, golf course and pro shop, bike rentals
Elevation: 123

Road conditions: Paved roads

Hookups: Water, electric, sewer

Sites: 2 premium RV sites with full hookups, 8 premium RV/tent sites with water and electric hookups, 33 standard RV/tent sites with water and electric hookups, 1 pioneer site, 6 cottages

Maximum RV length: 40

Season: Year-round, Apr–Oct peak season

Fees: Premium RV site with full hookups $38, premium RV/tent site with water and electric hookups $38, standard RV/tent with water and electric hookups $34, pioneer site $40, 2-bedroom cottage $155, daily parking fee $5, annual pass $50

Maximum stay: 14 days

Management: Georgia State Parks and Historic Sites Division, 2610 Georgia Highway 155 SW, Stockbridge; (770) 389-7286; www.gastateparks.org

Reservations: (800) 864-7275; www.gastateparks.org/reservations

Pets: Dogs on 6-foot leashes allowed

Quiet hours: 10 p.m.–7 a.m.

Alcohol restrictions: Unlawful in public areas

ADA compliant: Yes

Finding the campground: From the junction of US 23 and US 82 in Waycross, go east on US 82 for 7.3 miles. Turn right on GA 177. At 2 miles the park entrance is on the right.

Located near the northern edge of the Okefenokee Swamp, Laura Walker State Park is home to fascinating plants and animals.

About the campground: This 626-acre park and its 120-acre lake are both named for Laura S. Walker, a local writer, teacher, civic leader, and naturalist. The park offers a full range of activities for the entire family for day use or vacation getaways and is a short drive from the Okefenokee Swamp.

The park's championship 18-hole golf course is a favorite of local golfers and visitors alike.

The campground is composed of two loops, with the outer loop offering four sites on the lakefront. Most sites are closely spaced and offer at least partial shade beneath an overstory of pine trees.

Be aware that alligators are present in the park waters.

138 Skidaway Island State Park

Recreation: Hiking, fishing, birding, mountain biking, playground
Location: 15 miles southeast of Savannah; 52 Diamond Causeway, Savannah 31411
GPS: N31 94.93' / W81 05.37'
Facilities and amenities: Flush toilet, showers, laundry, water, dump station, hiking trails, playgrounds, picnic area, volleyball court, outdoor fitness equipment, geocaching, bike rentals, amphitheater, interpretive center
Elevation: 9
Road conditions: Paved roads
Hookups: Water, electric, sewers
Sites: 33 premium RV sites with full hookups, 59 standard RV/tent sites with water and electric hookups, 3 camper cabins
Maximum RV length: 70
Season: Year-round, Apr–Oct peak season
Fees: Premium RV site $54, standard RV/tent site $46, camper cabin $160, daily parking fee $5, annual pass $50
Maximum stay: 14 days
Management: Georgia State Parks and Historic Sites Division, 2610 Georgia Highway 155 SW, Stockbridge; (770) 389-7286; www.gastateparks.org
Reservations: (800) 864-7275; www.gastateparks.org/reservations
Pets: Dogs on 6-foot leashes allowed
Quiet hours: 10 p.m.–7 a.m.
Alcohol restrictions: Unlawful in public areas
ADA compliant: Yes
Finding the campground: From exit 94 on I-95, go east on GA 204 (Abercorn Street) for 6.6 miles. Bear right to stay on GA 204, which becomes Truman Parkway, and continue for 1.9 miles. Turn right on GA 204, which now is Whitefield Avenue but soon changes to Diamond Causeway. At 4 miles, turn left into the park on Skidaway Island Park Road.
About the campground: The park is positioned on the Skidaway Narrows, a section of the Skidaway River that separates its namesake island from the mainland. This is a very popular camping destination, due to its close proximity to historic Savannah.

The park hiking trails feature subtropical flora composed of marsh grass, cabbage-palmetto, live oaks draped in Spanish moss, and pines, as well as shell middens, destroyed liquor stills, and Civil War earthworks.

The campsites in the campground are closely spaced but often separated by the understory of palmettos. Most are shaded by the live oaks and pines.

Be aware that this is a location where bug repellant is a necessity in warmer months.

139 Stephen C. Foster State Park

Recreation: Hiking, fishing, boating, paddling, birding, playground
Location: 18 miles northeast of Fargo; 17155 Georgia Highway 177, Fargo 31631
GPS: N30 82.70' / W82 36.21'
Facilities and amenities: Flush toilets, showers, laundry, water, dump station, fire rings, picnic tables, picnic shelters, playground, hiking and fitness trails, photography, star gazing, swamp boardwalk, geocaching, boat tours, boat ramp, canoe/kayak/fishing boat rentals, fish cleaning station
Elevation: 115
Road conditions: Paved roads
Hookups: Water, electric
Sites: 6 premium RV/tent sites with hookups, 56 standard RV/tent sites with hookups, 1 pioneer site, 9 cottages
Maximum RV length: 50
Season: Year-round, Apr–Oct peak season
Fees: Premium RV/tent site with hookups $40, standard RV/tent sites with hookups $36, pioneer site $55, 2-bedroom cottage $175, daily parking fee $5, annual pass $50
Maximum stay: 14 days
Management: Georgia State Parks and Historic Sites Division, 2610 Georgia Highway 155 SW, Stockbridge; (770) 389-7286; www.gastateparks.org
Reservations: (800) 864-7275; www.gastateparks.org/reservations
Pets: Dogs on 6-foot leashes allowed
Quiet hours: 10 p.m.–7 a.m.
Alcohol restrictions: Unlawful in public areas
ADA compliant: Yes
Finding the campground: From the junction of US 441 and GA 177 just south of Fargo, go northeast on GA 177 for 19.2 miles. The road ends at the park entrance.
About the campground: Stephen C. Foster Park is located on an island near the center of the fabled Okefenokee Swamp's 438,000 acres of black water and cypress wilderness. It is the jumping-off point for visiting the "Land of the Trembling Earth" from the west. This park is a wonderland for photographers, birders, and anglers. It also is recognized by the International Dark-Sky Association as a Dark Sky Park, making it ideal for stargazing.

The campsites here are situated in two loops, with Loop 2 composed of pull-through sites. All the sites are shaded, and most are surrounded with vegetation, giving them a feel of privacy.

Be aware that you will see alligators in the park. Avoid feeding or throwing objects at them. Also, keep your pets leashed and away from the water's edge. The gators have been known to attack dogs.

140 Jekyll Island Campground

Recreation: Fishing, boating, paddling, biking, birding, playground, swimming, horseback riding, golf
Location: 15 miles southeast of Brunswick; 1197 Riverview Drive, Jekyll Island 31527
GPS: N31 06.39' / W81 24.73'
Facilities and amenities: Flush toilets, showers, laundry, water, picnic tables, fire rings, playground, bike rentals and trails, Wi-Fi in campground, camp store with propane pump, storage area
Elevation: 16
Road conditions: Paved roads
Hookups: Water, electric, sewer
Sites: 167 RV sites with full hookups, 12 tent sites with water
Maximum RV length: 60
Season: Year-round
Fees: RV site $51, tent site $36, island entry fee $8, annual pass $75
Maximum stay: 14 days
Management: Jekyll Island Authority, 100 James Road, Jekyll Island; (912) 635-4000; www.jekyllisland.com/authority/
Reservations: (912) 635-3021; www.jekyllisland.com/lodging/campground/
Pets: Dogs on leashes allowed; $4 per day pet fee
Quiet hours: 10 p.m.–8 a.m.
Alcohol restrictions: Unlawful in public areas
ADA compliant: Yes
Finding the campground: From exit 29 on I-95, go east on US 17 / GA 520 for 6.2 miles. Turn right onto the Jekyll Island Causeway (GA 520). At 15.6 miles and after crossing the bridge onto the island, turn left (north) in the roundabout onto Beachview Drive. At 4.6 miles the campground entrance is on the left, where the road changes names to Riverview Drive.
About the campground: The 18 acres of the Jekyll Island Campground are the gateway to Georgia's most popular family vacation spot on the Atlantic Coast. Just minutes from the miles of public ocean beach, fine golf courses, and the historic Millionaires Village, the campground also is within walking distance of the island fishing pier at Clam Creek and scenic Driftwood Beach. The island's paved bike trail runs past the entrance to the campground as well.

The full-service campground offers sites shaded by a mixture of pines and live oaks draped in Spanish moss. The RV sites are broken down into eight sections, with two more for the primitive tent sites. All the RV sites are closely spaced. Fifteen storage spaces for boat trailers or other gear are also offered.

141 Altamaha Regional Park

Recreation: Hiking, fishing, boating, paddling, swimming
Location: 23 miles northwest of Brunswick; 1605 Altamaha Park Road, Brunswick 31525
GPS: N31 42.86' / W81 60.74'

Facilities and amenities: Flush toilets, showers, dump station, laundry, picnic tables and shelters, boat ramp, boat docks, lighted fishing pier, lighted fish cleaning station, hunting, nature trail, horseshoe pits, camp store, bait shop

Elevation: 12

Road conditions: Gravel roads in campground

Hookups: Water, electric, sewer

Sites: 46 RV sites with full hookups, 10 tent sites with water and electric hookups, 2 cabins

Maximum RV length: 50

Season: Year-round, May–Aug peak time

Fees: Waterfront RV site with full hookups $34, RV site with full hookups $30, tent site with water and electric hookups $20, 2-bedroom cabin summer $85, winter $75

Maximum stay: 14 days

Management: Glynn County Parks and Recreation Department, 1725 Reynolds Street, Brunswick; (912) 554-7111; www.glynncounty.org

Reservations: (912) 289-9068

Pets: Dogs allowed on leashes

Quiet hours: 10 p.m.–7 a.m.

Alcohol restrictions: Not allowed in public areas

ADA compliant: Yes

Finding the campground: From exit 36 on I-95 in Brunswick, go northwest on US 341 for 14.1 miles. Turn right onto Altamaha Park Road and continue 4.4 miles to the park.

About the campground: Altamaha Regional Park is situated on the shore of its namesake river, with a historic, abandoned turnstile railroad bridge crossing the flow at the site. The campground has the feel of a classic fish camp, popular with anglers and hunters, who utilize surrounding wildlife management areas in the fall and winter.

The campground is rather open, with sites ranging from no shade to partial or full shade. The restroom/shower facilities have coded entry for privacy and safety, but no ground fires are allowed.

142 Blythe Island Regional Park

Recreation: Hiking, fishing, boating, paddling, biking, swimming, playground, horseback riding

Location: 3 miles west of Brunswick; 6616 Blythe Island Highway, Brunswick 31523

GPS: N31 15.44' / W81 54.57'

Facilities and amenities: Flush toilets, showers, laundry, water, dump station, picnic tables, fire rings, picnic areas and shelters, lake, swimming beach, hiking and biking trails, fishing pier, bait shop, boat ramps and hoist, canoe and kayak rentals, horseshoes, horseback riding, archery range, cable TV, Wi-Fi in campground

Elevation: 10

Road conditions: Gravel and sand in the campground

Hookups: Water, electric, sewer

Sites: 13 premium lakeview RV sites with full hookups, 84 standard RV sites with full hookups, 24 tent sites with no hookups

Maximum RV length: 50

Season: Year-round, May–Sep peak season

Fees: Premium lakeview RV site $45, standard RV site $42, tent site $19
Maximum stay: 14 days
Management: Glynn County Parks and Recreation Department, 1725 Reynolds Street, Brunswick; (912) 554-7111; www.glynncounty.org
Reservations: www.glynncounty.org/178/Camping
Pets: Dogs allowed on leashes
Quiet hours: 10 p.m.–7 a.m.
Alcohol restrictions: Not allowed in public areas
ADA compliant: Yes
Finding the campground: From exit 29 on I-95, go west for 0.7 mile on US 17 / GA 520. Turn right on Blythe Island Highway / Old Jacksonville Highway (GA 303) and drive 2.8 miles. Turn right on Sam Coffer Road. At the end of the road, turn right on Blythe Island Park Road and proceed 0.8 mile to the park entrance.
About the campground: Blythe Island Regional Park is an 1,100-acre facility sandwiched between freshwater Lake Cindee on the north and the saltwater of the South Brunswick River to the south, with access to both bodies of water. The park is truly a destination offering amenities and activities to meet the entire family's needs.

The campground is composed of a large one-way loop, with four smaller interconnected loops within it. Thirteen of the sites have views of Lake Cindee, with most all sites shaded. Though the sites tend to be close together, vegetation provides some measure of privacy between them. The primitive camping area is in a separate portion of the park.

143 Traders Hill Recreation Area and Campground

Recreation: Hiking, fishing, boating, paddling, swimming
Location: 4 miles south of Folkston; 1388 Tracys Ferry Road, Folkston 31537
GPS: N30 78.07' / W82 02.67'
Facilities and amenities: Flush toilets, showers, laundry, water, dump station, picnic tables, fire rings, hiking trails, fishing pier, fish bait, boat ramp, swimming area, canoe and kayak shuttles
Elevation: 40
Road conditions: Dirt road within the campground
Hookups: Water, electric, sewer
Sites: 46 RV sites with full hookups, 1 large primitive tent area
Maximum RV length: 60
Season: Year-round, Apr–Oct peak season
Fees: RV sites $20, tent sites $10
Maximum stay: 14 days
Management: Charlton County, 68 Kingsland Drive, Suite B, Folkston; (912) 496-2536; www.charltoncountyga.us
Reservations: (912) 390-9288
Pets: Dogs on leashes allowed
Quiet hours: 10 p.m.–7 a.m.
Alcohol restrictions: No alcohol allowed
ADA compliant: Yes

This scenic campground is situated on the shore of the St. Marys River, which forms the border between Georgia and Florida.

Finding the campground: From the junction of US 301 and US 23 in Folkston, go southwest on US 23 for 3.6 miles and turn left on Traders Hill Road. After 1.3 miles, turn left on Tracys Ferry Road and proceed 0.2 mile to the campground entrance on the right.

About the campground: The campground at Traders Hill is in a level area with dirt drives. It is situated on the shore of the St. Marys River, which forms the border between Georgia and Florida. The site is quite scenic and peaceful, resting beneath a canopy of pines and Spanish moss-draped live oaks, some of which are 350 years old.

The campsites are rather rustic but do have full hookups. The tent area is spacious, with no marked sites.

Kayak or canoe shuttles can be arranged at the office, where fish bait also is offered.

144 Okefenokee National Wildlife Refuge

Recreation: Fishing, paddling
Location: 7 miles southwest of Folkston; 2700 Suwannee Canal Road, Folkston 31537
GPS: N30 44.18' / W82 07.33' (Suwannee Canal Recreation Area entrance)
Facilities and amenities: Vault toilets, camping platform, picnic table, fire ring
Elevation: 154
Road conditions: NA
Hookups: None
Sites: 9 primitive paddle-in group camping platforms
Maximum RV length: NA
Season: Year-round, Dec–Mar peak season
Fees: $15 per person
Maximum stay: 1 night on each platform
Management: US Fish and Wildlife Service, Okefenokee National Wildlife Refuge, 2700 Suwannee Canal Road, Folkston; (912) 496-7836; www.fws.gov/sites/default/files/documents/Okefenokee WildernessCanoeGuide22-508.pdf

Alligators are quite plentiful, and camping is permitted only on the platforms along the paddling trails.

Reservations: To plan your itinerary, www.recreation.gov/camping/campgrounds/250860/ itinerary; Wilderness Camping Permit Reservation Line, (912) 496-3331

Pets: No

Quiet hours: NA

Alcohol restrictions: All federal, state, and local laws enforced

ADA compliant: No

Finding the campground: To reach Suwannee Canal Recreation Area, starting from the junction of US 301 and US 23 / 121 (Okefenokee Parkway), go southwest on US 23/121 for 9 miles. Turn right on Suwannee Canal Road and drive 4.1 miles to the visitor center.

About the campground: The Okefenokee Wildlife Refuge holds 438,000 acres of wilderness, composed of flooded prairies, lakes, and occasional hammocks of dry land. The only camping provided in this exotic landscape are nine platforms along the paddling trails that run through the swamp. From north to south the platforms are Maul Hammock, Big Water, Bluff Lake, Floyds Island, Canal Run, Round Top, Mixons Hammock, Cedar Hammock, and Monkey Lake. These campsites are limited to use by paddlers only. No motorized vessels allowed at them.

These are limited to just one group per platform and are made available for just one night. You can, however, book consecutive nights on several platforms for multiday paddling adventures. Thus, it is possible to cross the entire swamp in a single trip, which can entail paddling as much as 95 miles.

Some of the platforms are free-standing in the water, while some others are anchored into banks of dry land. At Floyds Island and Mixons Hammock, the platforms are entirely on land and fire rings are provided. At Canal Run the platform is built into the bank of the Suwannee Canal, and it has a fire ring on the shore as well. Each of these platforms is a group site, designed to hold up to 20 campers.

145 Brickhill Bluff Wilderness Campsite

Recreation: Hiking, biking, birding

Location: Ferry dock is 7 miles northeast of Saint Marys

GPS: N30 89.91' / W81 43.78'

Facilities and amenities: Nonpotable water

Elevation: 10

Road conditions: All island roads are soft sand

Hookups: None

Sites: 4 primitive tent sites

Maximum RV length: NA

Season: Year-round

Fees: Tent site $9, one week entrance fee $10, annual fee $35, round-trip ferry $34, add $10 to carry a bicycle, cash not accepted

Maximum stay: 7 days

Management: US National Park Service, Cumberland Island National Seashore, 101 Wheeler Street, Saint Marys; (912) 882-4336; www.nps.gov/cuis/index.htm

Reservations: For the ferry, (877) 860-6787; www.cumberlandislandferry.com; for camping, www.recreation.gov/camping/campgrounds/253730

A ferry carries visitors to the Cumberland Island National Seashore where the island's wild horses are a common sight.

Pets: Only service dogs allowed
Quiet hours: None
Alcohol restrictions: None
ADA compliant: No
Finding the campground: Ferry dock: From exit 3 on I-95, take GA 40 to the east for 9 miles. At the end of the road turn right. The Cumberland Island National Seashore dock is on the left at 0.1 mile. Parking is on the right just past the dock.
About the campground: Cumberland Island National Seashore is located on the most southerly of Georgia's barrier islands. The isle stretches for 18.5 miles on a north/south axis and has 17 miles of unspoiled, uninterrupted beaches.

Brickhill Bluff is the most remote of Cumberland Island's campsites. A hike of 10.5 miles from the ferry dock is required to reach it in the federally mandated wilderness area on the north end of the island.

No carts are allowed, and all gear must be backpacked in. Bicycles are allowed on the main road but cannot be taken into the campsite. They may be chained to a tree no more than 15 feet from the road. Thin road wheels on bikes will not work on the island's sand roads. Hammocks must be free-standing, and no fires are allowed. Camp stoves may be used. Nonpotable water is available from a pump well and should be treated before drinking or used for cooking. Food and trash should be hung, since raccoons are prevalent.

The bluff overlooks the East River and marshes beyond on the inland side of the island. It is the closest campground to Whitney Lake, a freshwater pond often frequented by the wild horses on this end of the island.

146 Hickory Hill Wilderness Campsite

Recreation: Hiking, biking, birding
Location: Ferry dock is 7 miles northeast of Saint Marys
GPS: N30 83.28' / W81 45.12'
Facilities and amenities: Nonpotable water
Elevation: 23
Road conditions: All island roads are soft sand
Hookups: None
Sites: 4 primitive tent sites
Maximum RV length: NA
Season: Year-round
Fees: Tent site $9, one week entrance fee $10, annual fee $35, round-trip ferry $34, add $10 to carry a bicycle, cash not accepted
Maximum stay: 7 days
Management: US National Park Service, Cumberland Island National Seashore, 101 Wheeler Street, Saint Marys; (912) 882-4336; www.nps.gov/cuis/index.htm
Reservations: For the ferry, (877) 860-6787; www.cumberlandislandferry.com; for camping, www.recreation.gov/camping/campgrounds/253730
Pets: Only service dogs allowed
Quiet hours: None
Alcohol restrictions: None
ADA compliant: No
Finding the campground: Ferry dock: From exit 3 on I-95, take GA 40 to the east for 9 miles. At the end of the road turn right. The Cumberland Island National Seashore dock is on the left at 0.1 mile. Parking is on the right just past the dock.
About the campground: Cumberland Island National Seashore is located on the most southerly of Georgia's barrier islands. The isle stretches for 18.5 miles on a north/south axis and has 17 miles of unspoiled, uninterrupted beaches.

The Hickory Hill campsite is located 5.5 miles north of the ferry landing in the wilderness area. It is positioned on the 2.1-mile Willow Pond Trail, which connects the main road to one of the most scenic areas of the beach in the midsection of the island. To reach it from the main road, head across a 1,000-foot boardwalk spanning the freshwater marsh between the New Swamp Field and Old Swamp Field. The boardwalk is a good location for birding or spotting one of the resident alligators.

The campsite also is at the junction of the Willow Pond Trail with the Yankee Paradise Trail approaching from the north and the Parallel Trail from the south.

No carts are allowed, and all gear must be backpacked in. Bicycles are allowed on the main road but cannot be taken into the campsite. They may be chained to a tree no more than 15 feet from the road. Thin road wheels on bikes will not work on the island's sand roads. Hammocks must be free-standing, and no fires are allowed. Camp stoves may be used. Nonpotable water is available from a pump well and should be treated before drinking or used for cooking. Food and trash should be hung, since raccoons are prevalent.

147 **Sea Camp Campground**

Recreation: Hiking, fishing, biking, birding, swimming
Location: Ferry dock is 7 miles northeast of Saint Marys
GPS: N30 76.91' / W81 46.46'
Facilities and amenities: Flush toilets, cold showers, water, dish-washing sink, picnic tables, fire rings with grills, food storage, swimming beach
Elevation: 20
Road conditions: All island roads are soft sand
Hookups: None
Sites: 18 tent sites, 2 group sites
Maximum RV length: NA
Season: Year-round
Fees: Tent site $22, group site $40, one week entrance fee $10, annual fee $35, round-trip ferry $34, add $10 to carry a bicycle, cash not accepted
Maximum stay: 7 days
Management: US National Park Service, Cumberland Island National Seashore, 101 Wheeler Street, Saint Marys; (912) 882-4336; www.nps.gov/cuis/index.htm
Reservations: For the ferry, (877) 860-6787; www.cumberlandislandferry.com; for camping, www.recreation.gov/camping/campgrounds/253730
Pets: Only service dogs allowed
Quiet hours: None
Alcohol restrictions: None
ADA compliant: No
Finding the campground: Ferry dock: From exit 3 on I-95, take GA 40 to the east for 9 miles. At the end of the road turn right. The Cumberland Island National Seashore dock is on the left at 0.1 mile. Parking is on the right just past the dock.
About the campground: Cumberland Island National Seashore is located on the most southerly of Georgia's barrier islands. The isle stretches for 18.5 miles on a north/south axis and has 17 miles of unspoiled, uninterrupted beaches.

Sea Camp is the most developed of the campgrounds on the island. The sites are situated under a canopy of live oaks, with full shade. It also is by far the most popular location for camping on Cumberland Island and often stays full. Additionally, it is the closest camping area to the ruins of the Carnegie family's Dungeness mansion on the south end of the island. The only portion of the island on which bikes may be ridden on the beach is from Sea Camp dune crossing south to the Dungeness crossing.

Carts are allowed for transporting gear the 0.5 mile from the dock to the campground. Bicycles are allowed on the roads to the south of Sea Camp that are not marked as private. Your bike also can be taken into this campsite.

148 Stafford Beach Campground

Recreation: Hiking, fishing, biking, birding, swimming
Location: Ferry dock is 7 miles northeast of Saint Marys
GPS: N30 81.18' / W81 45.05'
Facilities and amenities: Flush toilets, cold showers, water spigot, fire rings with grills, food storage (bear boxes, for raccoons; no bears on the island), swimming beach
Elevation: 25
Road conditions: All island roads are soft sand
Hookups: None
Sites: 10 tent sites
Maximum RV length: NA
Season: Year-round
Fees: Tent site $12, one week entrance fee $10, annual fee $35, round-trip ferry $34, add $10 to carry a bicycle, cash not accepted
Maximum stay: 7 days
Management: US National Park Service, Cumberland Island National Seashore, 101 Wheeler Street, Saint Marys; (912) 882-4336; www.nps.gov/cuis/index.htm
Reservations: For the ferry, (877) 860-6787; www.cumberlandislandferry.com; for camping, www.recreation.gov/camping/campgrounds/253730
Pets: Only service dogs allowed
Quiet hours: None
Alcohol restrictions: None
ADA compliant: No
Finding the campground: Ferry dock: From exit 3 on I-95, take GA 40 to the east for 9 miles. At the end of the road turn right. The Cumberland Island National Seashore dock is on the left at 0.1 mile. Parking is on the right just past the dock.
About the campground: Cumberland Island National Seashore is located on the most southerly of Georgia's barrier islands. The isle stretches for 18.5 miles on a north/south axis and has 17 miles of unspoiled, uninterrupted beaches.

The hike from the Sea Camp ferry dock to Stafford Beach is 3.5 miles. This campsite is the last one traveling north before you enter the wilderness area.

No carts are allowed, and all gear must be backpacked in. Bicycles are allowed on the roads not marked private but cannot be taken into the campsite. They may be chained to a tree no more than 15 feet from the road. Thin road wheels on bikes will not work on the island's sand roads. Hammocks must be free-standing, and no fires are allowed. Food and trash should be hung, since raccoons are prevalent.

149 Yankee Paradise Wilderness Campsite

Recreation: Hiking, biking, birding
Location: Ferry dock is 7 miles northeast of Saint Marys
GPS: N30 89.99' / W81 44.80'
Facilities and amenities: Nonpotable water
Elevation: 14
Road conditions: All island roads are soft sand
Hookups: None
Sites: 4 primitive tent sites
Maximum RV length: NA
Season: Year-round
Fees: Tent site $9, one week entrance fee $10, annual fee $35, round-trip ferry $34, add $10 to carry a bicycle, cash not accepted
Maximum stay: 7 days
Management: US National Park Service, Cumberland Island National Seashore, 101 Wheeler Street, Saint Marys 31558; (912) 882-4336; www.nps.gov/cuis/index.htm
Reservations: For the ferry, (877) 860-6787; www.cumberlandislandferry.com; for camping, www.recreation.gov/camping/campgrounds/253730
Pets: Only service dogs allowed
Quiet hours: None
Alcohol restrictions: None
ADA compliant: No
Finding the campground: Ferry dock: From exit 3 on I-95, take GA 40 to the east for 9 miles. At the end of the road turn right. The Cumberland Island National Seashore dock is on the left at 0.1 mile. Parking is on the right just past the dock.
About the campground: Cumberland Island National Seashore is located on the most southerly of Georgia's barrier islands. The isle stretches for 18.5 miles on a north/south axis and has 17 miles of unspoiled, uninterrupted beaches.

The Yankee Paradise site is 1 mile east of the Plum Orchard mansion and 0.5 mile east of the main road. The campsite sits on the 2.5-mile Duck House Trail, which crosses the island to the beach. It also is at the junction of that trail with the Tar Kiln Trail to the north and the Yankee Paradise Trail from the south. The hike up from the Sea Camp ferry dock is 7.5 miles.

No carts are allowed, and all gear must be backpacked in. Bicycles are allowed on the main road but cannot be taken into the campsite. They may be chained to a tree no more than 15 feet from the road. Thin road wheels on bikes will not work on the island's sand roads. Hammocks must be free-standing, and no fires are allowed. Camp stoves may be used. Nonpotable water is available from a pump well and should be treated before drinking or used for cooking. Food and trash should be hung, since raccoons are prevalent.

Campground Index

Help Us Keep This Guide Up to Date

Every effort has been made by the authors and editors to make this guide as accurate and useful as possible; however, many things can change after a guide is published—regulations change, facilities come under new management, and so forth.

We would love to hear from you concerning your experiences with this guide and how you feel it could be improved and kept up to date. While we may not be able to respond to all comments and suggestions, we'll take them to heart, and we'll also make certain to share them with the author. Please send your comments and suggestions to falconeditorial@rowman.com.

Thanks for your input!